The Manager's Job

The Manager's Job

INCLUDING PAPERS FROM

UTILITY MANAGEMENT WORKSHOPS

COLUMBIA UNIVERSITY, 1956 TO 1959

Edited by ROBERT TEVIOT LIVINGSTON

and WILLIAM W. WAITE

New York, 1960

COLUMBIA UNIVERSITY PRESS

GENERAL INTRODUCTION

THROUGHOUT THE AGES men have bemoaned "the times and the customs," and, while no Cassandra has ever won a popularity contest, there never seems to be a lack of people to predict the inevitable and unpleasant consequences of going on the way we are. Perhaps it is a cliché to say that this was never more true than it is today, but clichés are apt to be truisms, and truisms are apt to be overlooked and neglected. Orators like to say, in effect, that we are standing at the crossroads of history and ours is the choice, to follow the easy pleasant road with which we are familiar, or to struggle up the hard and unpleasant path which leads we know not where, even when we feel reasonably certain that the old familiar path will not lead where we want to go and may lead nowhere or to oblivion. But, long-time favorite of politicos or not, it is becoming increasingly apparent that many of the old ways are no longer good ways and that what is needed today is courageous, conscientious, and confident (as well as technically competent) industrial leadership.

Some years ago a group of leaders in the public utilities field, believing this was so, sponsored the Utility Management Workshop, which, in 1961, will celebrate its tenth anniversary. This volume represents an effort by the director and his associate to report on what was seen as a unique experiment and what has proved to be a powerful instrument for the development of the leaders of tomorrow—in a particular field, it is true, but the experience of those years which is presented here is as important and useful in any other field as it is in the field of regulated industry.

This is not the place, nor is there the time or space, to present the history of what has gone by or the plans and ambitions of the future; yet, it seems important to express briefly the basis upon which the Utility Management Workshop was founded and upon which it operates. Each year a volume of limited circulation is published and distributed, in part for publicity purposes but also, and perhaps in larger part, as a statement of principles. This volume is known as *New Dimensions for Managers,* and the following is abstracted from it to serve as an introduction to the papers which have been presented or developed at the Workshops. These are joined into an integrated whole by connecting sections from the Workbook, which serves as a basis for the participants' work.

A New Dimension in Manager Development

The man at the head of a public utility company knows that machinery, manpower and money are vital in the continuous and successful operation of his concern. He also learns that there must be supervision, control, direction, planning and all the other elements of what is defined as management. He also knows that a present supply of these factors is not the full discharge of his responsibility to perpetuate the business as a sound, continuous agency.

Machinery, equipment, and supplies come from manufacturers and vendors; manpower comes from the efforts of his Personnel or Employee Relations Department; and money is derived from the efforts of his directors, bankers and security dealers. The fourth and the controlling factor of management reproduction—expansion and improvement—is his personal and pressing problem.

This important process of insuring an expanding future for a utility company has been a subject of study by every executive of vision. Much has been done in providing ways and means to assure judgment, personality, humanity and vision in the men who are rising to posts of command in the utility industry—much more is still to be achieved before there can be any assurance of success in the promotion of the right men to the right places. Only by careful and continual attention to manager development can the industry assure itself of full performance of its responsibilities to the customers and the continuance of a free enterprise.

Requirements of a Program of Manager Reproduction

Any program of managerial reproduction must be based upon a program of manager development. A complete program of manager development will provide the following four basic components.

1. A panorama of the operation and its management, starting with the job and moving up through the unit operation, the function, the company, the industry, the environment and the society. The beginning of understanding lies in the ability to see and to recognize.

2. An understanding of the interrelated structure which is the company, starting with the
   a. Relationship of the man to his job
   b. Relationship of the job to other jobs
   c. Relationship of the special groups of men in associated jobs to the department and the company.
   d. Appreciation of the place and practices of the company both internally and externally, both as a company and as a group of men working together. The ability to do is based upon understanding of the process and the place of the manager therein.

3. The development of technical competence in the job, not only so that the job will be handled adequately in relation to all the other jobs, but also that the individual may learn the feeling of confidence which comes from a record of successful accomplishments and of faith in his ability to meet problems and emergencies.

4. The growth of the man as a mature individual who can see beyond the immediacies of the job and can exercise the necessary leadership is not only a requirement of every job but becomes increasingly important at the higher echelons and will be essential to meet the problems of the future.

An Analysis of the Operation

The Utility Management Workshops which Columbia's Department of Industrial and Management Engineering operates at Arden House are a unique experience in adult education directed to a specific problem—that of developing leadership for the future.

From California to Connecticut—whether electricity, gas, telephone, airlines, or railroads—the public service industries have certain common problems. Those who manage these industries experience the same kinds of forces and pressures. It is this membership of people with common interests and similar professional problems which makes possible the very real accomplishment which is an annual feature of the Workshop.

The Method

To discover and explore the new, to sharpen and expand the known managerial skills for the long-range improvement and total realization of managerial potential is the constant aim of the Workshop. The method by which this is achieved is the psychological involvement of each participant in order to bring into play the total personality of each, probing latent talent and discovering untapped personality assets in the area of leadership. In thirteen days there will be few profound changes of behavior, but a surprising number of men will be triggered into that process of growth in self-awareness that leads to self-development in management techniques, attitudes, and accomplishment.

People learn by doing—by participation. This is particularly true if they are interested in what they are doing and intimately involved. At Arden House each group takes on a project, the subject of which is determined individually by its members and which is related closely to the common backgrounds of the participants. At the end of the program each group makes a report on its project.

The Discovery of New Dimensions and Perspectives. The program as a whole is designed to give the participants a look at their problems in new dimensions. Working in a group brings a new dimension in itself, in that most managers have assistants at home and can delegate their work. Here they must do the work themselves; at the least, they will exercise mental muscles which may have become stiff through disuse. Being able to see the job from the point of view of another person is a major step in manager development.

Early in the group process each member of the Workshop is asked to describe his company, his job, and his relations with other departments in his company—in other words, how he sees the other departments. Here, each man may see how someone else sees his opposite number in another company, thereby gaining a new perspective—by seeing his job and himself as others see him. Since, as a manager, he must work through others, only if he sees himself as others see him can he motivate and stimulate them most effectively.

The Individual Development Program. The basic objective of the Workshop is the development of each person who shares in it. But every manager, indeed every man, sees two sets of objectives, different but related: the objectives of the company and the industry, and the objectives of the individual. And this is held definite: the objectives of the company and industry will only be fully realized if the objectives of the individual are realized.

THE PRESENTATION BY THE EXPERTS

A group of experts in the management field drawn from academic life, as well as from among business executives, speak to the conferees in formal sessions. The body of this volume is composed of papers selected from those presented at the Workshop over the past few years. Following their formal talks, the experts make themselves available to the various working groups in informal meetings where the discussions range the scale of the conferees' interests. It is here that new dimensions are explored and ideas shared most freely. Frank comments are encouraged, and experience has shown that people are more apt to speak up in a group of this kind than they would be if they were on their home grounds, surrounded by their day-to-day associates. As the Workshop approaches its tenth year it seemed wise to make a collection of papers which could be integrated into a coherent whole, representing not only the ideas of some of the outstanding writers in management, but also presenting what has happened at Arden House in the past few years as a suggestion of what the future will be.

ROBERT TEVIOT LIVINGSTON

Columbia University
in the City of New York
April, 1960

CONTENTS

Contents

Part One

THE JOB OF
THE TOP MANAGER

INTRODUCTION

THE TOP EXECUTIVE of an organization is the court of last resort in resolving the managerial problems that arise in the course of the concern's operations. He is the person who must decide between alternatives of action. His job is complicated by the accelerating rate of change in the industrial environment. New developments in labor relations, economics, governmental regulations, and international relations tread close on the heels of fantastic advances in the physical sciences and their applications to technology. The manager must simultaneously account for the past, operate in the present, and plan for the future.

To discharge his heavy load of responsibility the top-level manager must assemble and develop a staff of assistants capable of handling the various segments of the total job. He must delegate responsibility and commensurate authority to his subordinates in their respective areas. And he must set up procedures for identifying, selecting, and developing a reserve of potential replacements for himself and his managerial colleagues in order to perpetuate the organization. "Development" implies the process of allowing subordinate managers considerable latitude in making their own decisions on matters affecting their segments of the organization. It also implies watchfulness to correct any behavior by parts of the organization, or sub-systems, which may be best for themselves but which may have adverse effects on the management system as a whole.

In attempting to solve the problem of development, the top

manager and his immediate aides must form as accurate a picture as possible of the goals of the concern, translated into terms of executive manpower requirements. No development program can be justified on any other basis. Only when this objective has been determined can steps be undertaken to set up specific means for broadening and deepening the competence of subordinate managers—or for seeking qualified persons outside the present employee body.

Professor Erwin H. Schell, of Massachusetts Institute of Technology, has set down what he considers "Today's Ten Most Important Utility Management Problems." [1] They are:

1. How may we keep abreast of the ever more rapid developments in the art of utility management?

2. How may we increase creativeness and work improvement among the rank and file as well as the executives of our companies?

3. How may we obtain and prepare young men of ability for future executive positions in terms of the new industrial climate and environment in which they will function?

4. How may we improve the quality and unit costs of our internal operations in maintaining parity with advances made in the power generation field or the consumer facilities field?

5. How may we increase our knowledge of, collaboration with, and close relationship to the ultimate consumers of our products or services?

6. How may we cement and strengthen our constructive relationships with our communities and our local and national affiliations?

7. How may we shorten and refine those periods of transition and change in our operations which will grow in frequency in the future?

8. How may we institute better data processing in our opera-

[1] Address presented at the Sixth Utility Management Workshop, July, 1957.

tions, to the end that the facts essential to control may be precisely ascertained and quickly made available?

9. How may we build increasing reserves of trust, confidence, and loyalty among our employees, executives, customers, investors and communities, which are so vital to our security in times of emergency or rapid change?

10. How may we appraise our relative skill and effectiveness in the management of our business? How can we measure the quality of our own efforts as managers?

While these were specifically labeled as problems facing the managers of public utility enterprises, they are almost equally applicable to any institution—industrial, educational, or governmental.

On the following pages are reproduced selected papers presented at Utility Management Workshops from 1956 through 1959. Robert T. Livingston sets the pattern for a review of the field of top management and for the first presentations to the members of the Workshop. He describes the conceptual mechanism of the operation and the place occupied by the managerial system in carrying out the operation.

Chester Stackpole explores the reasons for the existence of either harmony or conflict among the several aspects of the manager's job, as well as various means of promoting or exploiting harmonious relationships for the benefit of all.

Donald C. Power and Allen Van Wyck present the picture of the top executive from the vantage point of experience. His is a lonely position because he must make the final decisions on basic policy matters. He must guide and help his subordinates in reaching their decisions without usurping the authority to *make* the decisions while, at the same time, guarding against the possibility of a serious mistake at the lower level. Both papers stress the necessity of teamwork and planning, and Power points out the executive's responsibility for public relations and the "good citizenship" of the organization.

Erwin H. Schell stresses the use by the executive of existing focus and situations to the advantage of the organization. He also emphasizes the desirability of insuring the future of the organization by insuring the quality of future management. Management is no longer equivalent to ownership, but is now a widespread social function in which everyone participates.

AN OVER-ALL LOOK AT THE JOB
OF THE MANAGER

by Robert Teviot Livingston

VOLUMES have been written on this subject, specifications have
been set up telling what a manager should do, and directions
have been prepared on how he should do it. This is not only
natural but necessary, and the basic assumptions that I am
making are that all the participants have been sufficiently interested to read a book or so, that almost everyone has taken a
course in college or in his company, and that everyone reads a
journal or two in which various specific problems of management are discussed. It is further assumed that most of the
people here have served on committes, either within their
companies or in one of the industry associations, which have
been concerned with exploring and reporting upon important
management problems.

All of this has advantages and disadvantages. This Workshop is very different from a class in college. Almost everything
that will come up will be in some way familiar to the group;
therefore, we on the staff do not have to spend time on many
of the things that one does in a college course. But it also has a
disadvantage since you are all, to a certain extent, set in your
ways and the main purposes of the Utility Management Workshop will be accomplished only if we can persuade you to look

Adapted from the UMW Workbook for 1957. Mr. Livingston is Professor
of Industrial Engineering, Columbia University, and Director of the Utility Management Workshop.

behind the "how" of what you know and to ask "why." In summary, let us say that here we will try to look at the basic problem, anticipating that each of you is more or less successfully practicing management right now.

Any job can be looked at in the terms set forth above, and at times we will, as all academic people tend to, slip into the general story of a job, any job. However, we all are basically interested in the job of the manager and we will only deal with jobs in general on the assumption that, to some extent, everybody is a manager. It is believed that by looking at a simple job, without the complication of injecting people into it, we can see some things about the job of the manager which are a little different. We start in by describing what the job of the manager is; then the natural thing is to think of what the things are that a manager has to work with. This immediately brings us up short, as it is obvious that there is a man in that job. So we can think of a job from two aspects: the job itself (which we define as a set of expectations) and the man who is trying to satisfy those expectations.

Both of these are, in a sense, independent, individual, internal viewpoints and so, because we want to be realistic, we will think of these two together—the man in the job, or the man/job system which is actually what an outsider sees.

ALL MANAGERS' JOBS ARE THE SAME—BUT DIFFERENT

It is natural to think of every management job as being different from any other, and so it is in certain ways. For example, running a utility company is a different matter from running a bank or department store. On the other hand, in the broader sense, there are certain things every manager has to get done. The difference between managerial jobs lies in what is worked with, rather than in the management itself; what kinds of things are important and what are not. It is probably

true, however, that there is more difference between managerial jobs at different levels of one industry than there is between
managerial jobs at the same level in different industries. For
example, a foreman *is* a manager, and so too is a vice-president
in charge of a function, or a chief engineer, or an assistant.
Each one is practicing the managerial art, and together they
are accomplishing the managerial function. One of the characteristic discoveries that everyone makes when he is promoted
is how little he really knows about the managerial phase of his
new job, even though he knows the technological aspects thoroughly. There is variation in the job of the manager at different
levels, and it is an important point that the success of a person
in any managerial slot is largely dependent upon his understanding of the problems of the managers above and below
him.

As one mounts the ladder of responsibility in a company,
one's perspective changes and one's values should as well. Perhaps the most disturbing change is the increased personal risk
which is associated with higher position. One may ask for advice from above and below, from peers and consultants; but
decision, within the increasingly widening area, is the lonesome
responsibility of the manager. There are certain barriers, as was
previously mentioned, and at these barriers this change is particularly to be noted. To press for a promotion without understanding what the promotion means in things other than status
and money is not the mark of a good manager.

The point of view of the job (which is perhaps a mechanistic
viewpoint) and the man in the job (which is distinctly a personal point of view) leads us to divide into two categories the
tools with which the manager has to work. Those that are
largely independent of the particular person who is in the job,
we will call managerial techniques. But there are other techniques which are not independent of the person in the job—
techniques that a given individual has to use personally with

other people; these are called human relations. This phrase has been used so widely, and so loosely, that we must approach the subject with caution. Because we believe human relations to be a very personal matter, our method of approach will be descriptive and interpretive rather than prescriptive.

We will, in effect, attempt to draw a road map for the practice of human relations. You will have the opportunity to review some of your own problems in human relations and submit them to our panel of authorities in the field. This attempt to make sense of human relations in general, the formulation of the problems you have met, or have avoided, and the reaction of the social scientists to your problems, will be the high point of the first half of the Workshop.

DIFFERENT APPROACHES

There are four aspects of a management job which we can study:

A Management Function: a set of expectations, things which must be accomplished.

A Managing Process: the method by which these things are done, and the expectations realized.

Managerial Behavior: in broad terms, the complex of roles which the manager must play in order to follow the necessary method required by the particular aspect of the management function which is uppermost at any particular time.

A Manager: a man whose particular problem is to select an appropriate role and play it well, with minimum frustration on his part.

Much of the literature in the field is confusing because it does not differentiate among these four approaches. In the Workbook for this conference, the first Workshop task (the job of the manager and how he does it) is studied in four steps:

Any Manager's Job

The Scope of the Job

Managerial Techniques

The Manager's Human Relations

The four sub-tasks are designed to follow each other sequentially. There is a general notion that in life there is a function known as management; this is followed by the concept that it is a universal function, and that an individual performs it in his own individual life. In organized life there is a basic difference in that the actor and the manager are not the same person, hence the comment that the job of a manager is to "get things done through others." Everyone, whether he is managing a group or himself, has to produce something for which the external world is willing to pay, and has to adapt to and live in that world. In order to do both of these he must have foresight, plan ahead, and prepare; and he must, to some extent at least, sell. It is, of course, true that he must work through others, but basically this is only because he cannot physically do all these things himself. There is nothing startling or new—in principle—about the job of the manager or what he does. The newness is in the products which he is responsible for producing and the means he has available to produce them.

In history we find examples of huge organizations of peoples (usually pursuing conquest), so size alone is not a new problem. There are new features in management today—among them the modern industrial corporation. The different levels in a modern industrial organization have very different viewpoints, use different sets of values, and require different skills. These differences are due, in part, to the function performed, but, more particularly, to the positions occupied by the different levels of managers and the power they wield.

In this increasingly technological age the manager has available to him many tools and techniques which, in certain ways, simplify his job and make it possible to do cheaply and rapidly many things which previously were not possible. In the modern corporation there tends to be a very high degree of specialization, and this necessitates an equally high degree of integration and cooperation. Just as in industry at large there are many units which produce only for the use of other corporations, so too, within a given unit there are divisions and departments whose existence is hardly known to the public and whose work does not appear directly in the finished product; they only serve other members of their own company.

In the end we return to where we began: "The job of the manager is getting things done through others," and getting things done through others is "human relations." A manager meets many different experiences; luckily, most of them can be sorted into categories, depending primarily upon the number of people involved and the formal occasion. While no cut and dried behavior can be specified, because there are always unique individuals and unique situations, the manager can assume certain roles, and thus have a guide for his behavior.

THE OPERATION

We may conceive of the integration of the four steps of the manager's job as "the operation." This will provide a fundamental way of looking at the whole first task. While the sections which follow may not be formally tied into the concept here presented, due in part to space limitations, the operation is assumed to be the basis of the discussion.

An operation can be considered as the meeting place of three elements: input, the physical system, and managerial stimuli. In Figure 1 these are represented by blocks which form a column. To the left is shown a block titled Resources, and four elements are indicated: material and supplies, men, machines and equipment, and information. These have different characteristics. Materials and supplies are converted and used in the operation, and they form one element of the input. Machines and equipment have a longer life span in their specified and useful condition. They are not converted in the process directly; they are the means by which the material is converted. On the other hand, they are eventually used up in their functioning. They wear out and must be maintained and repaired.

Men are of a different category. It is their effort that is used. The man himself remains; he gives up energy, it is true, but this energy is replenished routinely and his potentiality is not

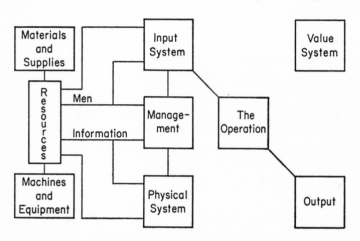

Figure 1. The Operation

decreased by use as a machine's is. It is of course true that, like the machine, he may be damaged by accident and may have to be physically repaired. Man's effort is used in two related processes: the physical process by which the materials are converted and the mental process by means of which information is treated. In the diagram the human effort resource is shown as leading into the input system and into the managerial system. It is not shown as going into the physical system except through the managerial system. That is to say, it is human effort which plans and designs the physical system of the operation.

Information is both a simple and a very complex concept. In the diagram it is indicated as going to the managerial system and the physical system, but not to the input system. Information is an input to the managerial system. It is an element of the physical system without going through the managerial system in the sense that every machine and process has built into it a large amount of information—information internal to the machine or process. With the increase of automation this is increasingly obvious. Information is not shown as feeding directly to the input system; rather it is suggested that one of the functions of the managerial system is to select and choose the proper set of information to be fed to the input. As will be shown when we discuss the input system, there is information which is not fed from the managerial system. It is of a variety of kinds, the principal ones being (a) information from the operation and the output or primary feedback; (b) information from the value system or social matrix; and (c) wild information.

One block is shown with no influence lines—the value system. This is done because we have not, as yet, figured out just how this system works. It seems probable at this time that the output of the value system will be largely information, but at two levels: as an input to the resource system, and as an input to each of the systems containing human beings—the input system and the managerial system.

The operation is a process of exchanging values. The output is at least indirectly determined by the value system.

THE INPUT

In the previous section the general concept of an operation was presented and the various elements involved were located. This presentation indicated flow lines but not directions. The model is not an operative one; rather it may be considered as potential. The word "resources" is used in the broadest possible sense to include everything which is included in the normal consideration of the problem (actor and that acted on) but to exclude all things which, to some extent at least, are not considered, selected, obtained, manipulated, and controlled by the manager. The connection with the value system was not detailed, but this acts upon the manager and he designs and operates his system (the total construction is called the operation) in accordance with his understanding of it. However, the value system acts upon the other elements of the system

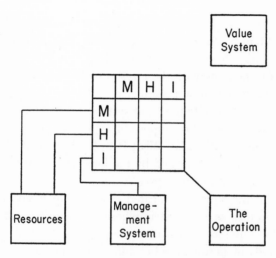

Figure 2. The Input System

(and other subsystems) and the manager may only be aware of, but not understand, this operation. There will also be other forces which influence the operation as a whole and its subsystem which he may not know about until they have taken effect. One of the marks of excellence of the manager is his ability to foresee the possibility of these forces and to provide the ability to adjust to them.

Figure 2 presents in enlargement a part of the total operation that is concerned with input as an array, indicating the primary source of the elements of the input system. Three elements have been included in the input system:

$M/H =$ action between materials and a man

$M/I =$ information about a material

$I/H =$ orders or directions given to a man

The vector which may be drawn from any point is defined in terms of these three variables. The point so defined is called the "potential point," as no action occurs until the operation is started.

As shown, materials (M) and men (H) are assigned to the input system by the management system. This is indicated by the line connecting the resources and the management system. What is to be done with these resources in respect to one another prior to operation is indicated by the line connecting the management system to the input system. This will include such matters as assignment of responsibility, purchasing and storage information, and the like. What is to be done to these inputs in the operation is indicated by the line between the management system and the operation.

Each of the squares indicated may be expanded and considered in turn as a subsystem whose characteristics should be understood. Before that is done it seems wise to attempt to see what kinds of pertinent subclassification can be made under each major classification. The list and discussion which follows is a first attempt. The point of view which is adopted as to these subclassifications is that of: identification, use in the process, managerial ability to effect.

MATERIALS AND SUPPLIES

There is a continuum from raw (natural) materials and supplies to complete operative subassemblies and including energy. Management's interest lies in (a) specifying them in kind, quality and amount, selection of a resource from the universe of all resources; (b) specifying how they shall be treated in order to have their value changed—in the operation; (c) specifying how they shall be treated before being fed into the operation.

Other classifications, of course, are possible, but it is believed that this is most nearly related to the internal needs of the grand system and of the operation. It is to be noted that materials can also be considered in respect to the output in terms of whether they appear physically in the output or only by their effect; the difference is between materials and supplies.

MEN

Human effort rather than men comprises the input. The resource H has already been divided into two classes at this point —managerial effort and productive effort. This means that we are dealing with a classification of the kinds of effort that are used.

INFORMATION

Operation-directed information is the only sort that we are basically interested in and, in consequence, the most helpful subclassification would be in terms of source, always recognizing that there is a great deal of information (or communication) being distributed which is not directly operative or organizationally directed; it may be individually directed and hence indirectly affect the operation, and it may, indeed, be hostile or negative to the operation.

As sources of information we can note (a) the management system, (b) the other elements of the input system, (c) the value system, and (d) wild information. In order to be used and to appear in the operation, all of this information must pass through the human element.

The physical system and its interrelations are shown in Figure 3. The array indicated is only 2 by 2, the two elements being *M* and *I*.

M is shown as flowing entirely from the resources. The particular items are selected from the world of machines on a basis of their fitness to perform in the operation. Information is

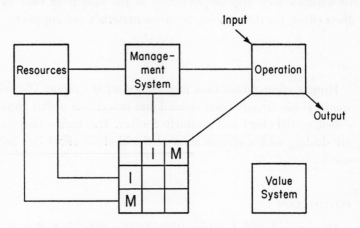

Figure 3. The Physical System

shown as flowing also from the resources, on the assumption that any machine represents in its design and manufacture the transfer of some information to raw material. It is an interesting side thought that a machine, in fact any device, represents a high degree of improbability by chance. Further, each machine carries with it a set of directions for use and these directions are information.

The rest of the information is shown as coming from the management system. Here is the design of the physical plant, including all processes, machines, and equipment, which operate on the material according to a set of directions (information) by men, using effort.

The management system is shown (see Figure 4) with three connections, one each to the input system, the physical system, the operation. These three connections represent three different kinds of information. For the present we will consider the

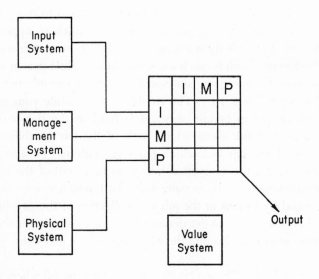

Figure 4. The Management System

management system as the focus. These connections are concerned with (a) selecting, locating, and obtaining resources; (b) caring for, assigning, and using consumable resources; (c) integrating, arranging, and caring for assets which are not entirely consumed in any operation within a definite time span; (d) specifying the interactions in kind, quality, time, etc. between the input system and the physical system.

By considering the question of "caring for" resources, a somewhat different point of view is raised. That is to say, storage and maintenance then become a function apart from the operation itself. This has some conceptual value, especially in terms of automation.

WHAT EVERY MANAGER SHOULD KNOW

Let us consider the points of view from which one may approach the total task and the sub-tasks. We begin to study the first task by questioning its basic premise which is, approximately, that everybody is a manager and that, in certain ways, every manager's job is much the same. Any sensible person will agree with the foregoing statement, but every sensible person will also say, "but. . . ." The trouble is that, while your jobs are all unique in certain ways, it is hard in the day-to-day operation to think about which parts of the job are different because of the job and which parts are different because of yourselves. So, the suggestion here is to move out of the little white rectangle in the organization chart which carries your name and try to look at the job as a collection of things which other people expect to get done or have done, which somehow or other must flow through the white box where, in a sense, you live.

All people are alike in certain ways, and it is useful whenever we worry about our individuality to see how much we resemble someone else. It is particularly useful to think of someone whom we don't especially like. In a similar way it is useful to think about the ways in which our job is like every other management job. If one does this he can begin to identify the ways in which his job is really different, and not just his own job, but the jobs above and below him, and the jobs of the other people with whom he has to work. If we can accept certain things as common to all management jobs, we can study how best to get these things done. Perhaps we can train ourselves and others to do them better and can then focus our minds on those things which are unique about our jobs—not about ourselves and how we now get the job done, but about the job itself.

Having looked at the job from the outside, we can study the job with a man in it—not any old man, not the other fellow, but ourselves. It is useful to hold the idea of the job as a set of expectations by other people, then to think of what a person should be like and how he should behave to fit the expectations best, and, finally, to observe how you perform. You will probably see that there is a difference between the way someone else "ought to" or would do the job, and the way you do it. Whether that difference is important or not, only you can really judge. However, it is often helpful to think of somebody else's job, preferably one to which you and your job are related and upon which you depend intimately, and figure out how much better you could do the job than it is being done at present. Another useful thing is to realize that the other fellow probably has some strong ideas about how your job could be done better. "Better" means more convenient for him. We can set down an aphorism here (an aphorism is a rule that we have no intention of following): Always look at your job and the other fellow's job from the point of view of the other fellow.

HARMONY AND CONFLICT IN THE JOB OF THE MANAGER

by Chester S. Stackpole

I WAS INTERESTED in the array in which Professor Livingston presented several aspects of the job of the manager: representing the company; expanding goals and policies and explaining them; allotting and assigning tasks; stimulating, rewarding (by penalizing and motivating).

	Representing	Expanding	Alloting	Stimulating
Representing the company				
Expanding goals and policies	R/E			
Alloting and assigning tasks	R/A	E/A		
Stimulating and rewarding	R/S	E/S	A/S	

Figure 1. Aspects of the Manager's Job

Address presented at the Eighth Utility Management Workshop, July, 1959. Mr. Stackpole is Managing Director of the American Gas Association.

I propose to concern myself with six of these relationships, which can be either in harmony or in conflict. Let us consider the R/E relationship—R for representing and E for expanding —the relationship between representing the company and expanding its goals. It can be expressed in just two ways: the factors can be either in conflict or in harmony.

I suppose many of you were in the military service and will recognize this as analogous to the commander's estimate of a situation. When a military commander is faced with a decision, he must consider each capability of the enemy and each capability of his own troops. He must match each one of his own capabilities against each one of the enemy's capabilities in order to make the proper command decision. The job of a manager is to strive constantly to make the right decisions. To do this, he obviously must be aware of all of the aspects of his job and their relationships to each other.

Furthermore, I think I can show you how each relationship can result either in harmony or in conflict. I hope to be able to show how you can exploit the harmony of a relationship to the benefit of your company, its employees and customers and, of course, of yourselves. I may even be able to show you how to take a conflict relationship and make of it a situation where, although you can not completely resolve it and turn it into harmony, you can go from conflict to anxiety. By anxiety I mean a situation of potential conflict with which a person can live without getting ulcers.

The R/E relationship can be in conflict or in harmony. Suppose we take an example of the relationship in harmony. I think you have harmony when, for example, you are called upon to speak before security analysts in your role as a corporate officer and you explain the results, practices, policies, and goals of your company. You can exploit the harmony of this relationship by the clarity of your expression in outlining, with practical optimism, the loftiness of the company's goals. You are not preaching and you are not coldly pragmatic either. You "hitch" your company to ideals and beliefs to which all your listeners can subscribe. This seems obivous. Now let us see what happens when your representation functions and your expanding functions are in conflict.

First of all, I think you can see that this kind of conflict occurs inside a company more often than in the public view. When we have conflicts in the public view, they may involve such things as proxy fights, public exposure of the real reasons for resignations, lower earnings, and so forth.

Let us take an example of the internal R/E conflict, and consider a company policy which you, as a manager, feel is unworthy of your company or is nonproductive. You can usually tell when there is a conflict here because you feel uncomfortable about this particular policy. When you try to explain it, you end by explaining it in defensive terms. This is a tough one. To resolve the conflict you can get the policy changed, if possible, or quit. I might say I suppose you could get a solution by becoming converted to the policy. But let us suppose, to make this a good example, that it really is a poor policy.

If the policy cannot be changed immediately, you, as a manager, might achieve a state of anxiety or tension. This could happen if you kept quiet in public about policies with which you do not agree, but engaged within the company in a vigorous, concerted, common-sense attempt to have the policy changed.

In my organization we had a problem like this a few months ago. We used to have a policy which forbade us from conducting any lobbying activity. Yet, we were expected to keep our members informed and alerted to the consequences of proposed legislation. Our lawyers told us that we could not alert or inform our members unless the Association was duly registered. You can well imagine that a policy like this reduced the effectiveness of the president of the Association and the staff in a very important area. On one occasion the President of the United States asked us to help him "hold the line" with a balanced budget. We had to tell his emissary that we could not do this in any effective way. As it turned out, we did write a rather innocuous letter to the President of the United States, copies of which we sent out to our members without comment. The President answered, and we mailed his answer out to our members, again with no comment. So, you see, we achieved a state of tension or anxiety by doing something which was not effective but indicated our desire to comply with the Presidential request.

Meanwhile, this question of legislative activity was being considered by our board of directors and executive committee. Just in passing, I am happy to say that our legislative policy has been changed so that we shall no longer be in a position threatening us with ulcers!

Now let us move on to the *R/A* relationship. We are still speaking of representation, but now I want to look at the relationship between representation and your job, as a manager, to assign and allocate tasks.

I suppose it is rather trite for me to say that you get harmony in this segment when you assign tasks so that the company is successfully represented by others as well as by yourselves. As a simple example, suppose your company has an active speakers' bureau. I am sure you know what I mean—a group equipped to furnish speakers to service clubs, professional groups, civic organizations, women's clubs, and all the other groups which meet in your community and are asking for good speakers. I think it is perfectly obvious that a good, active speakers' bureau is an assurance that your company is well represented *at the grass roots level!*

How about the other side of the coin? Representation and assignment or allocation can be in conflict when only the top executives can speak for a company. You can see, I am sure, how the so-called "company image" can be distorted and weakened. To take accident prevention, as an example, suppose one of your servicemen, while driving a company truck, is involved in an accident with a private automobile. Suppose, also, that a company policy forbids a driver to discuss the accident —even with the police. Suppose all he can say is, "You will have to talk with the claim agent when he gets here." I know of a company which has, or at least had, such a policy, so this is a real example; that company has not given its drivers even a small share of the job of effectively representing their company.

Just imagine the effect of such a policy on public relations! I am sure you are saying, "Why can't the drivers be trained to perform in such instances in the way all insurance companies suggest that all their policy-holders act, i.e., discussing the accident, but avoiding statements accepting or implying acceptance of responsibility?" They can be, and, in my opinion, they should be, with the assistance of the company's legal staff, the public relations' staff, and, possibly, the local police traffic department. Obviously, the manager's job is to assign goals which will result in everyone's representing the company in a proper, positive, and beneficial way.

Now let us look at the R/S relationship. Again, we are talking about representation, but this time as it affects stimulation, in the form of rewards, penalties, and motivations. When is this R/S relationship in harmony? It is in harmony when the people you manage have sufficient information that they can represent your company properly. We have harmony here because most people consider that being well informed is, in itself, a reward. Knowledgeable representation is a powerful motivation for people to do a better job for the company.

For example, the local manager of a telephone company not far from here has access, among other things, to a working model of a Vanguard Satellite as well as to a movie about rockets and space travel. Also, his company trains him in public speaking and keeps him informed regarding company activities. He is a member of its speaker's bureau. What's the result? He feels important and knowledgeable when he speaks to the P.T.A. or other groups. He is proud to be the voice of the telephone company. He is enthusiastic about it and his job. Now you know why the audience is impressed with the ability of this local manager—and this is important: the audience thinks the telephone company is a pretty good one, too. In other words, that telephone company has made an effective representative of its local manager by *rewarding* him with the necessary tools to exercise his public speaking ability.

As always, there is a less bright side to the relationship among representation and rewards, penalties, and motivation. You all know that unfair, unduly harsh, carelessly handled criticism or lack of discipline can cause conflict between representation and motivation. As an example that is perhaps all too prevalent, take the case of the manager who cannot face up to pointing out personal, supervisory, or managerial defects and shortcomings in the people he supervises.

Some of the people who work with you may not be making any progress and they may want to know the reasons why. It is a quirk of human nature that not many of them possess the temerity to ask you. Those who do ask do not always get answers they can use for self-improvement. Those who do not ask—and this is tragic for management—may "shrivel up" and become "dead-enders" and problems in the organization as the years go by. As managers, we should not let this sort of thing happen. We can resolve the conflict by telling our subordinates about their shortcomings—not by "bawling them out," but by telling them in a helpful, straightforward, and meaningful way. We can and should tell them, with specific suggestions which they can use to improve themselves if they really want to.

I realize it is not as simple as it sounds. Resolution of conflict

is the ideal. But, I insist that you can replace this conflict with
a bearable tension if, after proper discussion, you place your
subordinates where they can do the best jobs for the company and themselves.

When you do this it could be that the man whose job you
change to help him avoid inner conflict may come to realize
that the company, *through you as representative,* has decided
he may have reached his limit. But you will often find that,
through your willingness to face up to the, at times, unpleasant
task, the man himself will understand, for the first time, that
he has indeed reached his limit. When this happens, you have
a man who now knows himself and will not waste any more
time trying to become something of which he is incapable,
unless he is willing to set himself to the very difficult, arduous,
and challenging task of acquiring added education and/or
training.

Of course, it will not always work out this way, I am sorry
to say. A man who has once had a taste of executive privileges,
as it were, may not be willing to admit that he has come to the
end of any expectation of gathering to himself more of the
same. Let us not blind ourselves to this very difficult aspect of
the job which we managers should perform. We must, we find,
"seem cruel only to be kind."

Now let us look at the effect of expanding policies and goals
upon the allocation of tasks—the *E/A* relationship. First, we
shall review the harmonious aspects of this relationship. It is
a truism to say that turning policy decisions into practices and
procedures, in order to reach an expanded goal, requires many
hands. The well-rounded manager, to put many hands to work,
must allocate tasks.

Good policies, understood and believed in by all, are the
breath of life of a corporation. Organization and clearly defined procedures and practices make up the living body that
reaches the corporate goal. We can say that good organization

is an example of allocating tasks to make policy effective so that we can attain goals. Good organization leads to clearcut lines of authority which should, nevertheless, permit unequivocal freedom of cross-contact. So, we might say that the set-up of a well-organized and thought out organization chart which is actually complied with in practice is a good example of harmony in the area of the E/A relationship.

Expansion of policies and goals can also be in conflict with the allocation of tasks. Poor company communications can prevent policies—and sometimes even goals—from being known to and reached by the people to whom the tasks are allocated. The result of this situation is no enthusiasm, because of no understanding.

Here is an example right in our own industry. Suppose a company undertakes a tremendous sales promotion program which flops. And suppose the reason is that the salesmen did not know why it is important to them, as well as to the company, to make this promotion a success. Someone in the management area has failed, through neglect, lack of knowledge, or inexperience.

Let us look now at the relationship among expanding goals and stimulation. Expansion of policy and goals fits very well into the whole system of rewards, penalties, and motivation. Many of your own companies have dynamic, forward-looking policies, and you know at first hand what great motivating factors such policies are for all concerned. There are, for example, companies which have enlightened public and employee safety programs and policies. I think we can easily see that public relations people, safety supervisors, claim agents, insurance managers, and the operating people want to and actually do perform better under such policies.

Take another example; a policy might, itself, be a reward or provide for a penalty. An example of a reward is company support of self-education for its employees. As for penalties, many companies through their personnel departments' operations and functions have regular disciplinary policies so that each employee knows where he stands and for what he may be separated from the company and for what he may be otherwise disciplined.

Of course, we can have conflict in the E/A relationship. Suppose the manager, in his eagerness to achieve goals, rides roughshod over subordinates who attempt to cooperate with him but fail to live up to his high standards. Too often, we create a conflict situation in this area when we fail to realize the human limitations of our subordinates. Too often, we forget that we are managers simply because we are more valuable today, to our companies, than are our subordinates. We should remember that it is neither proper nor fair to expect them to possess all the capabilities that we ourselves possess.

Take a brilliant manager who wishes to change the format of his company's annual report. He wants to abandon the somewhat staid and unexciting style of the past and produce an annual report with illustrative pictures and interesting information about company subjects that are not purely financial and operational. He so instructs the public relations or information director. The latter, after making all the proper contacts with the company people concerned, presents a "dummy" of what he considers a workmanlike annual report. To be sure, this report includes all the subjects the manager wanted touched upon. However, the report uses "subheadings" in the text rather than "headline" headings. For this, and other reasons, the general appearance of the report fails to excite or satisfy the manager. This brilliant, though impatient, manager tells the P.R. man that the dummy is a failure. If something similar has happened to you, did you feel frustrated and discouraged?

The trouble here was that the manager saw, in his mind's eye, an annual report which he alone was capable of creating.

I am not saying that it was his responsibility to sit down and dummy up the annual report. I am saying, rather, that he instructed his subordinate to draft it without taking sufficient time to pass along his own ideas about the format effectively. Let us remember then, that we cannot always expect our dreams and aspirations to be those of our associates as well.

There is a resolution to this conflict. The manager could have realized his dream by making the necessary changes in the annual report instead of flatly calling the dummy a failure. In so doing, he could have worked closely with the public relations man so that the latter would begin to share his dream and ideas. Success in so sharing determines whether we get resolution, tolerable tension, or unresolvable conflict. Patience and understanding are so essential.

Now I come to the last relationship, allocation and assignment of tasks as they affect the stimuli of rewards, punishments, and motivations—the A/S relationship. I think you will agree with me that when allocation or assignment constitutes a reward or a motivation A and S are in harmony. We can say it better, perhaps, as "give a man a task he loves to do and he'll be motivated to do it in a manner above and beyond the call of duty."

You can all think of examples. I like to think of a warm-hearted little girl in the stenographic department who was selected to be chairman of the "sunshine committee," a rewarding assignment. In this capacity she is consulted by management on things the company can and will do for employees who are sick or have had a family tragedy. Such consultations are a part of the management job. Since it is so easy to do, we certainly ought not to overlook giving out assignments which, in themselves, are rewards.

Assignments and rewards and discipline can, of course, be in conflict. Conversely to what I said a few minutes ago, give a man a job he hates to do and, chances are, he will make a mess of it. Try, for example, to make a salesman out of a dedicated accountant and watch the man crack up before your very eyes. I am sure all of you have thought of dozens of examples, so I hardly need to add any more.

What I would like to talk about, rather, is an interesting and heartening aspect of this "allocation/reward" business. It has to do with the discovery of hidden talent. Allocate or assign a "dirty" job to a man who looks at undesirable tasks as challenges rather than as stumbling blocks, and you often find the key to the development of a talent neither you nor he himself knew existed.

Take an example; the industrial engineer with the scientific bent, who goes out reluctantly to persuade a hard-headed industrial customer to change a process over from one fuel to another. The engineer is all prepared with the facts and he is bound and determined not to let this unscientific industrial customer tell him off. You can see it coming; he's heading for the loss of a sale.

But, during the course of his visits in the customer's plant, he discovers some antiquated equipment in the plant cafeteria, and the hot water in the company washroom is cold. His interest is aroused. He forgets his industrial sales mission and points out to the plant manager the benefits of a properly sized commercial water heater for the washroom. He also outlines the need for and benefits of replacing the cafeteria equipment. Result? The plant manager buys the commercial cooking equipment and the water heater—*and the industrial changeover!*

This all looks accidental, but this industrial engineer, fortunately for himself and his company, saw the peripheral applications in this plant as challenges. I call this sort of thing "making a lemonade out of a lemon."

I hope that I have encouraged you to look consciously and carefully at the various aspects of your job as a **manager**.

Intuition and experience will not always do. Often we have to analyze what we are doing, with or without help, in order to make sure that we are still "on the beam." All of us need to take time out in our busy working day to reflect upon and analyze problems and situations which we, as managers, work with daily. I suggest to you that we must *make* ourselves do this thing, so that we do not tie ourselves up completely in "putting out fires."

Let me go further, and urge you to make a deliberate effort each day to spend a half or three-quarters of an hour not working, but merely thinking about your managerial performance. But, never forget that this thinking will be worthless unless it leads to action. Further, remember that action is sterile unless it achieves a worth-while goal. By all means, act as a result of the conclusions reached during these quiet hours of thought.

I know this sounds obvious. Reflect for a moment, if you will, on the manager who spends time thinking and identifies that troublesome conflict among representation and rewards, punishments and motivations. This may be the manager who discovers a need to point out the defects of a subordinate. His quiet hour of thought has indicated that he has an unpleasant action facing him. The temptation here to lapse into unproductive inaction is almost irresistible. Let us then use the quiet hours of thought also to help steel ourselves to take the action that our analysis tells us should be taken.

And now a final thought on the job of the manager. It is incumbent upon us to identify the aspects of our job, to analyze the inner relationships among the aspects of our job, to cultivate the thought habits necessary to check continuously on our managerial performance and—above all—to cultivate the habit of taking action on what the thinking indicates we must do. This is a simple process. However, the solutions to the problems to which our thinking turns require a great deal of involved and challenging day-to-day contact among human beings. And this is, of course, the reward unique to us managers, for ours is the magnificent privilege of helping to further the progress of the human endeavor while progressing ourselves.

HOW IT IS TO BE THE
PRINCIPAL EXECUTIVE
by Donald C. Power

BEING CHIEF EXECUTIVE of a great corporation is, in many respects, a lonely task. No matter how loyal, devoted, and efficient the principal executive assistants may be—no matter
how extensive their contributions—the ultimate decision on
most matters of important policy falls inescapably on the
principal executive. He could not and would not avoid this
responsibility, but the burden of meeting it is, indeed, a heavy
one. The chief executive, alone, must meet his board of directors. They look to him for guidance and recommendation
in helping him set policies for the corporation. They look to
him for leadership, and his opinions and ideas are the ones
which usually are embodied in the dynamic, working program
which ensues. He cannot escape the sense of importance of
his every act. His thoughts must be intelligent, his recommendations sensible. His knowledge of his company must be
vast. His background in his industry must be long and extended. He cannot be aloof to the economic and political climate of his area and of the country as a whole. He must be a
leader, a dreamer, a thinker, a man of action. He must be con-
versant with finance, although not necessarily a financial man.

Address presented at the Seventh Utility Management Workshop, July,
1958. Mr. Power is Chairman of the General Telephone & Electronics
Corporation.

The requirements of the principal executive of a large corporation are enormous and, I repeat, in many respects the position is a lonely one. The words which set policy in motion must be his—and exclusively so. The ultimate responsibility must necessarily be his also.

The full implementation of the program which the chief executive wishes to effect must come through action of the directors. These are important men, each important in his own right and by his own accomplishments. However, all are busy men, and they must concentrate the time, thought, and attention which they can devote to company matters in a very short interval—usually the relatively short monthly meetings. Therefore, they expect the principal executive to be brief, but they insist that he be right. Theirs is, to a great extent, a complete dependence on him. Their confidence in him is unlimited —their trust unremitting. Therefore, he must be right every time. He must not vacillate or procrastinate. His judgment needs to be infallible. If the important relationship of principal executive and directors comes to full fruition, it will be because the executive possesses, to a superlative degree, the requisites of his many tasks and is able to discharge those tasks well. In the final reckoning, he must make the decision, he must act— and there can be no substitute for his individual thought and his action.

The public contacts of the chief executive are vital to the success of the enterprise he heads. An informed public is usually an appreciative one—certainly an understanding one. His general press contacts may have a marked bearing on the results which he is able to achieve—on the climate in which his company lives. He must devote himself assiduously to the task of dealing with this important aspect of his work. The policies which he is able to effect will be implemented by action on the part of members of the staff. This is the natural development of the work of the executive. Yet the primary contacts—

and in some cases continuing ones—must of necessity be his, and there are certain of them that cannot be delegated.

One of the principal and important relationships is that of the chief executive and his stockholders. In these days of wide public holdings the confidence of the stockholders is a paramount consideration. This means that this group must be well informed. To the degree that they are, confidence in the management of the company will be sustained. The average stockholder does not pretend to know all that needs to be known properly to evaluate the usually intricate investment situation. What he needs to have is regular and sufficient information about the larger and broader aspects of the company's operations to give him the needed sense of participation.

To the extent that he feels that the principal executive tries to maintain this great avenue of communication, he expresses a full measure of approval for the results of the administration's actions. He not only holds his shares but, from time to time, increases his holdings. He and his many counterparts thus provide a great measure of stability to the public market for the company's securities. This is healthy not only for the company but for the economy in general. The wider the holdings of the capital stock of American businesses, the stronger the whole free enterprise system becomes. This is a matter in which we all have a keen interest, and it is an eventuality devoutly to be desired.

Communication with stockholders can be had in many ways. The usual press releases are one vital medium. The average stockholder watches from month to month reports emanating from the corporation with respect to earnings, dividends, and possible changes in corporate structure. Everything affecting his holdings interests him. Additionally, the leaflet accompanying the quarterly dividend check has the merit of bringing an interim report of some substance—covering as it does the longer period of the current year's operations to date.

Valuable as these media are, there is none to compare with the comprehensive annual report, issued soon after the end of the fiscal year. Readable, informative, and interesting reports bring to the stockholder the whole vista of the company's activities and financial position and progress. In the annual report the principal executive has an opportunity to talk directly to the stockholders. The intimacy of this contact, properly fostered, should produce the finest of results. The stockholder is brought close to the family and feels a part of it. He reads the executive's message with interest and satisfaction as being an important word from the head of an organization in which he is part owner.

One of the most important of the other external contacts of the chief executive is that with the security analysts. Particularly, in the utility industry is this true. These analysts are well informed and highly interested in a company's financial standing and prospects. They frequently consult the executive to ascertain new trends or confirm older impressions. They write intelligently and do much to create a climate favorable to the company—where it is deserved. To keep them informed, therefore, is to assist the company, for the major function of these analysts is to carry to the clients of their firms the most accurate word possible about the company being studied. No more important or influential group exists with respect to the public appreciation of a company's prospects or its securities. Far from ignoring them, it is one of the principal executive's major responsibilities to cultivate them. The analysts are accustomed to talking to the executive about these matters, and the latter has no more important work that he can do. Through them a tremendous public will be reached. Most important of all, however, is sympathetic understanding of the company's present position and prospects.

How then does the principal executive do all of these things, attend to a multitude of other duties not mentioned, make the numerous required public appearances? By creating and using a good management team. Every organization is different and certainly reflects the personalities of the people working in it. Therefore, there is no magical or standard form of top organization. The management team will have to be selected to meet the problems of the particular company in the way which the chief executive believes in the best. In my own situation, in a company which has enjoyed tremendous growth of late, I have been assembling a management team based upon what I think our needs are and are likely to be. This process goes on steadily, and we do not hesitate to study our needs—present and prospective—and to round out the organization accordingly. This is no standard plan of operation; it is tailored to fit our own needs.

Starting with the nucleus of devoted and experienced executives at the top who have served the company for many years, additions have been made to fill positions which we have come to consider as vital and necessary. Progress and success have brought us new problems. We need new hands to help us get the chores done. We are trying not to make the mistake of spreading ourselves too thin and thus do important tasks poorly or not at all. We are trying to do today's work today, thus avoiding the heavy costs of procrastination. Inertia, stemming from the overloading of even the best personnel, is a terrific problem to cope with. When inertia lapses into failure to act with reasonable promptness—or even failure to act at all— the cost in performance and money can be quite heavy. It is our plan to have no part of this.

The principal executive must study the needs of, then create the new posts in the organization. Selection of competent people follows, and this is, perhaps, the key to the whole process. Good men of top management calibre are not easy to find. It is difficult for some executives to recognize good men when they appear.

What do we expect of the people who are a part of our top management team? First, *we want them to be experienced and capable*. Throughout our whole organization we have people of promise, and we do not hesitate to promote them to top management jobs whenever it is desirable and important that we do so. We have not hesitated to add experienced and mature people from the outside, both to do the current tasks and to train the younger men who, in a few years, will take their places. Thus we are combining maturity and experience with youth and drive to meet the present situation with all of its attendant problems. We are also training and preparing adequately for the future.

Secondly, *we seek men of decision and the courage of their convictions*. Vacillation and indecision are no part of our plan and those who fall prey to these business vices do not belong with us. Growing as fast as we are, with all of the management needs and requirements attendant on that growth, our top personnel must wade into the daily problems and meet them promptly and effectively.

Third, *we need people who can plan for the future*. No matter how effective the execution of daily tasks the entire process can be meaningless without a careful blueprint of future plans and prospects. Here, long range vision is required and the members of the top management team must possess it to a superlative degree. To be able to plan for the future in the midst of vigorous current activity is a vital prerequisite for those who aspire to, and are selected to fill, posts in top management.

Fourth, *we need people who have a great sense of their economic environment*. The business enterprise of which they are a part will not long escape the vicissitudes of recessions and business slowdowns. Therefore, a full awareness of the economic factors—special and general—which affect the industry, the company, and the country, will certainly serve them well for the important decisions which must be made. Important decisions cannot be made in an economic vacuum. Success and progress do not stem from ignorance. Aloofness to the implications of the constantly changing economic scene certainly is to be avoided. Study, reasoning, thought, based upon data secured from the best information sources, are needed and needed badly. The ability to think and the energy to secure the information which makes the thought processes valuable are what we look for and, we think, find. No long-range planning will be valuable if the full implications of the trends are not noted and considered. Independent judgment and opinion here are of inestimable value and may point the way to the success of the whole enterprise. Certainly, lasting success or effective progress cannot be made by people who are literally unaware of the economic forces all about them which shape their destinies. Perhaps, in some cases, the end result cannot be changed. Prior knowledge, however, of what the end might be, may help to avoid the rigors at the conclusion. In other cases, intelligent and careful appraisal of the current situation with the portents of the future may reap direct and important benefits. The rewards are certainly worth the effort. This is another example where the race is truly to the swift— and, I might add, to the industrious and the astute.

Fifth, *we need men who are able to work as a team.* The brilliant man with the impossible disposition has no place on our team. Part of a man's success—and a great part of it—lies in selling his ideas to his associates. Close working relationships call for good interpersonal relations in the top management team. Listening ofttimes proves to be as great a virtue as speaking. Cohesion among top management personnel is a must—and cohesion is not possible without harmony. Where this obtains, individual talents are magnified and the resulting total is far greater than the mere sum of the parts.

What is the principal executive's responsibility to the management team? Leadership, of course; but, above all, sufficient contact to afford to every member of the team a great sense of belonging. The reward for this effort is to bring intense and proper loyalty and a keen desire to be about the work of the company. Communication plays a vital part in this endeavor, and, here, oral communication is as important as written. While time plays against too frequent direct contacts, yet a short visit by the president to the office of one of his associates is a wonderful way to build morale. Sending for an associate may, at times, be necessary or even desirable, but there is no substitute for the occasional, impromptu visit by the "Boss" to the office of a member of the team. The interchange of opinion and ideas among the executive and the management team is of the utmost importance. No lasting virility can result from the work and ideas of the staff if they are not seasoned by the judgment of the principal executive. Nor can the staff function well without the opportunity to have sketched for them the broad outlines of policy. The team works for and with the executive, and the most effective arrangement is one which brings the two together on as many occasions as possible. We have, as part of this working relationship in our company, no chasms to bridge. We try to walk the continually solid land of close contact and excellent communication. There can be no measurable progress without achieving a status such as this.

The principal executive is limited in what he can do directly and personally. There are many important things which he must do himself and which limit his time for other things. Therefore, he accomplishes what he needs to get done through the people with whom he surrounds himself. He transmits his ideas and policies to them for implementation and execution. He appraises the suggestions which they make and gives the counsel which they need. He keeps the lines of communication open—on a two-way basis.

To summarize the reactions of a principal executive to the

internal affairs of his own company, let me say that I find it:
—great—with a high degree of exhilaration;
—strenuous—with the fatigue factors which accompany high endeavor;
—interesting—with the challenge which stems from solving difficult problems;
—rewarding—for the accomplishments;
—absorbing—above all a challenge every working hour of every day; and, finally,
—fun—in our shop we have learned how to enjoy ourselves while making prodigious efforts to advance the company's best interests.

But what of the principal executive's broader economic and social responsibilities—his duties as a citizen in these uncertain days through which we are passing? It is true that his major and particular interest must always be that of the company whose affairs are under his direction. Can he, however, remain aloof from the political, economic, and social forces which provide the setting in which his company must do its business? I think not, and for these reasons:

1. I said earlier that no corporation can operate in an economic vacuum. To be informed is to be intelligent, and such intelligence provides the basis for making a constructive contribution to the industry as a whole. Decisions made in the great corporations of the country have a way of affecting large segments of the economy. The executive who makes the decisions cannot be unmindful of this fact. For example, our decision to proceed in 1958 with the greatest construction budget of our history was based upon two things: (a) the need for the facilities in our growing company, and (b) the salutary effect of such expenditures upon general business at a time when bold and proper action is certainly to be desired. Our plans to continue our construction in the next five years at an accelerated rate are based equally upon these two important

factors. It is our firm belief that we cannot make the major decisions which are vital to our company's welfare without considering fully our place in the nation's economy and the responsibilities which grow out of this position.

2. Much of the length and severity of the present business slow-down are based upon the unwillingness of the public to buy. In my opinion, the public feels too often that its interests have not been considered sufficiently in style, quality, price, and immediate availability. To the extent that this is true, the whole economy suffers. The great statesmanship of American business must assert itself strongly to eliminate the causes of buyer resistance. To do so will quickly provide the needed impetus to the upsurge which has already begun to manifest itself.

3. The social effects of unemployment are great—and can be exceedingly dire. No responsible executive can remain untroubled when any large segment of our population cannot find employment in work which it would like to be doing—and is qualified to perform. The principal executive, in weighing the profit considerations of lay-offs where they may seem desirable, must consider equally the broader social effects of the unemployment which will result. While the latter consideration may not be compelling in every case, it is a factor never to be ignored in any such major decision. While profit management strives to secure for the corporation the maximum of net return properly to be secured—nevertheless it does not overlook the fact that American business management has a deep social consciousness. The striving for profit, under the free enterprise system, is thus leavened by thoughtful appraisal of every act and decision in the light of their implications for the economy generally.

4. The more important an executive, the greater is his responsibility to be informed on, and alert to, the political acts and considerations currently affecting American business. It is

equally important that, in concert with other corporation executives, he take definitive action where it seems indicated. Who among us can afford to be insensible to the problems of the railroads? Can the economy long prosper if this great industry remains in the doldrums? Have we thought out the best form that help and assistance might take in aiding the railroads? Are we prepared to assist in securing that aid? And what of the copper and metals industries? Do we believe they should receive protective foreign aid? Or do we believe in government stockpiling and support of prices within desirable ranges? What of the lumber industry? The aluminum industry? There are many more, but these highlight the problem. My main point, here, is that the principal executive must have informed judgment in these matters, and he must be willing to take definitive action—as a citizen and an important one—whenever that action is required.

To be a principal executive is to have a great sensitivity to the country's problems and the country's welfare. It is to have the desire to do something about these matters and not merely sit back and complain of the results from the prodigious efforts of others. Certainly an awareness of the problems of every segment of our economy is part of the successful executive's makeup. He does not individually need to have all the answers, but certainly he should be able to identify the problems so that he may discover in what direction lie the sources of information upon which intelligent judgment is predicated.

Free enterprise brings a multitude of opportunities. It also brings equally great responsibilities. To be a principal executive is to maintain equilibrium between grasped opportunities and fully met responsibilities. This is the challenge and the reward. To me it is a matter of daily satisfaction.

WHAT A COMPANY PRESIDENT
SHOULD BE
by Allen Van Wyck

FOR SIXTEEN YEARS I have been a company president, and I am going to tell you some of the things that I think my job ought to be. I learned one thing early in the game—not to be afraid. You have a 50-50 chance of being right on a decision even though you flip a coin. If you do a little thinking your average ought to be better, but there is always that 50-50 chance. Nobody is going to be 100 percent right—you will make some mistakes and there is no advantage gained in worrying about them.

I think the chief job of the head of any company is leadership. He must know about company operations in order to make decisions when required and to be able to give advice. But he should always stay clear of the details so that he is free to meet emergencies whenever they crop up.

The president should be able to sit down with senior supervisors of his organization and discuss problems that are of major importance to them; not to solve their problems for them, but to let them talk it through with someone who can make suggestions to help them solve their problems for themselves. Everybody needs someone with whom he can discuss difficulties which he can not possibly discuss with his subordinates or his peers. This is one of the toughest problems of the

Address presented at the Fifth Utility Management Workshop, August, 1956. Mr. Van Wyck is President of the Illinois Power Company.

top executive himself. Many times there is no one to whom he can talk and it can be terribly lonesome. I have alleviated that difficulty for myself by getting several people on the board of directors with whom I could frankly discuss fundamental policies of the company.

But, in order to free himself for such activities, a president must delegate to others. By delegation I do not mean abdication. When I turn work over to a subordinate I expect him to do the job without running back constantly for advice or directions. I give him authority to do the job and stand behind him, but I keep an eye on the job so that if something goes seriously wrong and is going to do real damage to the company I can step in and call a halt. In delegating work to others, one of the hardest things to learn is to let a man do a job in his own way. One's tendency is to think that one's own way is best, but, providing the end result is satisfactory, a subordinate's own way of doing any job is the best way for him. I, personally, have stopped carrying pens and pencils in my pockets. I found that I was automatically reaching for a pencil before I had even read a letter someone brought me for my approval. I do not do that any more. Perhaps the letter is not worded just the way I would have had it, but if it is an adequate job, I let it go. When it becomes necessary to correct a subordinate, handle the matter in such a way that you will not scare him out of taking a chance another time.

A big part of that job of delegation is coordination. You have to give work out in pieces and your company is divided up into sections. Those sections have to work together. At one time, in my company, we had two departments which simply would not work together. Finally I had to replace the men who headed them, even though they were men who, in their own minds, had the utmost loyalty to the company. They had done wonderful jobs for the company in many ways, but they would not play on the team. These men were unable to understand that, although I had delegated to them the job of running particular departments, they had to do so within the framework of the fundamental policy set down by me and the board.

A president should find time to do a little dreaming, planning for the future, particularly in the matter of developing people who will be able to take over the jobs when the present top management leaves the scene. This is a matter to which I have given much thought. We have had industrial psychologists in to interview people; they are supposed to be able to help you make the best possible selection by discovering a man's good and bad traits. In my opinion, this means nothing. Sometimes it seems that a man's bad traits are what make him good in a particular job. Mistakes in judgment are easy to make when promoting people and, while it seems a hard thing to take a man out of a job to which you have just promoted him, it is no kindness to keep him on a job he is unable to handle. I think that management has a very serious responsibility to the people they promote, and mistakes should be corrected and corrected promptly.

What I want in a subordinate supervisor is the will to do the job; someone willing to take a chance and take responsibility. Too many young people nowadays have the "40-hour week" attitude; I think this indicates a lack of interest on the job. They would not be able to keep track of time so well if they were really engrossed in what they were doing. Lack of ability to express themselves is another problem with young people today. It seems that they cannot spell, or write, or express themselves in any way. This is a problem not only with graduates from the public high schools but also with the engineers we get from colleges. Ask them to write a memorandum and they cannot do it. They may know their job, but it is not much help if they cannot tell me, or their subordinates, or any of their associates what they are doing.

As to engineers, I think this shortage everyone is worrying

about would not be so bad if engineers were used for engineering. In our company we have forbidden our engineers to do any computation work or drafting. That sort of work can be handled just as competently by less highly trained personnel. If other companies would follow the same practise I think it would alleviate the problem to some extent.

I think a company's president should restrict himself, too. Public relations are an important feature of a president's job, but if you must neglect either management of the company or public relations then, I say, neglect public relations. If the affairs of a company are well directed, public relations will follow to a great extent. A president who tries to handle both usually accomplishes neither.

Concern for what people will think can lead to errors in judgment. Decisions should be based on the facts and can be made to benefit the company regardless of immediate bad reactions and the momentarily ruffled feelings of others.

The one thing I try to bear in mind, and that I urge you to remember, is this—do something! If you do something, you have that 50-50 chance of being right. If you do nothing you are sure to be wrong.

EVERYBODY IS A MANAGER
by Erwin H. Schell

MANAGEMENT has been defined as the judicious use of means to accomplish an end. That is a very broad definition. It has been argued that there is no formalized judicial function in industry; that we have the executive and the legislative, but not the judicial. This definition would infer the contrary. Every executive is in some measure a judge—he must decide.

Sometimes one finds oneself moving toward management by sheer assertion. I asked a colonel how he went about picking squad leaders. He told me that at his last assignment there was, in the middle of the parade ground, a big stone—so big that it took three or four men to move it. Whenever he needed a new squad leader he would select five or six soldiers and instruct them to move the stone forty feet due north and fifteen feet west. Then he would retire to his office, take a pair of binoculars, and watch. Within ten minutes there would be one fellow directing the others while the rest of them pushed the stone. He was the new squad leader.

Whenever there is effort consciously directed toward the attainment of a goal, there is management. Management appears in the behavior of animals and birds. A great flock of geese, as is well-known to ornithologists, makes regular migrations north and south. The day on which these geese leave one place for another is in some fashion established. They

Address presented at the Sixth Utility Management Workshop, July, 1957.
Dr. Schell is Professor Emeritus and Lecturer in Industrial Management, Massachusetts Institute of Technology.

land in certain very safe areas where hunters cannot easily get at them. But the one who interests us here is the leader. He decides where they go and when they go—he is watching out for his 17,000 charges. That is management.

Management is concerned with occasions. An occasion is something that rises in prominence, assumes temporary importance, reaches an apex, and then wanes and ends. A beginning—a rising—a decline—and an ending. Life is filled with these occasions. In endings are beginnings found. Management's problem is to capitalize upon them. Management makes use of the changing world about us. The best illustration I know is that of the surfboard riders—they do not try to change the wave; their interest is in riding it, in capitalizing on it. It moves very rapidly from time to time and is constantly dealing with transitions. It is a business of dynamics, of velocity and accelerations and decelerations.

Management is inherently related to time and timeliness. There are times when good management means delay. Queen Elizabeth I was said to have been the first great ruler to use delay effectively.

While it is possible that management applied to organization actually creates new dynamics, we yet find it convenient to view management mainly as being involved with the direction of the forces already at hand and in operation. I suppose the part of the country in which we live would change our emphasis. If we were on the west coast, or better yet, on the northwest coast where many new industries have recently been started, we should be more interested in the management of an evolving business, a new business handling a new situation, new markets, new facilities, new labor situations; whereas in older parts of the country we might appropriately be concerned with running those companies which are already established. At this point we must not forget that many, if not all, of the great industries in the United States will be continuing after all the men now in these businesses are dead. One of management's great problems is to assure the future by insuring the quality of future management.

Managements assume different colors. We remember the kaleidoscope—how each time we looked into it there were different patterns with no two ever the same. Management is like that; the patterns are constantly changing. There may not be anything fundamentally new, but the emphasis is new.

THE MANAGEMENT CYCLE

There is a round of activities found in management. This round proceeds in a sequence of activities which have now been generally accepted as normal. Of course, everyone has his own interpretation. He puts this in his own particular way. Here is mine.

The Determination of Objectives. This is one of the first tasks of all managers. What we want to find out is what we are up to. We may say, "Everybody knows what we are trying to do. We are trying to make money. We are trying to make a profit." My answer is that if there is anyone here whose company has not solved the problem of making a profit he had better go home and spend some time getting that straightened out. Then he can come back and talk about the really fundamental questions relating to the insurance of profits over the long term.

Objectives vary radically. I know of a concern which had for many years the requirement that it should not grow. If it developed anything which demanded growth, this was sold to another company. But between this extreme and the normal situation, there is a great range. I have made studies for more than one client to find out why they were successful. Why were they doing so well? There usually were completely erroneous ideas extant as to why the company was prosperous.

The Gathering of Information. After the determination of

objectives comes the gathering of information. Of what may we be sure? What are the facts? Frequently something will stand out that is indisputable, like a rock in the path of a brook.

May I illustrate. We lived in a double house many years ago when our neighbor's small boy—now a physician of note—was about four or five years old. His nurse was busy preparing him for bed one night when the telephone rang and she went to answer it. When she came back he said, "Nurse, I've discovered a law." Thinking that was pretty good for a four-year-old, the nurse said, "What is it, honey?" he replied, "You can't pull your pants off over your head." Well, we must admit to a certain immutability in his discovery.

Collaboration. Managers do not work alone; they are involved with other people. Let me give you an illustration of this often unrealized collaboration. We have, not too far from my home in Cambridge, a nursery school. A teacher told me that every once in a while those little tykes would just go berserk. They would raise eternal confusion—tear down pictures, pull off curtains, throw chairs around. She could find no reason for it until someone suggested that she should keep track of the dates when these eruptions occurred and see if any correlations appeared. She found that these periods coincided with the time when the fathers of these children were preparing for examinations and the situation at home was one of "Don't make any noise—your father's studying." So when the children got to school they pulled the walls down. Now this is what I mean by collaboration. Probably not one of those fathers realized that he required the collaboration of his small boy to get his degree—but each one did.

Solution. I speak here of solution as apart from action—a distinction that has been overlooked. To decide what you ought to do is one thing. To do it is another.

Verification. Then comes the verification of our findings. We study; we come to a conclusion and make a decision; and we should, at that point, verify that all the evidence is in—that the things which will really affect all of the action and reaction are there to be considered.

The Obtaining of Sanction. This is important for a special reason; managers need backing. They need psychic, moral, and other kinds of support when they move forward to do the thing that they are supposed to do. And the time to get sanction is before the action.

The Taking of Action. Let us say we have decided upon what we are going to do. At this point we lay aside our theorizing, our uncertainties, and our concerns; we go ahead and act. It is no secret that a poor plan well administered is better than a good plan poorly administered.

Evaluation. Evaluation is an aspect of management which has recently been receiving special attention—the responsibility for review, inspection, or feedback.

This managerial cycle has the widest of applications. For example, let us apply it to the lighting of a cigarette. There comes over us a feeling that we must have a smoke. The question presents itself: "Shall I smoke or shan't I?" And something says: "Yes." We now have an *objective*—to smoke a cigarette. Next we go through all our pockets in search of facilities (*assembly of the facts*). Then we come to the matter of amenities, of *sanction*. So we ask: "Do you mind if I smoke?" Then comes the ceremony of *action*, and finally, *inspection* and *review*. There is the cycle! We apply it constantly to all sorts of situations where we find forces which call for management.

ACCELERATIVE CHANGE

May I now mention an aspect of our present environment which is strongly affecting management. Change today is taking place much more rapidly than ever before. Someone recently said that if we take the life of the human race as twenty-four hours, there have been greater changes in the last five or ten seconds than in all the preceding periods. And these changes are revealing the necessity for new attitudes. We must learn to manage in a climate of rapid change—to live in a dynamic situation. Constructive change has become our insurance for security and continuity.

THE MANAGEMENT OF OTHERS

It was the philosopher Hegel who coined the phrase "to sink oneself in one's object." This is the first goal of management as it approaches the problem of group objective with its sacrifice of self-interest to the good of the whole.

Providing information for the group is difficult because the kind of data managers and groups need is varied and often hard to obtain. For example, one such body of data may be termed the *competitive unknowns*. In manufacturing, a manager cannot know precisely what a competitor is going to offer. Another has to do with moving data which change as they are being examined. Group collaboration calls upon the use of the artistries of management—namely, so to integrate the self-interests of people with corporate goals that they are also satisfied with the objectives of the corporation.

A problem for group solution and verification that seems to be cropping up everywhere is the prediction of human behavior. In the market, the shop, and the community, management is asking, "How will the customer, the employee, the neighborhood respond to contemplated changes." Group action with morale need not always infer unanimity. We may have morale in an organization even though complete agreement is not present. Group review and evaluation are important, not only objectively but also subjectively. Managers should give public credit to accomplishments of employees if they are to obtain highest motivation.

CONCLUSION

Management in the past has worked through various zones of influence. For a long time management was equated with ownership. The person who owned the company, or the person who provided the money, had the control. This situation has tended to disappear, and management has assumed a more professional status.

Again, the problem of management is a dual one. Management is a compound word. We have the manager and the managed. We have to consider what kind of people we are managing.

Finally, we have learned that in our home life too, we must be managers. We have become entailed in community functions of one kind or another, clubs and associations and other responsibilities to be shouldered. In other words, management is now being recognized as part of almost all aspects of our activities. This is one of the most extraordinary developments that has taken place in our time.

Suddenly it has become evident that management is a widely pervasive form of social activity—a kind of doing that is in no way the prerequisite of any single class; that management is an inherent ingredient in the lives of every one of us.

Part Two

THE JOB OF ANY MANAGER

INTRODUCTION

EVERY MANAGER, at every level of every organization, is responsible for the discharge of certain functions. This is a universal process and varies only in degree of responsibility and complexity from level to level. However, these differences in degree mark the boundaries set on the progress of individuals through the managerial hierarchy. Each of us has definite limitations—physical, mental, or emotional—which determine the maximum progress he can make in a given organizational situation. It is possible to define five rather clear and definite categories of tasks in a typical association, based on responsibilities involved in descending order of magnitude; they are:

1. Coordination of policy, setting over-all goals, assigning major responsibilities.
2. Planning general accomplishment within policy limitations, assigning specific responsibilities, designing and coordinating processes to accomplish goals.
3. Planning and coordinating specific accomplishments, designing the jobs.
4. Coordinating and directing the activities of others in accomplishing specified tasks.
5. Doing the actual work, as assigned.

Having classified the assignments in this way, we can designate the first four as manager-type assignments of different degrees of difficulty and responsibility. In many actual situations, size of the organization alone dictates the establishment of one or two additional levels, usually as parts of the second category, so that we might set up a "pyramid of power and performance," headed by a single person (the principal executive) and leading down to the nonsupervisory workers. This pyramid, with typical numbers of personnel found at each level, is shown in Figure 1.

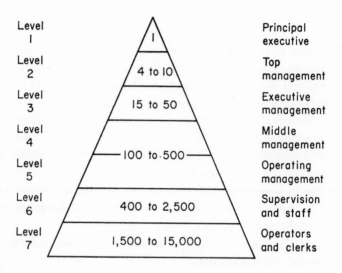

Figure 1. The Pyramid of Power and Performance

One of management's great concerns today is to find competent people to fill the vacancies occurring at all managerial levels. As already mentioned, there are limiting factors in the personalities of all people; many lack the education to solve the problems encountered; others lack experience; some have limited mental capacity or physical stamina; still others are emotionally incapable of assuming responsibilities.

Technical competence alone is not enough for a higher management job today. We must turn highly qualified specialists into generalists if we are to have competent control of the increasingly complex and diversified organizations we have built up. To technical knowledge must be added courage and self-confidence in dealing with finances, labor relations, governmental controls, and closely interlocking effects of economic changes in other industries and other countries. Today's manager must take the risk of making mistakes and getting into trouble—often not of his own making. He must be able to extricate himself and his organization from tight spots and, to an increasing extent, he must be able to operate his own unit at a profit, regardless of how well or poorly other branches of the organization are doing. Is it surprising that the job of any manager is a complex set of functions and responsibilities which can be carried only by well-qualified people?

THE PAPERS

Part Two contains six papers selected from those prepared for Utility Management Workshops for the years 1956 through 1959. In his first presentation Dr. Livingston explores the technologies which a manager applies in getting his job done. These include the identification of people who are capable of progressing as managers and the development of their capabilities for still further progress. He then considers the problems of internal management in terms of planning for the future, largely in terms of personnel requirements.

Kendrick Porter also analyzes the techniques available to the manager, but in terms of the requirements of business progress. He advocates a "unified management system" which includes, as components, planning, execution, and feedback and discusses each component at some length. Perrin Stryker discusses the survey of the executive job undertaken by *Fortune* magazine. He stresses the lack of uniformity both in the public images and the self-images disclosed in the survey and then goes on to point out that the chief characteristic of an executive is that he performs a variety of functions in combination.

Felix Wormser confines himself to the problems encountered by the manager in dealing with the federal government, but let no one misjudge the seriousness and complexity of this deceptively simple limitation! From inside the government as well as outside, the author has seen the difficulties and frustrations of these contacts and he cites case after case in illustrating his points. William W. Waite covers a number of the principal managerial tools, most of which involve, ultimately, reliance on subordinates to get the job done. This, in turn, requires delegation of responsibility (with concurrent authority) in large amounts to men who must be encouraged, corrected, trained, and developed to the point of being able to discharge their delegated responsibilities satisfactorily and, eventually, to take on the added burdens of higher-level positions.

Livingston's paper on functions discusses at length the four functions of the association:

1. Dealing with outside contacts
2. Internal management
3. Production
4. Planning for the future

He points out the manager's responsibilities for each of these tasks and shows that they exist at all levels.

MANAGERIAL TECHNIQUES

by Robert Teviot Livingston

IT HAS BEEN SUGGESTED by Fritz Roethlisberger at Harvard that a manager can be looked at conveniently from three different viewpoints:

1. The *role* he plays as a manager
2. The *skills* he employs in his human relations
3. The *technologies* he uses

This is interestingly true, but we are concerned with appropriate managerial behavior and, to understand the role a manager is playing, or to know how to play a role successfully, it is necessary to know what the expected role is and to recognize the particulars of the situation in order not only to select the best role, but to know how to play it. Here we shall concern ourselves with the question of internal management. Because a part of internal management is concerned with the specific actions of the manager, the principal concern of this section will be the problem of continuation of reproduction of the unit—in a word, on selection, training, and development.

Everybody in a managerial position is simultaneously acting in at least two quite different work groups: his own group, for whose production he is responsible, and a group of peers who are all responsible to someone else above—the boss. The manager's position and behavior in these two groups is, of course, different, but in both he plays one identical role—the role of a

Mr. Livingston is Professor of Industrial Engineering, Columbia University, and Director of the Utility Management Workshop.

responsible manager. As such he acts as a representative and a filter.

Let me present a brief summary of managerial technologies. Just as the journeyman artisan has a kit of tools which he carries to every job, so too does the manager; that set of tools we call managerial technologies. Tools are fairly standardized. Although they may differ slightly in detail, each is designed to do a specific range of jobs. For some kinds of jobs there may be several different tools available, and the tool selected will depend upon the worker himself. So, too, with the manager. He will select the tool with which he thinks the job at hand can be done most easily or most satisfactorily.

The skilled worker usually has a helper, and one of the jobs expected of him is to train the helper in the skills necessary for the jobs which will later be expected of him. After instructing him, he lets the helper do certain jobs and, in permitting that, he does two things: he lets him make mistakes, but he also watches carefully so that the mistakes made are not irrevocable and will not spoil the whole job. It is much the same with the manager; he too has the job of training his subordinates. He lends his tools, but he expects the subordinate to develop his own skills and abilities. These will perhaps not be identical with the ones his mentor practices, but it is expected that the result will be much as if the manager had done the job himself.

I shall not detail here all the managerial technologies which are available. A broad, convenient classification would be: operating technologies, engineering technologies, personnel technologies, and advisory technologies; and it is suggested— merely suggested—that the proportion of any one item which can be delegated decreases as one goes down the list. Thus, once the manager has made some definite decision, most day-to-day operations can be carried on by subordinates as long as the control feedback is good. However, as is well known, no matter how much the manager may delegate, he cannot escape from his managerial responsibilities.

A manager assumes responsibility for the accomplishment of a job or a function and, the higher up the manager, the less it is a specific job and the more it is a function. This function will change in time, with circumstances, and with the development of the technology. One of the most important, though seldom continuously thought of, duties of the manager is to maintain an organization of competent people—competent to carry on whether he is there or not and, indeed, to replace him. This requires selection, training, and development.

Selection. The first step is selection. This is a process which may appear to be quite formal; yet it is, to some extent, always a personal matter. It becomes more so the further one moves up the executive ladder. Selection, while not a guarantee of promotion, is, in a certain sense, difficult to revoke. Prior to selection, placement, confirmation, and promotion there is appraisal. Also, there is a constant appraisal of accomplishment. However, in the end a man is selected for promotion because of someone's faith in his potentialities.

Selection is a process which is going on continually. How do we select, not for this particular job, but for any job? What mechanisms do we have for making judgments? How do we make them? What are the factors involved and what happens after we do these various things?

Evaluation. Just as selection is going on all the time, so too evaluation is performed consciously or unconsciously when anybody is to be selected. Also, in a large part of our lives we evaluate people, not just the new people we meet, but the people we know well. We often make estimates of what their behavior will be under certain anticipated circumstances. This involves an evaluation of the person.

In practice there are five formal ways which we use to make evaluations beyond the informal and usually involuntary procedure through which we go all the time: performance, personnel record, reputation, interview, tests.

Performance. Generally speaking, a person is judged for a new job or situation, at least in part, by his performance on his present job. This is valid only so far as it is possible to get an unbiased report on his accomplishment, and when performance in job *A* is an indicator of probable performance in job *B*. This method is perfectly natural and will always be used, even though performance of a man/job system depends upon the man, the job, the interaction, the situation, and the occasion.

The first three of these are quite obvious. "Situation" is intended to include all surrounding factors such as the physical environment, the other people who are associated (especially the superior), the climate of the job in respect to the company and to society as a whole, and all the intangibles including the individual's life outside the job. "Occasion" is intended to take cognizance of the fact that immediacy and urgency are important factors in the doing of a job. The behavior of an individual in an emergency, if very good, will be highly rated. If he falls down, he may be excused because of the emergency. On the other hand, in routine day-to-day going, better than average performance does not seem to get immediate recognition although, in evaluation, it may be recalled in a rather neutral manner.

Personnel Record. The personnel record is of most use as a means of identification and as a record of *what* a person has done, although it seldom tells how well he has done it.

Reputation. Everybody, every day, with every person whom he encounters, makes judgments. He assays other persons, judges his purposes from actions, and governs his own actions accordingly. The manager judges his subordinates. He also, incidentally, judges his peers and his superiors. There are six kinds of evaluations of reputations which should be recognized:

those made by superiors

those made by peers

those made by subordinates

those made by the individual himself

those made by society

those made by technicians and specialists in the field

The following may be helpful: What is the relation of the evaluation to the person evaluating? What is the competence, knowledge, and training of the person making the evaluation? What kind of a person is the person making the evaluation, and what kind of role is he most apt to assume while he is making the evaluation? Finally, it would be a good idea if we knew what side of the bed the evaluator got out of on that particular morning.

Interviews. One of the common methods by which we make judgments of people is upon the basis of what they say. This has both a short-time as well as a long-time aspect. Here is where we (a) fasten stereotypes on people, and (b) isolate them in certain areas.

Tests. Three types of measures can generally be obtained about an individual. A measure can be established from his present characteristics, such as weight and height, reading comprehension and speed, or ability to do arithmetic. Past performance can also be measured. Finally, his future potentialities can be assessed. In this latter respect, measures related to potential success on the job are estimated. Various techniques are employed for obtaining these measures. The psychological tests are perhaps the most common devices. Such tests are really paper-and-pencil measures of aptitudes, interests, and attitudes. Performance tests are also employed. Another technique is the clinical appraisal. This is generally a series of organized reflections given by skilled technicians. Lastly, there is the personal judgment which is a rating given by one's subordinates, peers, superiors, and even oneself.

Training. This is usually thought of as a mass transfer of information and skill, or is concerned with developing skills in the performance of specified tasks. It is much more than this. Every job requires some specific training, for, if nothing else, one has to "learn the ropes." Besides training for a specific job, there can be training in useful skills such as reading, reasoning, thinking, and behavior toward others. Training is useful for correcting faults, for expanding abilities, and for broadening concepts. It is definitely a company responsibility, and it is rightfully the expectation of every employee at every level. But higher up in the company it becomes more a personal responsibility of the superior.

In every company, no matter what the industry or how it is organized, there is a job of training to be done. It is thought of as a fourfold process of (1) introduction; (2) instruction; (3) training; (4) information—job relative location, purpose and reason for job. This process occurs at every level, whether recognized or not. Training is also required for every job transfer, whether across or upward.

Almost anybody, if he is willing to invest the time, trouble, forethought, planning and expense, can be trained to perform any desired act or acts leading to an expected performance upon receipt of the designed stimulus. A person can be trained if he has available the means and necessary competencies, and if the proper stimulus is applied.

The Fundamentals of Learning Applied to Training. It has been generally accepted that a manager requires four skills: personal skills, technological skills, human relations skills, conceptual skills. There is no doubt that the relative importance of these varies with the position in the hierarchy as well as the kind of business. There is also a difference in our ability to transmit information about them and to learn them. The important points are: *interest* in, *knowledge* of, *ability* to transform knowledge into *skill,* and finally, to *use.* The points to be explored here are:

1. What are the differences in the kinds of things to be trained in at different levels? This involves a consideration of how the jobs at the different levels really differ.

2. How much can pretraining be used (that is to say, training without real relation to the job), and how much must be done after the transfer or promotion?

To question the importance of skill is unrealistic. However, it is not improper to question whether the possession of skill is enough. Another way to look at it is to say that there is (a) a certain minimum acceptable level of performance, and (b) a facility. There is probably a complicated structure involved in the second, for example, facility in reading speed, comprehension, retention, and understanding. There are doubtless some other things involved, such as ease of recall and personalization (that is to say, is the material read absorbed into self or does it remain a quotation).

In designing and operating a training program, a comprehension of what training can do and what must come before training is important. Actually, training is basically directed toward developing whatever level of skills is deemed necessary.

The mere possession of skill is not enough. There must be the desire to use it and respect for the purpose of the association. This requires appreciation, comprehension, and understanding, as well as knowledge. Knowledge is recognition and identification. Appreciation is forming an estimate of the worth or meaning of that which is known. Comprehension includes not only the inherent appreciation, but also the relations between the thing understood and other things which are in some ways related to it. We may summarize as follows:

perception $\longrightarrow$ recognition and identification

recognition and identification $\longrightarrow$ knowledge

knowledge and aptitude $\longrightarrow$ capability

capability when limited $\longrightarrow$ ability

ability when used ────────────────────────→skill
skill when used ────────────────────────→ experience
skill and aptitude ──────────────────────→ cleverness

While training is important, it is only a means to an end. It is performance in which we are really interested, and in the prediction of performance. In the case of a machine this involves:

a knowledge of all the component parts
a knowledge of their interrelation
a differentiation as to direction of action
a differentiation as to internal and external
an understanding of the pertinent external forces

With a machine it is possible to predict results. With an individual, it is more difficult. We can recognize three determinants of performance:

1. competence or ability: capacity to use something specific
   skill: having practical ability
   cleverness: capacity to do and also to select
2. attitude, willingness to try
3. motivation, drive to do

Development. Development is always for the future. It is impossible to develop a man; he must develop himself. But it is the responsibility of the company to provide the opportunity and stimulus so that management will reproduce itself. People are seldom taught anything but simple responses to obvious situations, and learning must be self-motivated to be effective. Today management development programs, both inside and outside the company, are very common. What do they try to do, and is it the wise thing to do? How effective are they and what do they cost?

A development program may be thought of in four categories:

correction

strengthening: adding to assets, decreasing liabilities

expansion: depth, width

management: internal, external

This classification is made on the assumption that there is also a training aspect to every job at the point where a person is promoted and assigned to a new responsibility.

As far as the manager is concerned, while he is characterized as someone who "gets things done through people," that is only part of his task. He has to establish what things are to be done, and this requires "conceptual skill." Human relations skills are required to get the people to do the things which have been decided through the use of conceptual skills. Behind each skill is the need for ability. There are three obvious activities behind conceptual skill:

perception: ability to recognize a situation
and its importance

analytical ability

understanding, or comprehension

Perception of a situation leads to classification. Some people have a sense of the important and an ability to sense the unusual—to smell something wrong before it occurs or, similarly, to feel when an operation is under way that little moment when you know it is going to be all right and you can relax. Analysis means breaking down and figuring out the relative importance of the elements and their relation to one another; therefore, the word does not comprehend the whole process. The process consists of (a) analysis, (b) synthesis, and (c) invention and/or transfer. To be specific, a manager is faced with a five-step process:

to analyze a situation

to estimate the rationale

to evaluate the performance and locate
the weak links or bottlenecks

to conceptualize solutions

to synthesize the parts into the most

probably successful whole

It is to be noted that conceptual ability is only one (though a useful) step in the total process. Conceptualization without rationale is unproductive and probably dangerous.

As far as the requirements of the manager are concerned, the important abilities for him are deductive and inductive, or, more specifically, the ability to analyze and synthesize. These must be conjoined with understanding and feeling in order really to solve the manager's problems. It is important to realize that skill, no matter how great, is, in a certain sense, a technique; hence, skill alone is not enough for a truly successful manager. He must understand and feel as well as know.

SCOPE OF VARIATION IN THE JOB

The Physical Structure and the Relation of the Manager to It. In order to understand thoroughly the job of the manager, it may be useful to consider the mechanics of the situation and to note what studies have been made. Here we look at the total subject of management from the point of view of the areas, in order to suggest the kinds of problems which need to be comprehended, what is available in these fields, and what remains to be done.

Figure 1 shows eight levels:

1. The task and the man
2. The task/man combination called the man/job system
3. The combination of man/job systems which is called the associatron
4. The combination of associatrons which is the minimum association and which may be a process or a function
5. The collection of processes or functions which is called the company or association

6. The industry
7. The economy or social unit
8. The culture

These levels may be studied either horizontally or vertically. For complete understanding, both must be done. The former is somewhat related to disciplinary or subject research; the latter is the more pragmatic engineering study. To understand the

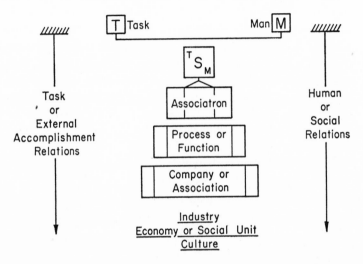

Figure 1. The Areas of Management Studies

one, the other must be kept in mind. A horizontal study is, in effect, a search for similarity amidst apparently dissimilar phenomena, and for an explanation of the dissimilarity. A vertical study would comprehend sequential relationships in some manner. We are interested primarily in the vertical study. This implies a hypothesis that man and his activities are basically always organized sequentially and to some extent in the same manner, and our interest is in the basic common inter-relationships which exist. Obviously, not all activities are identically organized and pursued, but the premise admitting this searches for those universals, even though it is realized that the accents, interest in, and apparent importance will differ.

Considering the vertical dimension, there are three courses of study which may be pursued: (1) structural relationships and goal-directed activities, (2) human relations and activities, (3) associational relations and activities.

The first may be considered the physical aspect in which the human aspect is recognized, but the basic assumption is that the human being should adjust himself or be adjusted to the organization requirements. The second is the humanistic, perhaps sentimental, aspect, where the starting point is the psychological entity which is man in all of his genius, but also all of his peculiarities. The focus here is primarily but not entirely on the individual, but if organizational life is taken into account, it is usually at the expense of the individual.

There is a central path which has not, to my knowledge, previously been organized as a study: the notion of the association as an entity which man perforce forms for his own advantage. It starts in the simple concept of an individual and a task, self-imposed or externally imposed. The hypothesis is that there is an exchange or trade of values within the individual. The path then moves down (or up) through the simple work group which has been termed the associatron (a supervisor plus four subordinates), through the process or function which may be basically considered a continuation of (largely) homogeneous groups, to the company or association which is a collection of non-homogeneous functions.

Beyond this point are a series of less specifically organized, but well recognized concepts: the industry, the economy, the state or social unit, and, finally, the culture.

Taking this middle path, we start with a task, which we have previously defined as a set of expectations, and a man. We have discussed these and how they form a man/job system. A group of related man/job systems forms an associatron which we consider as the basic building block of human organization as it is related to both the set of physical relations and the human relations.

Some aspects of this associatron have been studied in both of the vertical areas. From our studies we have concluded that a unit of five (four "workers" and one "supervisor") may be called the complete associatron, and practically all of the interrelations which it is necessary to comprehend can be understood from studying such a group. Smaller groups have been called "unsaturated" associatrons, to indicate that with less than five members certain fundamental and basic relationships do not occur. Larger groups have not been specifically named. Studies indicate that groups of six or seven start to deteriorate or break up into subgroups.

The next step is the process or the function which is formed of any given number of relatively similar associatrons, and which has come to be called the minimum association. Here, certain new internal relationships appear. There are three "levels" of authority rather than the two indicated in the associatron. Formal internal intercommunication becomes important, and general face-to-face relationships become less common although, of course, individual face-to-face relationships remain important. It also introduces the basic problems of allocation and production analysis without the immediacy of the individual, heterogeneous groups, and conflict.

The association is the basic vertical or managerial unit. In perfect form it consists of 21 people and five associatrons, four on one level and one on a higher level. Obviously, if the work demands it there will be duplicate associatrons and the number will be larger. Typical of such associatrons are the work associatron and the top management associatron. It is interesting to note how close to the number 21 are the group who are generally considered top management.

The ultimate of complete organization is the company or the association. Here non-homogeneous processes or functions are combined and there may be both processes and associatrons. This introduces a minimum of one more level of authority, but actually in real life—because of the multiple external relations —there are two added levels, and, if the company is of any size, a staff appears.

The corporate organization is considered to consist of three levels of associatrons: top management, middle management, and operating management; but, because there is overlap both at the top and bottom of middle management, there are seven levels in the heirarchy rather than nine. It is suggested that in any but very small or very large companies seven levels can be identified. Where there are more, it is usually due to special conditions which determine an extra level.

The situation up to this point is shown in Figure 2. Here the seven levels are shown with the three categories of management indicating the overlap. Four double lines are drawn to indicate points at which there are serious problems as far as promotions are concerned. It is suggested that the manager's job is quite different above the line than it is below; different not only in kind but also in expectations, required point of view (including values), and, finally, behavior—both necessary for accomplishment and expected by others.

Beyond this point formal organization breaks down, especially in the United States. An industry may form trade associations, but not cartels as abroad. Each company or association may be considered as an example of an "institution" which is a cultural pattern, usually specified by law, and any given economic or social unit will consist of a number of examples of each of these different institutional forms. The actual social or economic unit may be identified by the particular combination of these, all of which are encompassed by the culture.

It is suggested that the role an individual plays and is ex-

pected to play at these various levels differs, and that the
problems of training and development are correspondingly different—so different that general methods of training and opportunities to develop must be considered in light not only of
the level, but also of the particular combination of physical

	N	ΣN	Number of peers	Number for whom responsible	Number above	
1. Principal executive	1	1	0	5,460	0	Top management N=21
2. Top manager	4	5	3	1,364	1	
3. Administrative manager	16	21	15	340	5	Middle management N=334
4. Middle manager	64	85	63	84	21	
5. Supervisory manager	256	341	255	20	85	
6. Foremen and group leaders	1,024	1,365	1,024	4	341	Operation N=5,376
7. Operators	4,096	5,461	4,096	0	1,365	

Figure 2. The Factors in the Corporate Organization

and human relationships which exists at the different levels.

Internal Management in Theory. From the point of view of
any individual manager there are four areas of vital interest:
the management of the particular unit for which he is responsible, the management of the department of which his unit is
a part, the total internal management of the company, and the

management of the total company in respect to its purpose. Each of these involves the manager in a different manner, and in each case he plays different roles.

One of the basic laws of evolution, whether it is a biological species or an industrial organization, is specialization and task division. In the biological entity, specialization seems to follow fairly closely the six basic biological needs. It is quite probable that the list of needs evolved from an observation of the organs and the behavior of the organism. It is not so simple with an industrial organization to set up a rational basis of task division. These biological needs have been reconsidered in the light of observed industrial organizations.

When we go down to the associatron, three basic functions can be postulated: (1) receipt and disbursement, which corresponds with "trading with the world"; (2) the production activity which identifies the associatron as an entity; and (3) the management activity, which includes both internal management and whatever forecasting a unit of this size engages in. Between these two there seems to be no particularly sound basis of task division, although any number of rational ones can be found.

A company is much more than a collection, even an integrated collection, of the facilities which are producing the product or rendering the service. It is more than the people, those who are keeping the wheels moving or those who are the managers. It is the people and the equipment, but it is the dynamic interrelationships of those people who are not only doing different things, but also different categories of the same thing. Thus, different people performing different functions and playing different roles are simultaneously competing for, and cooperating in, the use of the resources which are available to render the service, not just today but from now on. One of the most crucial problems of the manager is adjudication among his subordinates on the one hand, and making claims upon his superordinate on the other. The allocation and distribution of rewards is one of the key points in modern management.

Provision for the future is, of course, the responsibility of top management, but preparation and performance is almost entirely delegated. However, it is never delegated as a complete function, but rather is parceled out on a basis of compatibility of the skills or uniqueness such as is the case with legal services or, in some companies, research. Provision for the future may be considered both on a defensive and an offensive basis; defensive to meet situations which have arisen, offensive to prevent situations from arising. Data collecting, forecasting, planning, and general design are in one class; engineering design and construction are in another.

Service functions are of two types: routine and intermittent. Accounting, employee relations, housekeeping, transportation, and public relations may be considered as routine; auditing, preparation of financial and other reports, reorganization, and procedure studies are intermittent.

In order to understand the job of the manager and how it varies depending upon the function and the position in the hierarchy, it is useful to try to escape from the biases of the familiar and to attempt to abstract in order to consider the problem in broad general terms. If that is done and an understanding is obtained, it is often possible to understand more thoroughly the familiar in terms of the basic.

Any biological entity has a set of activities which it must perform to persist: self-defense, reproduction, learning and adapting, homeostasis, consideration, and thinking. These have been adapted from the behavioral science literature and probably represent action for which there are recognizable organs, effectors and, usually, systems.

Any association made up of human beings must, to some

extent, perform these activities. These have been categorized into: trading with the world and interaction with the world; internal management; production; forecasting; providing for the future; insurance against risk. In our society any industrial association must perform one other activity: it must produce something for which society will pay.

These functions which apply to a total association or company, also may be applied to any sub-unit of the total association and, in the end, to the individuals who comprise the sub-units. Obviously, the titles will have different connotations. Thus, "trading with the world" means every world external to the unit being considered. When we reach the ultimate unit, the individual, it means all other people but himself. Internal management usually becomes less self-conscious as the size of the unit decreases. However, it is suggested that as far as the individual manager is concerned, he must assume a conscious consideration of this problem.

But the manager is concerned with external relations as well as internal management—external to his own operation even though that means, in large part, internal to his company. The interrelation among the various functions is indicated in the following array:

	W	P	I	F
World, external problems				
Production				
Internal relations				
Forecasting, providing for future				

There is also a universal rational process which, as we shall see, applies to all acts in which human beings are involved and

is the basic internal process of the company. It is shown in the
next array:

	I	C	D	A
Information				
Consideration				
Decision				
Action				

Much of what follows in the second task of the UMW is an
expansion of this basic process applied specifically to the decision process. These two arrays may be usefully combined.
For convenience in study, it is arranged as a threefold array in
which not only the interactions between elements of the two
different vectors can be identified, but also the interactions
among elements of any given vector.

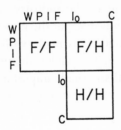

VARIATION OF THE JOB

The first two parts of this sub-task were on the general side.
At least, while you may have read and understood them and
perhaps seen how you could use them in general, to what extent
did you specifically relate them to yourself and your job? Perhaps they are not applicable to your job. If you do not think

they are, then at least you can amuse yourself by thinking about how good a job your boss does. Because development is a largely personal matter, let us look at selection and training.

Selection in the utility business is perhaps more important as a policy and process than it is in almost any other industry. This is because of the general tendency in the industry to promote from within. This makes the selection policy and process all the way down of great importance, perhaps more than we have acknowledged. After the first adjustment to public service life, the pathway to promotion is open all the way to the top. This has both good and bad aspects. Morale should be much better than it often is, not only because of relative security of employment, but also because most utility companies have excellent retirement, insurance, and other benefits. However, one bad point is that the choice available when making a selection is definitely limited. There is not much cross-transfer at lower levels; we say that is because of the highly technological characteristics of the industry. This is one of the reasons why courses to turn specialists of relatively high status into generalists are so important to the industry. Whatever the reasons, when one promotion is made at the upper levels, a whole series of lower-level promotions is made with relatively few people from whom to choose. This makes the problem of training and development more than usually important, and it often is necessary to train and develop *after* promotion. Let us here consider two points:

1. How do you select to fill an opening in your group?

2. What are you doing to increase the probability of your being selected for promotion *from* your present job?

How Do You Select Subordinates? Let us assume there is a vacancy in the next level below you. What do you do? To make it a little more difficult, let us assume that the former incumbent was "satisfactory" but was killed in an automobile accident. Or, if you would rather, assume that he was marked "promotable" and a vacancy occurred in another department that he could fill. You are faced with the job of replacement. I do not know what you would do, but I should be very interested to learn.

Are You Preparing Yourself for Promotion? To what extent have you really figured the game? Where can you go and how soon and under what conditions? How much of an emergency does it mean to you? Of course, we all want to make more money, be more important, have better offices, prettier secretaries, more expensive cars, longer drapes at the window and all that, but what have you done about it? What have you done to increase the probability that *you* will be selected? Also, selected for what?

It would seem that there are three fairly obvious things to think about:

1. Could your job be done better and, if so, how? If not, what is it—a sinecure or a dead end?

2. What jobs are going to be open and when?

3. What do these different jobs take that you do not have?

It will probably take a good while to think about each of these points, and having thought about them will probably lead you to do a lot of work as well as thinking. A person is always judged for selection on the basis of how well he is doing his present job. There is nothing much more satisfying than the confidence that comes from knowing you are doing your job not just acceptably, or even well, but superlatively. Do not be afraid that you will be thought of as an irreplaceable man where you are. Then again, perhaps you have made yourself into that. How about a bit of delegation? Perhaps your subordinates will not do as good a job as you do, but they can hardly learn any sooner than now.

Your Responsibility for Training. Some training is needed for the satisfactory performance of every job. Of course it is true that if you wish you can write a job description, but a job

description only tells part of the official story. It is useful as a
mechanism, but it is not training. Nor is training, however we
may come to define it, the total answer to getting a job done
right, although it definitely is a part. Not only must a person
know how to do a job (that is the job description, etc.) and
have the skill to do the job (you get that by training), but he
must also have the desire to do the job. All of these are important and they are different. What we should do is to look at
it from at least two different viewpoints.

1. What training does a person need when he is transferred
(or promoted) into a new or different job?

2. What experiences in the existing job can be considered as
training for another job and how can such experiences be designed into a job and how can they be used as a training device?

But let us assume a personal viewpoint and ask ourselves
what we can do for the new fellow in the job, or the fellow in
the new job, which will help him fit into place in the least time
and with the least trouble to him and to the rest of the gang
and the job. As well as that, we might think of what experiences
we can force on our subordinates which will train (or is it
develop?) them for higher jobs, greater responsibility.

You will not find it in all the books, not even in the company
manual. There are people who go by the book and they are
useful (most of us met at least one in the armed services and
most of us can remember a situation where going by the books
fouled things up). But it is not entirely that—there is the book,
and there is knowing when to go by the book and when to
throw it away, but there is an awful lot that is not in the book.
Some of the things that are not in the book are just as apparent
as if they were; others apply to the particular group and still
others apply to the individuals, and you are one of the individuals about whom the new man in the new job will want to
know. There is no doubt that when a new man comes to work
with you, you talk to him, take him around to meet the other

boys. You may even make a point of going out to lunch with him and talking to him informally about the things you think are important, the problems your group meets and are up against, the personalities that are useful or difficult, and so on. That is good, but it is only a part of the problem: the personal part, and only a part of the personal part. You have told him how you see the outfit; maybe the people in the outfit see it differently and there will never be a better opportunity for him to "get to know the ropes" right off. The new man is new. Everybody is anxious about him and, unless there has been too much office politics in his selection, they will be surprisingly glad to help him. Give him something to do but give him time to get his roots down.

"Giving him something to do" is where you have a chance to show your understanding of men, of the situation within your group and, indeed, of the place of your department in the whole picture. It may be that you will feel it wisest to show him his desk, his office, and his secretary, if he has one, and to dump him in—to sink or swim. Sometimes it is wisest, but it *may* be wiser to do all this and then give him a special job that will involve him with everybody in the group and outside as well. It had best be a job that you have to do and that you could do in no time at all, and it should be known that it is "only" an emergency. This will give him an opportunity to settle in and if his specific job has not been done for a couple of days or weeks, it will seldom be too serious.

All of this may not go under the formal name of training but certainly you will get a man into the group sooner, and make him a member of the team. There are a lot of other things, personal idiosyncrasies, yours as well as those of the other members of the group. Watch him. The skill with which he finds these things out and adapts himself to his new surroundings is one indication of his "feel" for human relations and his potentialities as a manager, for the old cliché is often right that in order to be a good manager you must have personally experienced the frustration of being managed.

If you have tried to train your subordinates to carry on without you, you should be able to relax here at Arden House and really get something out of it. Relax in the certainty that the routine will be carried on satisfactorily without you, and that emergencies will be handled in one way or another. Perhaps the new problems will not be solved in the way that you would have solved them, but is that bad? Perhaps you will have to rescue somebody, perhaps you will find out that some dust has been swept under your rug, but all of this will give you perhaps the best chance to evaluate the people who do your work for you. Or do you do their work for them?

AN APPRAISAL OF AVAILABLE MANAGEMENT TECHNIQUES

by Kendrick Porter

MANAGERS and management techniques are not new phenomena in this world in which we live. The first managers probably were early forms of birds and mammals. They applied their managerial techniques to train and discipline their offspring in ways intended to enhance the likelihood that their kind would survive. I like to think that their good management helped them to outlast the dinosaurs.

Certainly, managers and their techniques had undergone a long period of development prior to the time that the original troglodytes joined together to slay ground sloths. If we accept recent dating estimates, human managers have been exercising their influence for approximately a million years. Over that time the importance and interest attaching to the work of managers appears to have shown no evidence of abating. On the contrary, all evidence points toward acceleration of such interest, especially during the age of civilization.

That acceleration is attested to by the indirect evidence offered by ruins of wooden, clay, and stone villages stretching back 6,000 years or more in time. We have the written evidence that managers and their methods were a prime concern of Egyptian pharaohs, Hittite kings, and Chinese emperors. They

Address presented at the Seventh Utility Management Workshop, July, 1958. Mr. Porter is a management consultant with Wallace Clark Associates.

were discussed at length by Herodotus; Virgil's *Georgics* is a manual of management methods. Machiavelli produced another such manual fifteen and one-half centuries later. Roger Bacon, often credited as the innovator of modern scientific methodology, produced his three major works in 1267–68. It was in that same thirteenth century, according to Oliver Sheldon, the British philosopher of management, that "Walter of Henley, the earliest protagonist of modern scientific management," flourished. Yet, despite all that has gone before, here in the twentieth century we are deluged with additional management literature (including this presentation of mine) which shows no sign of even beginning to form a crest.

Parents comprise approximately 60 percent of the adult population of the United States. Incidentally, in the course of unearthing that statistic I learned that nearly 100,000 more American women than men profess to be married. But, to return to parents—without doubt the majority of them consider themselves to be able managers with somewhat effective techniques for training and disciplining children. Surely the entire child population of our country tries to manage parents.

Thus we see that the biological concept that "ontogeny recapitulates philogeny" clearly applies to management. For, as I have pointed out, the human race has had managerial experience ever since the first simian was born with a malformed pelvis that condemned him to walk upright. And, each member of that race, including us in this room, has practiced managerial techniques almost from the hour of his birth. Is it not natural, therefore, that we all consider ourselves to be management experts?

Dr. Jeffries of the General Electric Company once said, "Our progress depends to a considerable extent on seeing to it that simplification forces move forward in approximate balance with complicating processes. If this can be accomplished, then individuals with given ability can expect to go forward indefinitely without becoming casualties of their own complexity." It is in an effort to obtain some simplification within the literary and practicing fields of management techniques that I am going to employ three devices in my presentation.

First, I will describe what I believe to be the primary relationship of the manager to the business enterprise. I will adorn that description with a title, "A Fundamental Postulate of Business Management." I select this title because I believe that the relationship I will describe should be the original source of all management techniques that apply to at least one type of management system.

Second, I will list a series of management techniques in the form of major components of one unified type of management system.

Third, I will discuss and appraise selected features of a few of those components.

Thus, my approach will be "blue sky." My justification for it is threefold: (1) by providing a specified frame of reference, it simplifies concepts concerning the processes of management; (2) where it has been used the harvests have become very bounteous; and (3) it may help you to look at your own jobs with wider perspective.

PROGRESS AND PURPOSE, A FUNDAMENTAL POSTULATE OF
BUSINESS MANAGEMENT

I submit that the primary obligation of employees to the enterprise which employs them is to seek to improve the ability of that enterprise to survive under any tolerable conditions that may be encountered. Each action of employees, acting singly or in concert, that increases the adaptability of the enterprise to present or future conditions increases the survival power of the enterprise and represents "progress." Any action which does not result in progress dissipates the resources of the enterprise.

I further submit that the job of the managers is to train and discipline themselves and their subordinates to discharge their primary obligation and thereby enhance the likelihood that the enterprise will progress and, hence, survive.

Progress Involves Profits and Futurity. It has been reported that the charter of possibly every incorporated business enterprise obligates the management to "preserve the assets of the corporation." This obligation can be discharged only if the enterprise progresses. A similar obligation must be assumed, implicitly or otherwise, by the head of every noncorporate business enterprise unless dissipation of resources is intended. Thus, the actions of each manager *qua* employee should be initiated only after the question "Is this progress—does this increase the ability of the enterprise to survive?" has been answered affirmatively.

The foregoing concept of progress is not widely recognized. Many persons, especially the president's maiden stockholding aunts in a privately owned business, but also others who should know better, are prone to evaluate progress solely on the basis of current and immediately foreseeable earnings or, worse, dividends. This is roughly analogous to evaluating the status of a war on the basis of an individual battle. However, while such appraisals may be unbalanced, they are not superficial. A business enterprise must earn profits in order to survive, and an army must win battles in order to win a war.

Furthermore, if a business enterprise was founded for the sole purpose of serving meals at the Brussels Fair, current profitability could be the overriding criterion of its ability to last until the fair is closed. However, if an enterprise represents large investments in fixed assets and in the talents of its employees, its current rate of profitability might best be subordinated to its potential rate ten or twenty years hence.

Progress Presupposes Purpose. Through this presentation I am going to talk a lot about "purpose." It may be worthwhile to pause now and indicate the sense in which I will use that word. By "purpose" I mean the specific function that an enterprise can and should fill. That function usually will be unique for a particular enterprise. "Purpose" typically will be a continuing state or matter, analogous to destiny or the Hindu dharma. It will not be an end product or a goal that is reached. It will be more like the pot of gold at the end of the rainbow which is ever there and which ever recedes as it is sought.

One of the most famous statements describing the purpose of a business enterprise was that made by Theodore N. Vail, the president of AT&T, when he said that the business of that corporation was service. Have you ever seen a public release of the telephone company, whether in the form of advertising, promotion, or information, which did not emphasize that purpose? Progress for that company has meant creating and satisfying subscriber wants for service until the service is considered by many to be as essential as food, clothing, and shelter. Mr. Vail's statement, from hindsight, appears to be a truism. However, this is because he had the foresight to select a sound purpose for his company, and then to make that purpose become the symbol of his enterprise, and vice versa. Macy's, General Electric, Inland Steel, and Sears Roebuck are other examples of enterprises wherein the management was astute in selecting the purpose that permitted progress, and in putting all their resources to work for that purpose. Marshall Field, Montgomery Ward, and Packard are obvious examples of enterprises which lost sight of their proper purpose somewhere along the way.

The purpose which will permit an enterprise to progress often is neither obvious nor easy to determine. If it were, I suspect we would consider our present standard of living in America to be submarginal by comparison to what might have been achieved.

As an illustration of the difficulty, consider the present con-

dition of the suburban service of the New York Central or New
Haven railroads in the New York city area. Fares are skyrocket-
ing; reliability of schedules and profits are plunging; the presidents are publicizing their needs for subsidies. The purpose of
the service is the same as it has been for a hundred years or
more: hauling commuters between New York city and West-
chester or Fairfield County twice a day. Is it not conceivable
that these services would be thriving businesses today if the
managements of ten or more years ago had conceived of other
constructive purposes, and then acted in consonance with such
conceptions?

Assuming that the present purpose of those services is faulty,
how long do you think it would take you to formulate a better
purpose for them? In making your estimate, please be aware
that it is easier for an informed outsider to identify proper
purpose than it is for an insider with his very difficult problem
of perspective.

The correct answer to the question "What is the purpose of
this enterprise?" is essential for progress. Most desirably it
would be investigated periodically, and previous answers either
confirmed or amended. Unfortunately for all of us, the question
itself is too rarely asked, and superficial or apparently obvious
answers too easily accepted.

Progress, Purpose, and Techniques. Let us now return to my
opening remarks. I suggested that early forms of birds possibly
followed a managerial pattern of behavior similar to that which
we observe among modern robins and sparrows. That is, they
trained and disciplined themselves and their offspring in ways
that enhanced the likelihood that their descendants would become modern robins and sparrows. I observed that managers
of business enterprises legally have a similar obligation with
respect to themselves, their subordinates, and the survival of
the enterprise.

As objective observers we have no difficulty in identifying
the challenges to which robins and sparrows must respond cor-

rectly and, hence, the purpose toward which their training and discipline must be oriented. However, as subjective observers we usually have great difficulty in thinking timely, deeply, creatively, and courageously enough to identify the really critical challenges to which our own enterprises must respond and, hence, to define the purpose our training and discipline must serve.

If the management of an enterprise selects the wrong purpose to be served, will it not select the wrong managerial techniques to train and discipline itself and its subordinates? Also, if so few enterprises are pursuing their correct purpose, why do not more of them fail? There are valid answers to these valid questions.

Without going into detail, it is my observation that many enterprises pursue what someone trained in game theory might call "mixed purposes." That is, they pursue several at once with the hope that one is right; or, they pursue different ones from time to time. Such a course of action led Columbus to find America, even if he did not know what he had found. However, a group of airplane passengers leaving London for America would hardly consider the trip successful if America meant any place between Cape Horn and Point Barrow to the pilot, and he flew accordingly.

Concerning techniques, I suspect that Peter Drucker comes close to the truth when he says that most of them are so unreliable that they always serve the correct purpose occasionally, merely on the basis of statistical probabilities. He then remarks that improved reliability is the greatest danger inherent in the new methods which now are becoming available. Usually they will answer the questions asked and, hence, we must expect an ever-increasing number of right answers to wrong questions. Thus, if our errant pilot employs these techniques, he will never land his passengers in New York on the basis of statistical averages. He will only land them there if he heads for New York.

Everything I have said up until now is preamble. Like most preambles, it is probably more philosophy and less of a guide to action. But action can have no meaning unless it has purpose, and can result in no progress unless it seeks the correct purpose. Therefore, I submit that the most critical job of the manager is that of establishing the correct purpose for his specific enterprise. With the correct purpose established, the selection of proper techniques readily follows.

A UNIFIED MANAGEMENT SYSTEM

When I speak of a "unified management system" I am not referring to some "black box" method of management. I mean simply a system that is consistent with the purpose of the enterprise and one that includes only what is both necessary and sufficient for that purpose.

Many types of more or less unified management systems have endured and been successful over extended periods of time in various historical areas. Both from frequency of occurrence and length of tenure, slavery appears to be the most persistent and durable system. From the viewpoint of lofty ideals and ephemeral existence, we have the Platonic, Fourier, Rochdale, and analogous systems.

In present day industrial America I observe two predominant systems, one that is declining and one that is growing. The salient characteristic of the declining system is that all authority is retained by the chief executive officer, except that which is specifically delegated to subordinates. This philosophy is repeated in each level of the organization. As a system it is practical and workable. Enterprises in which it has been used have made great contributions to the progress of America, just as the concept of the divine right of kings made great contributions to France as a nation. The decline of this system has been hastened by many influences. Surely one of those influences is the increase in the size of business enterprises. Just as surely, another is the increased opportunities for employment in enterprises using the other currently predominant type of management system.

The other system, the one which is increasing in favor and acceptance, may be described as follows: Each managerial employee has full authority to take any action that he deems to be suitable, except as authority may be specifically withheld. This system is sometimes termed "management by objectives."

COMPONENTS OF THE SYSTEM

It was indicated previously that the function of management is to train and discipline itself and its subordinates to achieve progress in serving the correct purpose of the enterprise. The major types of tools or techniques available for the conduct of that function, irrespective of the system of management used, are: planning, execution, feedback.

Planning, of course, is the preparation to initiate action. Execution is the action and its consequence. Feedback is the reinforcement or modification of plans and actions as experience is gained in their use. Those three major types of tools may be likened to final assemblies, consisting of subassemblies, sub-subassemblies, and parts. The subassemblies may be identified as:

$$
\text{Planning}
\begin{cases}
\text{objectives} \\
\text{policy} \\
\text{organization} \\
\text{programs}
\end{cases}
$$

$$
\text{Execution}
\begin{cases}
\text{movement} \\
\text{communications} \\
\text{results}
\end{cases}
$$

$$
\text{Feedback}
\begin{cases}
\text{appraisal of progress} \\
\text{utilization of results}
\end{cases}
$$

The unity underlying those component subassemblies is this: (1) each is the logical next step following completion of the previous one—that is, the performance of any component involves the waste of resources unless the prior components have been completed; (2) the last component logically precedes the first in a continuing enterprise; (3) the sequence is dynamic and, taken as a process, can be aligned to achieve progress toward the purpose of the enterprise; and (4) managers and their subordinates require continuous training and discipline with respect to each component in order to achieve such progress. Let us look at each of these components and examine some of them in part.

OBJECTIVES

A concept of purpose, such as "service," "mass distribution," or "power generation," is an operative concept for the conduct of planning, execution, and feedback activities. However, it may be too broad and fundamental to be of maximum help in the normal conduct of affairs.

In order to increase the operative effectiveness of "purpose," it has been found worthwhile to subdivide that broad concept into component "objectives." One of the best known statements of objectives for an organized endeavor is that contained in the Preamble to the Constitution of the United States:

We, the people of the United States, in order to form a more perfect union, establish justice, insure domestic tranquility, provide for the common defense, promote the general welfare, and secure the blessings of liberty to ourselves and our posterity. . . .

In less interesting prose this could have been phrased as follows: "We, the people of the United States, seek to establish the following objectives for our country: a more perfect union, justice, domestic tranquility, common defense, general welfare, and the blessings of liberty to ourselves and our posterity. . . ."

These statements illustrate many of the following six characteristics, each of which contributes to the operative effectiveness of the technique named "objectives":

1. Objectives should stem directly from, be consistent with, and describe the essential characteristics of the purpose to be served by the enterprise.

2. Objectives should permit progress.

3. Objectives should be simply stated.

4. Objectives should be published.

5. Objectives should be officially promulgated and adequately distributed.

6. Consistent objectives, individually shaped to specific needs, should be established for each unit of the enterprise.

Let us look briefly at the operative aspects of these characteristics.

Objectives should stem directly from, be consistent with, and describe the essential characteristics of the purpose to be served by the enterprise. Inasmuch as objectives are an expanded form of purpose, it is obvious that these two devices are a long and a short way of saying the same thing.

To the extent that objectives describe the essential characteristics of the purpose, as illustrated by the Preamble to the Constitution, they provide a firm and stable foundation for conducting the affairs of the enterprise. Conversely, to the extent that they are concerned with faulty purpose, are inconsistent with purpose, or concern superficial aspects of purpose, they tend to defeat their own realization in either of two ways: (1) they become subject to frequent modification or change; (2) they lose their significance when relatively slight changes occur in prevailing conditions.

When the first of these situations occurs, progress is severely impeded or blocked by lack of stable direction. This is true in any enterprise but especially in large and dispersed ones, where each change in objectives requires the difficult and

seldom fully successful reorientation of all personnel toward
the new direction. With respect to the second situation, an
enterprise loses its vitality for progress when its objectives cease
to provide direction. When activities become purposeless, they
become wasteful.

Objectives should permit progress. Unless the purpose of an
enterprise permits progress, the enterprise will not survive by
reason of its unattractiveness to owners, job seekers, and customers. For the same reason, objectives must permit progress.

Objectives should be simply stated. The objectives in the
Preamble to the Constitution are stated in very simple form.
They are addressed to the people of the United States in words
that have meaning for them. Their simplicity surely has contributed to their stability in guiding the activities of the federal
government for 170 years.

It is granted that oversimplification may lead to wider differences in interpretation than will overelaboration. However,
experience has shown that when simple, over-all objectives are
supplemented by simple objectives for various subordinate
organizational units the processes of management are facilitated. Conversely, when a rigid superstructure is imposed upon
statements of objectives, the processes of management are
impeded.

Objectives should be published. In any undertaking, and
especially in undertakings which are large and widely dispersed geographically, uniform and widespread understanding
of objectives is not easy to obtain. Oral definition and trans-
mittal provides multiple opportunities for error, misunderstanding, and even deliberate misstatement. These opportunities increase proportionately with the literacy of the people involved.
Publication of objectives does not, in itself, overcome the foregoing obstacles. It does lessen the extent to which the obstacles
are encountered.

Objectives should be officially promulgated and adequately distributed. The Constitution was an official recommendation, as attested by the signatures of the legally qualified representatives to the Constitutional Congress. It was officially adopted by each of the thirteen original states. Such procedure lent dignity to the contents of the document and clearly established its official character for all. Analogous procedures used in connection with the objectives of a business enterprise lead to analogous results.

Consistent objectives, individually shaped to specific needs, should be established for each unit of the enterprise. As previously indicated, over-all objectives usually are too broad to guide the activities of a maintenance, billing, or district sales unit. Also, the objectives for a maintenance or sales unit in one area may differ from those for a similar unit in another area. Accordingly, the need is indicated for each organizational unit of the enterprise.

POLICY

A concrete example of the relationship between objectives and policies may be obtained by referring again to the Preamble of the Constitution. The objectives in that statement have been identified. In order to define how those objectives are to be sought, the policy was adopted to "ordain and establish this Constitution for the United States of America." In addition to broad and controlling policy of this type, which may be explicit or implicit in an enterprise, derivative policy also is used. This derives from the broad policy. It comprises the detailed rules and regulations for the conduct of affairs.

Both of these types of policy should embody legitimate, necessary, and experience-proven guidance. Thus they serve to reduce the area of independent thinking and to simplify the conduct of management processes. They are of material aid in creating a desirable element of uniformity that can lead to a resultant consistency in progress. While policy means confinement to uniform channels, that need not and should not lead to uniform mediocrity. Instead, it should release managers from repetitive decisions about recurring matters and make their energies thus released available for more constructive contributions.

Several of the characteristics contributing to the operative effectiveness of the technique named "policy" are the same as those described for objectives, thus:

1. Policy should be simply stated.
2. Policy should be published.
3. Policy should be officially promulgated and adequately distributed.
4. Consistent policy should be established for the over-all enterprise and for each organizational unit therein.

In addition, two other characteristics are pertinent.

Policy should provide for the conduct of all activities necessary for progress. It is obvious that progress cannot be achieved unless provision is made to conduct those activities essential to its realization, and to avoid those activities that are not conducive to it. The enunciation of policy concerning such activities is the initial step in inaugurating those activities.

While policy should be reasonably stable, it should be modified to meet new and changing situations. Whereas sound objectives should be subject to only infrequent change, policy should reflect current needs and conditions. Obviously, too-frequent policy change may be the symptom of faulty policy formulation. However, there are many situations in which this is not true. For example, policy relating to or deriving from current market conditions may change frequently if rapid fluctuations occur in those conditions. On the other hand, policy concerning the establishment of a public relations function or a pension program may change not at all over a period of several years.

Policy may also require change as progress is achieved. To illustrate, we often see the pricing policy of a company change as the enterprise grows from a small operation to a dominant one in its field.

SUMMARY IN MIDPASSAGE

We started out to discuss and appraise techniques available to a manager. Here, at midpassage, it must appear to many of you that I have done little except wade through matters which usually are taken for granted or else dusted off pretty quickly. I have made a multitude of ex cathedra assertions with almost no corroborative evidence. I have presumed to use this large proportion of space in that way because, in my experience, most of the faulty practices of managers and most of the faulty techniques they have used spring directly from faulty purpose, objectives, and policy. Yet we have merely touched upon some of the problems involved and lightly sketched some of the techniques which lead to successful solutions to those problems. That those techniques are very worth-while is evidenced by three well-known examples: the return of the United States Steel Corporation from near bankruptcy in 1934, and the dominant and strong leadership positions of the General Electric Company and AT&T.

If any single one of you acquires from this study a questioning attitude toward purpose, objectives, and policy which usually are taken for granted, I will be satisfied that progress has been achieved. Now let us take up some of the other tools.

ORGANIZATION

The literature on organizing groups of people to conduct the affairs of a business, government, or other undertaking is, I believe, unique. That part which has been written by practicing managers typically puts forth general principles that do not work very well. That part prepared by scholars is seldom more than a compilation of examples which demonstrate that almost any organization plan is sound if the enterprise in which it exists is big and successful.

This literature has, in my opinion, another unique quality. I find the writings that were completed between five hundred and fifteen hundred years ago to be superior to those completed subsequently. Modern authors can not hold a candle to Plato, Cato, Virgil, and Machiavelli. The ancient and medieval writers first asked and answered the question "Organize for what and with what?" Modern writers tend either to ignore that question or to give it only passing notice. Yet, unless it is asked and is answered adequately, any dissertation or action concerning organization has little significant meaning or usefulness.

If you had accompanied me to many of the hundreds of meetings on organizational problems that I have had with clients over the past sixteen years, there would be no need to emphasize the importance of knowing what you are organizing for. Typically the client personnel attending those meetings are informed, intelligent, sincere, and frustrated men. Often they have spent months fretting about whether geographic, functional, product, or goodness knows what other type of organization pattern should be applied to their situation. Many of them have thought I misunderstood their problem when I have refused to discuss organization and have insisted instead upon an examination of the purpose and objectives of their enterprise. Many, also, were astounded when they saw how simple it is to develop an appropriate organization pattern once purpose and objectives are clarified. My experiences have been no different than those of other workers in the field of organization.

Let us now look at that aspect of organization known as job

description. The principal organizational purpose of job description is to define a specific job so that the incumbent and his associates will know what he is supposed to do. At least three forms of job descriptions are now in use. These are exemplified by the old tale concerning the three stonemasons engaged in the construction of the cathedral at Chartres. They were asked what they were doing. The first replied that he was earning a livelihood for himself and his family. The second boasted that he was performing the finest stonecutting in all of France. The third submitted that he was helping to build a house of God.

The first answer parallels those job descriptions emphasizing the skills and responsibilities which are significant in differentiating jobs for pay rate purposes. Frequently these serve a collateral or incidental use in connection with organization. The second reply is analogous to those job descriptions which indicate the function of each job and then list, often in considerable detail, each duty and responsibility of the job. This is the most common form. The third answer illustrates the description that is based squarely upon the purpose and objectives of the enterprise and the employee's obligation with respect to them. Let us skip any discussion of the first type, for it is generally recognized as unsatisfactory and is gradually disappearing from use for organizational purposes.

The second type can trace its ancestry straight back to job descriptions originated for hourly paid factory employees prior to the First World War and, beyond that, to the itemized listing of the time-studied elements those employees perform. It is the proper type of description for use in all enterprises wherein the president retains all authority other than that specifically delegated. Under that type of management system, the proper concerns of most managerial employees are procedures and duties.

The third type of description has been designed for mana-

gerial jobs in organizations where the philosophy of management by objectives obtains. Its focus is on results and progress,
rather than on procedure. Its format contains three sections.
The first section includes the job title and other elementary
identifying information. The second is headed "obligation" and
states that the incumbent has the obligation to make specific
contributions to the progress of the enterprise, division, or
other organizational unit of which he is a part. Those contributions are identified. Naturally, for a department or division
head, his contributions are essentially the same as the objectives of his department or division. The third section is labeled
"freedom." It sets forth the freedom granted to the incumbent
to make decisions.

Presumably each manager in an enterprise is hired to make
contributions to the progress of that enterprise. In accepting
his job and its compensation he accepts the obligation to make
those contributions. The description explicitly sets forth that
condition.

The obligation of the employee ceases if his freedom is so
curtailed that he cannot discharge the obligation he has accepted. In such a situation a restatement of obligation is required if his employment is to be tenable. Properly, every
manager's freedom in a system of management by objectives is complete, up to the point where the exercise of his freedom prevents others in the organization from exercising their
freedom and discharging their responsibility.

Why are the terms "obligation" and "freedom" used instead
of responsibility and authority? There are two reasons: (1)
they better describe the relationship of a manager to his job
and, hence, are more operable; and (2) they are not charged
with the many and diverse meanings of the latter two words.

In some companies the second type of description is being
reshaped towards the format of the type just delineated. This
is being done by adding a section termed "accountability" at

the end of the description. The contents of that section are somewhat similar to those of an "obligations" section. However, the title of the section in itself is ambiguous, and the contents tend to be focused on results rather than objectives.

The work required to define the obligation of a manager in terms of the contributions expected from him often is very difficult, painful, and time consuming. This alone should indicate how badly such efforts are needed. Incidentally, the third type of description usually is easier to read and understand than the second type because simpler language can be used and because it is shorter.

It is common practice for job descriptions to be prepared by incumbents, edited by supervisors, and then, after some hocus-pocus by the personnel department, authorized as approved. In other words, the organization pattern is developed from the bottom up. Pursued to a logical conclusion, this worm's-eye-view approach could leave the president either jobless or overburdened with all the work no one else wanted to do.

The "obligation" type of description is not susceptible to this method of preparation. The description of the president's job must be prepared first and those of other jobs follow in sequence down through the organizational hierarchy. The reasons for this are obvious. The president has the obligation to achieve progress toward the purpose of the enterprise. The objectives of everyone else in the organization stem from those of the president, as do obligations. How can any subordinate manager know what he is supposed to contribute unless he knows what contributions are expected from his boss?

There is one more matter relating to organization on which I want to touch briefly at this point. That is compensation. If a chief executive officer is completely scrupulous in discharging his obligation to "preserve the assets of the enterprise" he will see that all payments made to employees are based, as closely as possible, on their contribution to progress. For, in our society, contribution is the only basis for pay that makes any sense. Translated into organizational terms, this means that a subordinate would make more than his boss if he made a greater contribution.

In a management system where all authority is retained in the upper organizational echelons, it is customary to find that all payroll information, as well as payroll control, is confined to those echelons. In those situations it is also customary to find that pay rates in the lower echelons tend to reflect contribution.

With the advent of increased management by objectives it became customary to delegate at least partial control of pay rates to subordinate managers. And, with this trend, grew the practice of paying the head of an organizational unit more than any of his subordinates. The result has been that organizational status rather than contribution has become the criterion of an employee's pay rate.

Under those conditions an employee can improve his economic status only by becoming a manager, and then a manager of managers. Thus the reward to an outstanding engineer, accountant, or salesman is to become a boss of engineers, accountants, or salesmen. This has turned thousands, and perhaps tens of thousands, of good technical and professional men into bad managers. It has condemned an equal number of potentially good managers to continue making second- and third-rate technical contributions.

Fortunately, in some companies a much deeper understanding of management by objectives is being developed. In those companies all practices may be subject to critical examination in order to evaluate their impact on progress. When compensation practices have been scrutinized, contribution has gained or regained its rightful place as the criterion of pay rates.

That "pay based upon organizational status" phase of American industry illustrates well the dangers inherent in the use of any management technique not consonant with the purpose and objectives of the enterprise. I venture, without fear of contradiction, to presume that in every large company there are critical management techniques which, through misdirection analogous to the example just cited, are resulting in very substantial drains on the resources of the enterprise.

Those losses cannot be stopped until they are identified. They cannot be identified until purpose and objectives are set into their proper controlling position, and all practices of the manager are critically examined against them.

I like to think that the status of management today is not unlike the status of mathematics in the late eighteenth century. Mathematics has undergone thousands of years of development with many great ancient and medieval achievements behind it. The analytical methods of Newton, Leibnitz, and Descartes were being turned into a flood of brilliant new contributions by Euler, Lagrange, Laplace, and Gauss. Then came the critical reappraisal, the demands for sounder foundations and more binding unity. The sweeping changes that ensued led to what Eric Bell calls the "explosive growth of physical science since 1900." That writer then points out "the universally acknowledged fact [among professional mathematicians] that the nineteenth century, prolonged into the twentieth, was and is the greatest age of mathematics the world has ever known. Compared to what glorious Greece did in mathematics, the nineteenth century is a bonfire beside a penny cradle."

In management, we have the material and the opportunity comparable to that of the nineteenth-century mathematicians. More important, we have the challenge of another management system to which we must respond successfully, or perish with our institutions. It is most timely for managers to think critically of their jobs and their practices, remembering with William Blake that "Damn braces, bless relaxes."

PROGRAMS

These comprise the goals, maps, strategies, and tactics within the framework of objectives and policy by which the manager seeks to achieve progress. Programs take a multitude of diverse forms such as sales campaigns, wage incentives, product design, and budgets.

This is the area where techniques flourish: consumer motivation, media evaluation, executive development, time study, inventory control, operations research, accounting, personnel management. This is the big circus tent with many times three rings, and with experts whirling and gyrating about in each ring while their apprentices stand at the side to handle the props. Now hang on tightly while I negotiate a sharp curve here. We shall "drop that metaphor" with the circus reference and pick up a more constructive one.

Let us think of those experts as "map makers," for that they truly are. They use their training and skills to scout the territory. They go out in survey parties to measure and plot the terrain, to observe climate and weather phenomena, to locate wells, springs, and other sources of sustenance, and to identify possible enemies and competitors and the dangers that they represent. They then compile their findings into some form of map.

An adequately prepared map enables a manager to set goals for what he wants to accomplish in the territory, and to develop his strategies and tactics for achieving those goals. Each goal is an expression of the specific progress that is anticipated within a definite period of time and toward specified objectives.

Wherever there are objectives they should be supplemented by such goals, including the maps and other paraphernalia required to meet the goals. Thus, goals should be set at regular intervals for the enterprise, for each organizational unit within the enterprise, and for each of the contributions that a manager is obligated to make.

In all of business there are only eight territories to be mapped. That situation comes about in this way; there are only eight characteristics of purpose which are pertinent to progress. Hence, there are only eight objectives for which to set goals. Ergo, there are only eight territories to map. This octad of objectives, goals, and territories includes: market standing, innovation, productivity, non-human resources, profitability, managers, nonmanagerial employees, and the public.

The relative importance of each of the eight territories varies from business to business. The importance of a few of the territories may be nil in a small number of businesses, but all of them are vital to progress in most businesses. While there are only eight territories, there is a vast multitude of forms the eight objectives and eight goals may take. Similarly, there are a multitude of types of appropriate maps. Let us look at a few common features of maps and see if they are instructive with respect to our managerial maps.

First, we all know that the map is not the same thing as the territory mapped. We can fold a map up and put it into our pocket. Some of us may think that we can put New York city or Texas in our pocket, but we would be a bit hard pressed if we had to prove it. Similarly, we can carry a statistic representing a customer into the president's office, while it would be a very different matter to carry the customer into that office. We could go into more serious and complex comparisons, but it would not change the fact that the map can never become the territory. Hence, a good map maker will exercise his imagination and foresight to include all that is pertinent to passage through the territory. He will omit from the map everything that is not pertinent, for he recognizes that there is no end to the possible extraneous detail. Can you say the same about the map makers in your company?

Different kinds of maps of the same territory will have many things in common. A weather map, a structural map, and a topographical map of a territory will all show various political boundaries, land and water boundaries, latitude and longitude, and magnetic north. How often does a productivity program even include all employees, let alone utilize proven factory productivity know-how, in sales and office operations?

A map is never more accurate than the data used in its construction. A map of a map suffers by reason of its further removal from the source data. I have seen a large and reputedly progressive company employ thirty accountants and pay $60,-000 annual rental on tabulating equipment to analyze its productivity and costs as shown in accounting statements. Those statements were prepared from data compiled by three shop timekeepers. Fifteen timekeepers would barely have been adequate to compile reasonably accurate source records. Few companies think quite that "big" when they waste manpower resources, but many waste them in the same way.

Let us move on from maps to map makers. I have spoken of the job of the manager as that of "teaching and discipline." The job of the map maker is that of "teaching and research." But is this what map makers do? Apparently not in most business enterprises. As an exception, I will cite the case of the personnel manager of one of the largest and best managed financial institutions in this country. He supervises one secretary. He performs no so-called "personnel administration." His time is spent completely in thinking and counseling. The benefits that result in terms of the progress of that institution are obvious and outstanding.

By contrast, I suggest that you review the annual study of personnel departments issued by the University of Minnesota. From that study I find that the average personnel expert spends a third of his time talking to other personnel experts in his own organization. He spends almost two thirds of his time in routine personnel administration. Less than one percent is spent in research. Is it any wonder that personnel management can be accused of bankruptcy? It appears that our managers have defaulted in their obligation to manage, and that personnel experts have defaulted in their obligation to be experts. I know of no other explanation for the prevailing type of personnel program.

I have singled out the program area of personnel because its practitioners are such a vocal group. However, I rarely see other types of experts pursuing more suitable programs.

EXECUTION

I am going to shortchange this important phase of the manager's job by pausing merely long enough to define two of the techniques, and to discuss only one aspect of the other technique.

Movement. This is physical travel: in the office, among offices, between plants and offices and among plants. Observing things and conditions and going to see people constitute a large part of the manager's life.

Communications. You undoubtedly will hear a lot about communications during this Workshop, and I have no wish to duplicate what others will say here. Accordingly, I am going to limit my remarks to that aspect of communications commonly known as clerical procedures.

I am not at all sure that clerical procedures would have been discussed had we been gathered here for a similar Workshop fifteen or twenty years ago. However, with the inexorable approach of automatic communications equipment it is now one of the most important phenomena on the manager's horizon. It is important because managers, scientists, and equipment salesmen have formed an *entente* to besiege the clerks. That siege will not be fully lifted until the last clerk is gone. Of course, there will be "die-hards" and they will die "hard," but they will surely die. There probably will be law suits before a punched tape or some more unlikely piece of material will be accepted as a legally binding commitment.

With automatic communications, the office as we know it today is going to disappear. I believe that you would have found it interesting to accompany me on a visit to a relatively new company a few weeks ago. All of that company's growth has been achieved in the past ten years. It started unhampered by precedent and clerical empires to be defended. More than 90 percent of the volume of clerical work is performed by a few people and a few machines.

It is likely, too, that with automatic processing facilities much of the supercargo surrounding the experts will disappear, so that the experts will be once again available to go about their business of being experts.

I am fully aware of the disappointment accompanying the installation of nearly all large-scale computers for clerical procedures purposes. However, one such installation has shown in-pocket savings at a rate of $800,000 a year since the fifth month after its delivery two years ago. Omitting that exception, those computers are glamour stuff, like the automobiles in the Indianapolis race. A typical car owner would be just as disappointed as the managers with large scale computers are if he were to obtain one of those racing cars for everyday use.

Nevertheless, experiences gained with those racing cars have contributed many of the *sois disant* improvements in the automobiles you and I buy. So, too, equipment such as the Flexiwriter, developed for use with the large computers, is now gaining acceptance at a rapid rate in hundreds of companies which have no computers.

In summary, let me repeat what I tell my clients. Within five years, perhaps, every company with six or more clerical employees will be able to reduce costs, improve services, or both, through the use of low-cost automatic communication equipment. It will take time to prepare for the installation. Often substantial benefits can be realized during the preparation period. The pattern is there for anyone who wants to see. I suggest that you look at it and act upon it.

Results. These are what happen after all the preparatory work I have discussed and the execution I have not discussed are completed.

APPRAISAL OF PROGRESS

For many years various management experts have extolled the virtues of "management by exception." In its ultimate form, which I have seen promulgated but not used, a manager would receive only reports of results that were worse than or better than expected. He could rest assured that all other results were "routine." Of course, if he used the airlines frequently he might not rest so assured that "routine" was a desirable condition.

The real purpose of "management by exception" is to conserve the time of the manager by making it unnecessary for him to wallow through a bog of paperwork, statistics, and charts in order to appraise a situation.

I submit that "management by exception" is too narrow a concept and should be abandoned. The job of the manager is not to emphasize exceptions but to keep his eye on objectives. "Management by exception" emphasizes that each result is a part of the whole management system and can be dealt with best as such.

A manager using a system such as described here has little need for a lot of reports to help him appraise his results. He is close to the situation and he has the obligation and freedom to discharge his obligation. His boss, in turn, needs only such information as is required to indicate the progress being made toward the planned goals. If he insists upon complete details

of matters within the obligations of his subordinates he is re-
leasing them from their obligations.

Recently a leading business executive spoke out against the
prevalence of "too much information." He is right, but unfortunately "he ain't seen nuthin' yet." Wait until automatic
equipment starts to spew forth information and some irrespon-
sible equipment supervisor starts to show you all the interesting data he can supply to you. Some of the data will be very
attractive and difficult to refuse. However, I suggest that,
unless you have already combated the spread of that virus by
some eager tabulating supervisor, you begin now to discipline
yourself and your subordinates to say "No." That discipline
will pay off when the equipment gets into operation. Production of the information you need will not be delayed by production of the information you do not need.

Discrimination in the selection of material and economy in
its use have characterized the majority of people who have
contributed most to our world's progress. This trait seldom
seems to be acquired naturally, as attested to by the files of
most business enterprises. Therefore, it should be taught as
part of the art of self-defense against waste and dissipation of
resources.

UTILIZATION OF RESULTS

A manager's appraisal of a situation may be worth-while if it
leads to the prompt repair of a machine and thus prevents delay
in the delivery of a specific customer's order. However, if all
of his subsequent appraisals under similar situations merely
result in more prompt repairs of machinery, his contribution to
progress is likely to be nil. A more constructive manager will
use his appraisal to initiate the emergency action. He will also
use it to initiate improved maintenance of the machinery so
that emergency repairs are not needed in the future.

Thus, each appraisal of a result that leads to a particularized corrective action should be fed back into the whole management system to determine whether and what preventive activities are desirable. Such feedback may take place within a manager's own organizational unit, or it may be referred to his boss or an expert. The corrective program may, of course, enter into the system at any appropriate point, from objectives downward in the list of components.

CONCLUSION

I have spent more time on the planning tools than I have on the execution and feedback tools because the planning tools must be used first. The application of the tools in an incorrect sequence can be dangerous, as illustrated in the example of "pay by organizational status."

TOWARD THE DEFINITION OF
AN EXECUTIVE

by Perrin Stryker

FORTUNE's survey of the executive job was undertaken in the fall of 1955 because we had heard many definitions of what an executive is and wondered whether anyone had really nailed it down. We had seen a good deal in the textbooks and elsewhere, but decided to try to define the executive job in terms used by executives themselves. First we had to find out what an executive is. We went down to Charleston, West Virginia, which was selected as a sample town because there are a number of big plants of big companies there, plus numerous small businesses and public utilities. A considerable amount of time was spent there in talking to a great many men, asking them to define an executive. What does an executive actually do, in his own terms? We also interviewed many top management men and wrote to others, receiving rather lengthy replies from the heads of large corporations on the subject "What does an executive do?"

Of all these replies or interviews, none agreed in specific detail as to what an executive does. However, by putting them all together we did arrive at a consensus of opinion as to what the executive functions are. We were surprised to find that so many of these functions could be described specifically. The

Address presented at the Fifth Utility Management Workshop, July, 1956. Mr. Stryker is a member of the Board of Editors of *Fortune*.

whole area seemed so extensive when we began the interveiws that it seemed this would not be possible.

Before I name the five areas of executive functioning turned up by *Fortune's* survey, you might be thinking over your own ideas of a good executive. What does he do? We were surprised that so many men who are executives had not really thought about this—so far as we could discover. If they had thought about it, they had not sat down and figured it out by functions. The first thing many of them did when we questioned them, was to answer the question "Am I an executive?" Some admitted they had worked at the problem a bit and finally pushed it aside, because they concluded they were not executives after all. I am not suggesting, of course, that any of you might come to such a conclusion.

The images of the executive which exist in the public mind are not much more varied than those existing in businessmen's minds. For instance, the man who is on the executive payroll is one order of executive. Those executives who are allowed to eat in the executive dining room are another breed, while those who sit on the executive committee are still another kind. Wherein lies the difference? There are many intangibles, and some of the thinking about executives found outside management ranks seems to have affected the thinking of management. Very often when we asked a man who the executives in his company were he would say, "Oh a few men at the top." Then he would start thinking specifically—we might sit there two hours with him—and he would start naming the men in his organization who, in his opinion, really performed the executive functions. One man who found himself spotting executives down to the divisional level, and even below this, had to stop and think what he was looking for. He finally concluded an executive was basically a man who had several responsibilities and, in addition, had the potential to reach a top job.

I have mentioned these experiences to make it clear that

we were not trying to arrive at any stereotyped definition. We were simply trying to report on what the men themselves said.

Another question was: Is there any difference between an executive and a manager? Here the term "manager" is being used inclusively, which I personally prefer. "Manager" is a good and honorable word and has not gotten any of the puffery that goes with the use of the term "executive." There is some pomposity in the term "executive" which I think is avoided by the use of the term "manager."

We finally condensed the definitions of an executive which we obtained from these people to five functions. I want to emphasize some words in each one of these five functions so you will see that they were not simply tossed in loosely. The first function involves setting objectives and over-all policies. The words generally used were "directly helps set over-all policies and objectives." It was mentioned more often and more emphatically than any other by every executive to whom we talked as *the* function of the executive. This means that the executive actually says "We will do such and such next year."

Function number two is decision-making. Specifically, this second most important function required of an executive is to make or approve decisions which have a significant effect on profits and future plans. The key words used by executives here were "he is required to make" such decisions. In other words, he cannot pass these decisions on to anyone else, and the decisions themselves must "significantly affect profits and plans." For practical purposes this eliminates the other managers, all the way down to the foreman level, who could in one sense be said to be performing this function.

Function number three is that of coordinating several functions or those of a major division or department. The key words here are "several functions." In other words, the executive may be responsible for personnel selection, training, and industrial relations, for example.

The fourth executive function is to "maintain and develop an organization of trained subordinates to achieve the company's goals." This is a function recognized most clearly in recent years, and it includes the technique of executive development. But responsibility for maintaining and developing both the organization and the calibre of the men in it is recognized by executives as a typically executive function and responsibility.

Executive function number five is to "delegate responsibility and authority to the organization"—you are all familiar with that—and also to "control performance and results through at least one level of supervision." This we found to be a minimum separation. The president of a great oil company, for instance, said that an executive has to operate through at least two levels of supervision.

Now the distinctive part of this collection of five functions, so far as *Fortune* is concerned, is this: An executive does one, two, three, four, *and* five. He does them all, not any combination of two or three, but all five. Obviously this makes quite a stringent definition.

One of the questions raised by many men to whom we talked was, "What happens to the staff man? Is he an executive?" The answer, according to this definition, comes back "No," because a staff man does not often *directly* set policies; he helps to set them. Also, he does not often make decisions which significantly affect profits; he suggests and recommends but he does not make the decisions. This may not be very flattering to a staff man who places a great deal of emphasis on the word executive. It is not to say that the staff man cannot be a manager who is superior in ability to a man who performs all five executive functions but, by this definition, he is not included in the executive ranks.

Some of the definitions of an executive were very short. The late Ralph Damon tried to cover it in these few words: "An executive is a man who can select, train, and lead others as a team to a successful objective." The words "select, train, and lead" obviously cover much ground, and Mr. Damon probably knew what he meant by them. But, when one begins to press executives for further definition, they begin to explain what they mean by the word "lead," and this extends into many ramifications.

One of the more amusing definitions was supplied by a radio commentator in Charleston who said that an executive is "a man who walks around with a frown on his assistant's face." This is not quite such an idle joke as it sounds, as I think I can show in a moment when I talk about the last of these five executive functions—delegation and control. I want to go into delegation and control at some length because, next to decision-making, this is probably the toughest of all the functions to perform and one which is, apparently, the least understood or recognized.

Decision-making is still, of course, almost totally indescribable. A colleague of mine spent a long time trying to find out why and how executives make decisions, and he concluded that the majority of them do not know the answer themselves. But I am not going into decision-making today.

I would like to report more of the findings *Fortune* made in the course of its survey, because I think they may help you to understand what is involved in the top level jobs. The predominant concept, for one thing, is that executives include only a few at the top; that phrase, "only a few at the top" was used over and over again. They did not define this by title or even by salary level. Those men who actually had the responsibilities and performed these five functions were considered executives.

Another point the survey revealed was that the executives operate on a higher level than the managers. It seemed pretty generally understood, semantically at least, that a "manager" is not as high as an "executive" in the corporate hierarchy. A third point, which is a corollary to the second, is that managers carry out policies made by executives. In the opinion of a great many of the men with whom we talked, this in fact is the clearest distinction to be made between a manager and an executive.

To clarify the replies of about 100 men on the value of the executive jobs, we tried to find out how many functions were really being talked about. Some men, like Damon, condensed them all into a one-line sentence. Others, like the president of a large railroad, wrote three and a half pages in reply and named something like a score of functions. The variety was extraordinary. These 100 men described about 115 executive actions which we condensed into five principal categories. We put them in order of the number of times each was mentioned; the ranking order follows: (1) "achieving the company's over-all objectives"; (2) "setting policies and objectives"; (3) "thinking and analyzing"; (4) "coordinating functions and people"; (5)"organizing and developing subordinates and advising other executives and managers"; (6) "handling subordinates, controlling operations"; (7) "improving our capacities, leading, setting an example"; (8) "delegating, giving orders, working through others"; (9) "exercising business judgment; performing a specialty in a field connected with technical ability"; (10) "handling public and community relations."

Some presidents said the number one job of the president is to deal with the public. This should interest you people in public utilities. However, we did not put too much weight on the ranking order of these functions; they were frequently summarizations of a great many phrases and whole paragraphs. "Setting an example" covered a whole variety of phrases like "motivating and inspiring others."

But the major point of the survey was that none of these functions or acts was uniquely characteristic of executive work, in the terms of the men to whom we talked. Such work is a *combination* of acts. No matter how you divide or describe it, you cannot evade that fact. An executive does several things. In other words, if a man is responsible for making the decisions about all capital investments in a billion-dollar corporation and he does only that, he is *not* an executive. He is a technical manager, in the opinion of the men we visited.

It is understood, of course, that we are reporting what the majority of managers say. There was quite a significant minority who objected to some of these definitions and categories. Some did not agree that an executive ranked any higher than a manager. Some—a rather vocal minority—said executives are "everybody right down to the foreman." Well, perhaps they are, theoretically, since the functions of an executive are found in some degree at every level down to foreman. But it was obvious that none of the men who were executives really thought in those terms. I do not know why so many men insisted that everybody down to the foreman is performing executive functions, but a good many did. But when they said they had lunch with some executives the other day, and we asked them how many foremen were present, they answered, "None at all." Well, what do they mean?

Their meaning is quite clear when it is possible to talk to them confidentially. The size of the company they manage makes a significant difference. We found, pretty generally, that executives thought executives could be found in companies with 1,000 or more employees. The corner grocery store manager is not considered an executive, although he may actually perform all five functions I mentioned earlier. There must be an organization, however, with several departments and at least 500 to 1,000 employees before executive work is considered possible.

Finally, there are one or two interesting points about supervisors' and workers' opinions on the subject. I would guess that we had about 1,000 questionnaires turned in from immediate subordinates and employees. We found that the description, "only a few at the top," and the function, "over-all policy setting and major decision-making," were the two most immediately recognized marks of the executive. The functions of over-all policy-setting and major decision-making were recognized right down the line, not only by supervisors but by workers on the bench.

There were some curious footnotes to all this. In Charleston, for example, we asked nine plant managers whether they thought they were executives. Three of them said they supposed they were. Three said they were not sure. And three said they were managers, not executives. These men handled anywhere from 2,500 to 10,000 people. Moreover, businessmen in the town who dealt with many of these men had very definite opinions on the status of these plant managers. Nearly two thirds of the local businessmen said "These men are managers, not executives."

This brings us back to a point I mentioned earlier to the effect that the term "manager" is still a very honorable term. In Charleston it seems to be applied generally to men running very large factory organizations. Only one of the major managers there was generally thought of as an executive. His attention to civic, social, and community work had brought him to the attention of local businessmen, and this apparently gave him an executive overtone.

By the somewhat stringent definition of an executive that we have presented, could you make a guess as to how many executives there are in the United States? If you could arrive at such a figure, and could get the names of those who were really executives, you could probably sell such a list for a million dollars tomorrow morning. However, there is no way to do this except by going around and talking to every one of the managers of every one of the large companies in the United

States, and finding out who was really thought to be an executive in each company. The men in top management know quite accurately the men who are carrying the weight of executives. While some may say there are two or three executives in their companies, there are others who say "there are a lot more who think they are executives."

However, just playing around with statistics we derived several different figures. On the basis of using 41,000,000 people as employees in industry, we arrived at one figure of 75,000 executives, another figure of 315,000, another of 430,000, and another of 250,000. The maximum is not over a half million men, you can be sure, and we figured that, if the strict definition were applied, the figure would fall well under 100,000. Compare this with hordes of people—some estimates have run into the millions—who are loosely considered to be executives and are referred to as such by advertising agencies, press agents, and management associations.

I would like to return now to the fifth function—delegation and control—which I think might be helpful and, I trust, not embarrassing to anyone here. This is a subject we dug into a while ago because of the furor that has arisen over decentralization. You know the major tenets of this theory; it is not the decentralization of plants, but the decentralization of decision-making. Decentralization has been considered one of the major methods of developing executives, i.e., that the man down the line will develop if he makes the decisions. "Let him stand on his own feet and make mistakes. Get rid of detail at the top. Have time to think and plan. Put your feet up on the desk." All these recommendations have become cliché—which is why we suspected that there was not as much truth in them as there appeared to be.

Once again I ask you to think briefly about whether you really know how to delegate, or do delegate, and whether you think you really exercise authority in your own job. It was apparent after we finished this study of ours that many men at first thought they did know how to delegate and then, when they began to think more about it, they concluded they were not making their own decisions or exercising their own authority, and yet they were perfectly happy about this. The ideal of democratic decision-making has certainly been given a great deal of lip service. It is probably a carry-over from the concept we have of democracy as a good thing, the idea that everybody should participate and help make decisions. It turned out in our study that management simply cannot make democratic decentralization work the way so many men have said it does work, or should work. And most of those who know this have never said it aloud.

A second point is the paradox that the more you try to decentralize decision-making, the more you must centralize control. It is a two-way action. If you give out the authority to make decisions, you must put a line on it and tie it back to profit. There are all grades and categories of decisions. There are those routine decisions made without reporting to anyone, such as when buying company supplies and paying bills. There are those decisions made without reporting to anybody until after they are carried out, such as when hiring and firing men, for example. And then there are those decisions that require constant checking and approval by your superior before the decision is made, in order that you may make sure, and your superior may make sure, that the decision you make can be approved by top management. This, of course, is a large part of top management's job: constantly to coach and guide and preshape and shape the decisions of everyone down the line so that, after a decision is made, top management can approve it.

This finding stuck out like a mountain in our survey. Decision-making is shaped and preshaped by top management, and it must be if the company is going to move effectively in one direction. Everyone has to know what kind of decisions can be approved. Needless to say, this was embarrassing to a good many of the men to whom we talked when they suddenly realized that the decisions they made had been preshaped for them; they felt they were puppets. For example, one executive vice-president who nursed the illusion that he was really making his own decisions, suddenly realized that the president had been molding his decisions for a good long time, so that the decisions he made were just what the president wanted him to make. To anyone with a highly sensitive ego, this might have been offensive. But he also realized that part of the executive job is to grow up and to recognize that one is working for the company and not for oneself. So this fact of executive life was pretty well accepted by him.

The ways in which the control operation works after the responsibility has been delegated are many and varied. There are direct controls, such as procedure manuals and policies that serve as restrictions. You cannot spend, say, more than $25,000. Then there are all the communication systems, the telephones, squawk-boxes, and so forth, to carry information up to top management and decisions down. These are controls; in fact, that is the main function of these tangible communication systems. But, while there has been a whole literature built around communications, very little has been said about the informal controls involved in the preshaping and shaping of decisions in the course of delegation and control. Many of these controls are at work in conferences, not in spoken directions, but in the opinions and decisions and arguments that shuttle around the table until everyone has a general idea of what they would agree to. Then this concensus is discussed some more, until the boss says something, or states a fact, and everyone then knows that this is a decision which he would approve, or would not approve. So the decision is finally shaped to gain his approval. I am oversimplifying it, but you all know what goes on. Most of this is known to any man who is an organizer, though nobody says much about it.

Interlocking committees are another neat device for shaping and preshaping decisions. Harlow Curtice, I recall, wears six hats at General Motors and Henry Ford II and Ernest Breech each wear seven at Ford Motors. They serve on committees all the way down the line; policy, coordinating, administrative, executive, etc. The necessity of control all the way down is obvious in a big organization where many able men are making decisions which affect profit. The decisions may affect only the shape of a mud guard, but an unsatisfactory result could mean millions of dollars in lost sales. Curtice changed the styling of the Chevrolet, for example, a few days before the designs were frozen for 1955. This business of keeping a finger on all operations seems to be typical of the most able managers in business today. You can call it meddling, but it seems to result in good management.

These informal controls are fascinating, I believe, to anyone who really gets into them. There are the controls exercised by just moving around and getting the feel of a situation, by a conversation here and there. No one has ever defined what the "feel" of a situation is, but Lucius Clay searches for it continuously at Continental Can. He visits each of the company's 80 or so plants once a year, and when he goes around he does not by any means limit himself to the top plant manager. He goes down often to lower-level managers, seeking to find out what is going on down in the works. In this way he says he gets the feel of what kind of management is really taking place.

Clay presented a very interesting paper at Harvard last June on the art of delegation and, in the course of it, he made a very extraordinary statement. He said, in effect, "I wouldn't hire a man who isn't always sticking his neck out and assuming responsibility, and who isn't actually making decisions when they have to be made, if they aren't being made by someone above him." So we asked Mr. Clay, "General, do you really believe that statement?" And he said, "Of course, if any manager takes too much responsibility and authority, I stop him." The point was that he was trying to encourage managers to think, to develop their decision-making powers, but he knows he must always be on hand with the stopping process and other means of checking up.

There are more subtle controls, too. For example, control by compatibility, which is the business of picking men who are agreeable to you so that you can get along with them, and, in this way, you may control the kind of management going on in your company. And there are at least four different techniques for delegating decisions. One is the pressure method, e.g., you do not promote a man unless he has trained a man to succeed him. Another way is to ask questions and never give answers; in this way you may frustrate managers into making decisions. A third way is to give completely free rein to a manager; sometimes this has to be done when a new president takes over a company and knows nothing about the men he controls. Then there is the technique of model-setting, inspiring by example. This is a very intangible kind of control and is one way, of course, to win personal loyalty. The hardest thing, though, is to win loyalty to the organization, which, in our observation, can greatly outweigh loyalty to a personality at the top.

This brings me to a major point, and I wish I had more time to deal with it. We have been interested to observe the emergence of a new kind of manager. He is a man who is able to manage nonpersonally. He makes the job the center of things and, while he uses human relations skills, he does not use them simply to avoid friction. He is able to convince his subordinates that he is sincerely after better work, and not really driving for his own advancement. The president of Electric AutoLite

Company, James Falvey, is an excellent example. He is a lawyer who moved into an "executive suite" situation with twenty vice-presidents, several of whom seemed hopeful of getting the presidency. They had worshiped the former president, Joyce Martin, who was a two-fisted rugged individualist. Martin had kept everything in his back pocket and had made all decisions. He had the loyalty of his vice-presidents, but, when he died suddenly, there was not a single man prepared to succeed him, though he had left some uncertain hopes in several minds. Falvey moved in impersonally, and put all the emphasis on getting his job done. He did this very quietly, and the vice-presidents have all shifted very quickly around to giving the company much more loyalty than Martin's personal management over twenty-five years was able to win from them.

This nonpersonal kind of management takes the minds of managers off themselves. It works the way an interesting object does when it is brought into a room where everybody has been arguing. Usually you will find that people will turn and look at the object and the personal bickering stops. It was something like this at Electric AutoLite; everybody got interested in the job and the personal animosity subsided.

At *Fortune* we are inclined to think that many managers are oversold on techniques of all kinds, especially those such as communication, human relations, and participative management. I am just completing a study of participation in a small company which has been working at it for seven years. It has been a very interesting experiment. The president, who had an ideal setup for experimentation, is a young man full of new • ideas about management and sociology. He had the authority to apply a great many techniques and he has worked hard at it. He is getting some results which are rather surprising. For example, he is finding that, after he worked hard to get them to participate, to argue, and discuss all their problems (and he has had participation right down the line to foreman), some of his men who are developing the ability to make decisions of their own are getting less participative and more authoritarian. They are not the same managers they were; they are making decisions and seem to be tougher managers than he would have wanted five or six years ago. They keep their minds on the job and minimize some of the human problems. The less these men think of their own ambitions, and the more they concentrate on the job and think of developing other men, the smoother and better job they do.

This is not new at all, of course. It is related to the old idea of "service" that has been talked about for years. It has been talked about in utilities companies especially. To you in the utilities field, the idea of service is old stuff. But if you could think of it in terms of service to the job, as well as service to the public, it might help you manage better. This is the sense of other-mindedness, thinking of the other fellow and the job and not thinking of what is in it for you. Its opposite is the emphasis on human aspects, which I think has bogged down a good many potentially capable managers. I find that most men who really are big managers at the top possess this faculty of impersonality. It is not coldness; it is an objectivity. It is, "Let's get the job done and let's not worry so much about what happens to me or you." Perhaps you can use this fact in your own introspective appraisal of whether you really *are* an executive.

FEDERAL GOVERNMENT RELATIONS TO BUSINESS

by Felix Wormser

IN A RECENT PAPER, Professor Livingston commented upon the importance of government relations to business as part and parcel of the knowledge which an industrial engineer must possess if he is to consider himself at all well equipped in his profession. I fully agree.

Certainly, as one goes up in the scale of management responsibilities, the enormous importance of government in the day-to-day decisions of business becomes increasingly clear. I daresay your company presidents and managers devote as much time, nowadays, to Washington affairs as they do to their own local problems. It was not always so, and the contrast between today's methods of conducting business and those of, say, thirty years ago is marked. We shall not have time to go into the reasons for this development; they are well-known to you. All of us have lived through this important period in American history, characterized apparently by a never ending, and still growing, intervention by government in business. The end of the road is either complete socialism or communism. Fortunately, we are still a long way from that goal.

The utilities industry has long been the target for the socialists. The reason is obvious; the generation of electric power is absolutely basic to our prosperity. The control of power is

Address presented at the Eighth Utility Management Workshop, July, 1959. Mr. Wormser is Vice-President of the St. Joseph Lead Company.

the control of life or death for industry and for society. I saw for myself, while in official Washington, serving in the Department of the Interior, the great inroads the government had already made in the public utility field largely as an offshoot of reclamation or flood control projects. As you know, the federal government now accounts for about 14 percent of the electric power generated in the United States, and there is a constant drive to increase this percentage. Remember Hell's Canyon? That battle is still going on, incredible though it seems. You may have noticed that, in an area not supervised by the Department of the Interior, the Tennessee Valley Authority is attempting to widen the scope of its operations in pure power generation. I have long felt that many of Interior's great projects, such as Bonneville or Grand Coulee, are eminently worth-while and must be financed by the government; but, it always seems to me that, as a matter of principle, the power should be sold at the generating station. However, Congress has had different ideas. It has introduced all kinds of preferences for the distribution of power, with industry last on the list, subordinate to numerous public authorities. This illustrates what I mean: Should the government control all electric power generation in the United States, it could very easily control the destiny of any industry or corporate enterprise by making it difficult for the company to obtain its essential basic electrical requirements.

At the same time this trend towards socializing electric power in the United States is progressing, I am glad to report forces operating in the other direction. Two of them are quite noteworthy. The first was the opposition to the federal drive to nationalize Hell's Canyon. This was a great battle while I was in the Interior and, to my mind, a very crucial one. If the Hell's Canyon battle had been lost, public power advocates would have been flushed with victory and would have made drives elsewhere in the United States to duplicate their success. The forces favoring private power and free enterprise won a great victory in the Hell's Canyon affair.

The other illustration I have in mind is the fact that the City of New York actually is divesting itself of power plants which it owned, selling them to private industry; I am amazed at this step. This is certainly socialism in reverse and will, undoubtedly, prove to be a good move. But it is discouraging to see the grip which socialistic ideas have in the United States and which emanate, no doubt, from the feeling that the government can operate business enterprises more satisfactorily and more beneficially for the public than private enterprise. This is one of the world-wide fallacies of the period in which we live. The lure has been the profits which private corporations are alleged to have been making. Socialists feel that these profits belong to the public. This view permeated the thinking of those who wanted to nationalize, and did nationalize, coal abroad and those who wanted to nationalize, and did nationalize, oil in Italy. I also believe the socialists have made a great mistake in not realizing that there are business risks involved in any business enterprise. There are losses as well as profits to be considered in any industry and, certainly in my own field of mining, the business risks are terrific. One has to find oil before it can be profitably extracted from the ground. The risk is so great that in areas of the world where petroleum has been nationalized, as in Mexico, Argentina and Italy, I note that production has not followed an upward trend or has done so only slightly. Contrast this record with what has happened in Venezuela or in the Middle East, where private enterprise has been given full play. Certainly, it is much wiser for government to allow private industry to take the risk of finding mineral wealth and then to share handsomely in the profits, either through profit-sharing arrangements or taxation. They then reap the benefits without the headaches.

I need not dwell upon the political difficulties attached to any government-run enterprise; they are manifold. It is likely that payrolls will be enlarged politically or more than is required for efficiency, that salaries will not be competitive with private industry, and that the future of the enterprise will be in constant jeopardy; it will then be necessary to lean upon Congress for any basic and time-consuming decision. The utility industry is, of course, quite conscious of all these fundamentals, and must submit not only to federal regulations but to state or local regulations. Therefore, if any industry is aware of the result of government intervention in business, it is utilities. It is quite proper that any public utility should be regulated in the public interest, for Americans have an abhorrence of monopoly and feel that, where monopolies are in existence, they must be regulated. I know that a great many businessmen chafe under the restrictions of the Sherman Anti-Trust law, but, to my mind, it is one of the soundest statutes Congress has ever adopted. It clarifies and formalizes our conception of free enterprise, which has made this nation great and is unique in the world today.

Even though the public utility industry has a monopolistic position, I am reminded of the fact that, from my own company's experience, this monopolistic position may not always be too secure. To illustrate: my company, being the second largest user of electricity in the Pittsburgh area, felt it could generate its own power more cheaply than it could buy from the local public utility company. Failing to get agreement on a reduction in rates, my company proceeded to build its own 250,000-kw. power plant, and the results have borne out the company's original view.

I recall some years ago talking to M. Jean Monnett, who, as you know, is the architect of the common market in Europe. He deplored the prevalence of cartels and monopolies abroad and said he hoped the common authority in Europe would pattern its rules and regulations after our own Sherman Anti-Trust law. If you have followed this important development abroad, which means so much to mankind, you will notice that there has been a tightening up of the laws affecting competition, and the curbing of cartels, even though Europeans do not go as far as we do in this country.

Of course, the utilities industry has not had to face the struggles in the market place as have ordinary manufacturing or other enterprises, and, as a result, its financial reward is generally circumscribed by law. Those in the industry do not complain too bitterly about this, for there are offsetting advantages. There is a certain amount of competition of an important nature, namely, competition from federal, municipal, or cooperative projects. I am sure this would be welcome if it were on an equitable basis, but, considering the tax-exempt edge given these governmental or semigovernmental agencies, the competition is certainly not equitable.

Perhaps it is trite to call attention to the inexorable rise in the consumption of electric power in our country, a fact well-known to all of us. However, in examining the statistics illustrating the *relative* growth in privately owned and governmentally owned generating facilities over the past twenty-five years, I was struck by two things: (1) the comparative decline in the generation of electric power from privately owned generating facilities, and (2) the startling growth of federal, municipal, and cooperative power plants. I notice, for example, that 94.5 percent of the power generated in the United States in 1930 was from privately owned establishments. The small balance was from government-owned units. Twenty-seven years later, in 1957, the last year for which I was able to obtain figures, there was registered a seven-fold increase in the amount of power generated in the United States. This is startling growth, but more striking is the fact that privately owned establishments generated only 76.2 percent of this power whereas the greatly expanded federal plants accounted for 16 percent, municipal plants for 4.5 percent, and cooperatives about 2 percent. Such has been the trend toward socialized power in the United States. I derive a certain amount of satisfaction from the examination of these figures, however, because the administration with which I was recently connected kept the proportion of privately owned power at around the current rate whereas, previously, the trend to socialization of power had been rather sharply upward. I hate to think what the result would have been in a year or so had we lost the Hell's Canyon battle!

Any businessman going to Washington to occupy a high position in government soon becomes acutely aware of the tremendous political machine we Americans have generated federally. As you know, we have concentrated in the federal government many activities which used to be considered largely the function of the states. These include labor legislation, education, and social security legislation. Hence Washington has developed an enormous bureaucracy, and there is still no end in sight to the trend. It complicates the job of a high official in Washington since federal decisions, on a high-policy level, almost always have to receive the concurrence of all the departments at interest and that is generally three or more. After this, Cabinet action is required. Endless hours are spent by Cabinet officers studying matters of high public importance before a decision can be made. Anyone who has the popular impression that government workers of high echelon are idlers will soon be disabused on taking office. The higher the office the longer the hours, is an almost invariable rule. The President, of course, is never away from his responsibilities, night or day.

I got a great lift in seeing for myself the industry and intelligence displayed by fellow Cabinet officers endeavoring to serve the public interest. But remember, the administration, under the direction of the President, is only one arm of our government. The legislative and judicial functions are equally important, and they, too, have to be considered in any decision that the administration or government may make. This adds to the complexities and explains the slowness with which government decisions are often made. The government can afford to take its time, and it always does.

I mentioned a moment ago the centralization of our federal responsibility—much of it accomplished over strenuous opposition and all of it extremely difficult to undo. No matter what your views happen to be about social legislation, you will quickly realize that it is not easy to undo the social legislation which has already been adopted by the people. As a matter of fact, would you, today, if you had the power, do away with social security, unemployment compensation, SEC legislation, labor legislation, and the like? This is not an easy question to answer, now that these activities have become so deeply entrenched in our economy.

There is one thing, however, you can be sure of. No matter what action the government takes, it is not immune from economic law, and, as we have noted in the past, whenever the government intervenes in markets in an effort to cure an unsatisfactory situation, such as we find in agriculture from time to time, the cure is generally worse than the disease. Economic laws function regardless of government edict! Look at the difficulties of agriculture today with gigantic crop surpluses worth over $9 billion! What to do with huge surpluses has indeed puzzled Congress for years. No one has yet offered a satisfactory answer for the farmers or for Congress. The issue is not only economic; it is moral as well. I think the average farmer is an honest, fine, American citizen. If you were to ask him whether he thought it would be right for him to pass the hat among his fellow townsmen, asking for a contribution from each so he could get a better price for his products, he would indignantly reply, "Of course not." Yet, that is the very thing he does, through the instrumentality of government, when he accepts a subsidy.

Everyone in the utilities industry is, no doubt, acutely aware of the indirect subsidies that the government has paid which enable the TVA and many of the Department of the Interior's public power projects to operate and charge rates lower than private enterprise, only because they do not pay taxes or obtain their capital from the government at artificially low interest rates. I suppose subsidies have long been part and parcel of our American economic system. I do not condemn all of them, because, appropriately applied and removed at the right time, they can serve the important function of giving a government incentive where it is needed, either in peacetime or in wartime. It is the abuse of the subsidy principle to which I object.

If you agree that subsidies have an immoral implication and should be discouraged, you will be appalled at the moral principle that government after government has violated in recent years through monetary policies that are now freely accepted throughout the world. I am referring, candidly, to the action by government after government, freely changing its monetary standards without any notification or warning to its citizens, allowing its monetary unit to depreciate, and thereby, in essence, stealing from its citizens. This is technically known as "devaluation of currencies." To my mind, this is disguised thievery. Yet it is accepted widely as a common, honorable practice. The departure from high moral standards in fiscal matters, and the departure from fundamental principles that have proven sound since biblical times, largely accounts for many of the difficulties in which governments, including our own, find themselves today.

I attended a meeting last month at which Senator Byrd of Virginia was honored. He told us that he was the only Senator left in the Senate of the United States who had voted against the TVA at its inception, and that he had voted against the Wagner Act. He said this quite pridefully, for, undoubtedly, he had in mind the serious problems both pieces of legislation have created for the American people. He took a stand on principle, and I think that is a guide for all of us, even though the temptation among businessmen is primarily to serve their own interests, regardless of whether the action might unknowingly violate some cardinal principle of good business judgment.

I am reminded of this by the fact that during the days of the deep depression in the thirties, many businessmen rushed to Washington, requesting a modification of our statutes so that they would have more liberty to control prices and production—a power which they felt would enable them to get together with their competitors and arrange matters so that the depression would soon be over. Congress acted and gave them the National Industrial Recovery Act, but you will recall that each code of fair competition, when finally adopted by the government, carried its famous Section 7A, which compelled industry to bargain collectively with labor. When the whole National Recovery mechanism was declared unconstitutional and erased from the statute books, the only thing that remained was Section 7A, which became the genesis of the Wagner Act. That was the price business paid for its folly! I know my own industry, at that time, was also imbued with the thought that it might be able to get together and solve its problems through some power bestowed upon it by Congress. I called upon Senator Borah, at that time, and he told me the scheme looked very attractive, and he would be very glad to help put it through the Senate of the United States. He said, however, that I should remember there would be a price tag attached; namely, the fact that the government would control the industry. He thought the price was pretty high to pay. We all agreed and, I am glad to say, we never took any step to implement our original thinking. Indeed, if there is any one lesson I have learned from my experience in Washington, and my observations of business history outside of Washington, it is that we make a great mistake when we ask the government to do anything special to assist us. The price of government control is too high to pay.

While I was in Washington the coal industry experienced rather difficult times. Some companies were desperate, and I remember presiding over a meeting of coal producers. I was shocked to hear one of them suggesting that the government take over the industry, believing the government operation would solve the problems of the operators. If anything, this step would make matters worse.

I agree with the conclusion of the Hoover Commission, which made a painstaking study on the organization of the executive branch of the government. It came to the conclusion that the present trend of our federal power policies would ultimately make the federal government a predominant producer of electric power in the United States and, in many sections, a sole and monopolistic producer. This would place an unnecessary financial burden upon the federal taxpayer to finance construction costs of the rapidly expanding power facilities of the government. It would also discriminate among regions and states and between users of federally produced and privately produced electric power.

In summary, may I repeat what I said in the early part of my talk. The managers of the utilities industry must look forward to spending an increasingly large fraction of their time in appraising and deciding problems of relationships with government—particularly the federal government. It behooves them to keep themselves adequately and accurately informed in order that their decisions, and the actions which flow from the decisions, may be effective.

THE TOOLS OF THE MANAGER
by William W. Waite

OTHER CONTRIBUTORS to this volume have emphasized the decision-making process and mentioned the effects which decisions made at one level of management have on other segments of the organization. These effects will be felt, and problems will be solved, to the extent that decisions are implemented. The implementation is accomplished by the manager through the use of all or part of an array of techniques and tools available to him. These include his subordinates, his knowledge of the job, and auxiliary services within his organization. The degree of effectiveness of problem solution is dependent on the manager's understanding of these techniques and his skill in utilizing them. Some highly successful managers have depended on their own judgment and ability in meeting every situation and being personally concerned with the details of every problem. Others of us, not so blessed with ability or energy, have been forced to content ourselves with reliance on subordinates or staff people to do the detailed study and data-gathering work, on the basis of which we formulate our decisions and take appropriate action.

I am reminded of an excerpt from Rogers, Slade, and Hill's *Management Briefs* which illustrates the point in terms of one man's experience a number of years ago. He had been "supervising" the members of his group in great detail and taking

Address presented at the Eighth Utility Management Workshop, July, 1959. Mr. Waite is Professor of Industrial Engineering, Columbia University.

home a briefcase full of work every evening. One day he arrived at the office garbed in the jacket and trousers of two different suits. Realizing that, as a dignified manager, he could not possibly appear among his subordinates, he telephoned his tailor for an emergency replacement and was told that he could be re-outfitted by two o'clock. Meanwhile, he confined himself to his own office, where his desk effectively hid the offending trousers. In the ensuing several hours he made a startling discovery—"I ceased doing other people's work and found time to do mine."

The transition from engineer to manager, or from worker to supervisor, is a difficult one. It involves a drastic mental and emotional readjustment. And it also involves rigid adherence to the managerial adage of letting subordinates carry out the actual work of the job. The engineer or scientist is trained to work on his own, to know and handle all the aspects of a problem. The manager, on the other hand, must learn to delegate responsibility and authority. The need for delegation has beset managers since the dawn of history. The Old Testament (Exodus 18. 12–27) records the plight of Moses, who spent all day, every day, hearing the complaints and petitions of his flock, settling quarrels, and giving advice. Progress toward the Promised Land was at a snail's pace and bade fair to cease altogether after many years of wandering. Jethro, the leader's father-in-law, advised him to reorganize on a line-and-staff basis, delegating to subordinates the authority to handle routine problems. Then, only the most serious and difficult decisions would be presented to Moses. Jethro's advice was accepted, the delegation was made, and the Bible tells us of the startling increase in the progress of the Children of Israel toward their goal. The transition from technical expert to manager is difficult in all parts of an enterprise—research and development as well as operating—and is a source of serious concern to every organization.

In order to gain some perspective in ways and means of utilizing managerial talent more effectively, it may be well to look for a moment at some of the major functions the manager performs in discharging his responsibilities and the processes or acts through which he must accomplish these functions. These functions and processes can be set up in an array (see Figure 1) and their interrelationships studied. For example, we may consider the gathering of *information* from *outside contacts,* which may be designated as Relationship 1/5.

	Process			
Function	Information 1	Evaluation 2	Decision 3	Action 4
Outside contacts 5				
Internal management 6				
Learning and planning 7				
Production 8				

Figure 1. Functions and Processes of a Manager's Job

We can break this function down into two major subheadings —"external relations" and "supporting services." The former includes (but is not limited to) long-term financial considerations, stockholder relations, labor relations, public relations, and legal matters.

The second major subheading can be broken down, in turn, into two minor listings. Supporting services are functions available within the total organization but outside the particular

manager's own department or division. Planning for the future
includes such activities as research and development, engineering and design, budgeting and forecasting, and market surveys. Regardless of the particular manager's niche in the total
organization, his job is vitally affected by what is done in these
collateral divisions, and he must take their work into consideration in his own planning and decision-making. For example,
many a manager's plans have been upset upon receipt of information that a cut has been made in his operating budget;
and there are many who feel that the market research information on which design of the Edsel car was based could well
have been somewhat more accurate.

The members of the second supporting group are the "routine and service functions," which supply the manager with
such needs as accounting and personnel administration, housekeeping, quality control, and purchasing and inventory. To
summarize the outside contacts, we may arrange them in tab-
ular form:

External Relations	*Supporting Services*	
	Planning for the Future	*Routine and Service Functions*
Long-term financial considerations	Research and development	Accounting
Stockholder relations	Engineering and design	Personnel administration
Labor relations		Housekeeping
Public relations	Budgeting and forecasting	Quality control
Legal matters	Market surveys	Purchasing and inventory

In most organizations these groupings complete the roster of
contacts outside the line manager's own sphere from which he
must seek information to aid him in making his decisions.
Without adequate use of outside contacts, the manager will
probably be groping in the dark on many important aspects of
his job.

In dealing with each of these sub-functions the manager must have information, usually obtained for him by others on request. Both the type and amount of data which can be assembled will vary with the source from which they must be obtained and the purpose for which they are to be used. The manager cannot afford to accept all information at face value, and he must evaluate (relationship 2/5) whatever he gets in the light of experience and corroborative evidence from other sources before he decides what to do about each problem.

Parenthetically, it may be said that the average managerial employee is grossly unappreciative (because he is generally uninformed or misinformed) of the problems of his boss and his colleagues, even though he understands, from personal experience, the problems of those he supervises. Also, communication between the engineer or scientist and the manager is often difficult and unsatisfactory because the latter must have his information in black and white, to make his decision, while the former wants to give the information in shades of gray, with numerous alternative choices involving different courses of action and potential results. Without discussing decision-making in detail, either as to theory or practice, let it be said at this point that a manager must evaluate each pertinent bit of information, from whatever source, to set up the alternatives in the clearest possible black-and-white terms, so that he can make a decision which, once arrived at, can be translated into action.

Moving down the array to the next function shown, we come to *Internal Management*. The manager is directly responsible for (1) functionalization and decentralization, (2) job division and delegation, and (3) the span of control. Like the man in the excerpt from *Management Briefs*, many of us have, at times, been too busy "putting out fires" all over our organizations to have had enough time to devote to internal management. The manager's function is to see to it that his unit is properly organized to accomplish its mission and not to try to accomplish the mission single-handed. We might express the latter philosophy as, "If you want something done, get a servant to do it; if you want it done right, do it yourself." Unfortunately, there are times when the urge to "do it yourself" is well-nigh irresistible, but this usually reflects inadequate internal management and the questions then arise, "Have we set the span of control of the subordinate too high? Has insufficient authority been delegated?" And so on.

The manager's job is a living, changing, evolving, developing thing, and its proper working depends heavily on his ability to learn from experience and plan for the future. The tools or processes which the manager uses to perform this function are, again, *Information* (Relationship 1/6), *Evaluation* (2/6), *Decision* (3/6), and *Action* (4/6). In this function, the process portion of the array is often discontinuous. Once a course of action has been decided upon to meet a particular situation, it can be incorporated in a program and the manager is saved the time and effort involved in going through the entire decision-making process each time the situation recurs. A program is as good or as bad as its author. It involves as much detail as the author sees fit to put into it. But, once developed, a program is fed into a human or mechanical computer and results begin to emerge. Too often the author blames the computer for unexpected or unsatisfactory results, when it is the information fed in by the program which is incomplete or inaccurate. As a case in point, we have a fairly specific program worked out for the Utility Management Workshop, and we expect you to provide some results. You are, in this instance, the human computers and it is our responsibility to give you, by every means possible—the Workbook, the experts' presentations, the panel sessions—all the information required to produce the desired results. If we fail, we cannot logically blame you for failing in the satisfactory completion of your tasks.

When programs are incorporated into operating manuals, they remain in effect until the manager finds it advisable to modify them on the basis of new information or a different evaluation of existing information. Routine changes can arise through the use of routine sources of information and, if provided for in the operating programs and manuals, require no action by the manager. For example, feedback from quality control indicating decreasing adherence to production standards results automatically in adjustments to restore the quality without specific decision and action by the manager. A seniority increase in the rate of pay for an employee can be handled under a wage administration program without specific approval by the manager. However, if it is learned that competitors are underselling the organization because excessively close tolerances are keeping production costs high, the whole array of supporting services may well be involved in gathering data for evaluation as the basis for a decision to change the operating program. Can market research find out whether customers really need and want components meeting the close tolerances? Will engineering and design state the changes necessary in the product and the resultant savings? Can research and development suggest less expensive substitute materials? Will labor relations be able to handle the repercussions from a reduction in piece rates or in the evaluation of certain jobs? Unfortunately, there have been instances where failure to receive information, or to evaluate properly the information received, has resulted in no decision being made or no action being taken.

One such situation, which occurs with discouraging frequency in the United States, is the failure by management to provide a fool-proof channel for advising job evaluation supervisors of changes in job content or requirements. If these are increased, the Union sees to it that a grievance is filed and ratings raised. But, if the job requirements are reduced, it is up to management to initiate downgrading before the end of the grace period or lose the opportunity entirely. Such changes can be made only if proper information is passed along promptly.

We can set up a series of actions by subordinates which incorporate the principles of programming and delegation of authority and which are fundamental to smooth and efficient functioning of an organization. In the first instance, the subordinate takes action appropriate to the situation on his own authority and need not even report such action to his supervisor. The next level is that the subordinate takes appropriate action and, later, reports the facts to his boss for the latter's information. Third, the subordinate decides what action to take, reports to the next higher level and asks for concurrence. Finally, there are the problems on which the subordinate goes to his boss and asks for instructions. These are the really tough ones—the ones for Moses. They cannot be handled either under established programs or by delegation of authority. Actually, these four types of managerial decision-making and action are carried out at each level of the pyramid of power.

All these preliminaries lead us to the raison d'être of the organization—*production.* All the executive's planning, organizing, internal management, and outside contacts are wasted unless he can translate them into that continuity of operation which is essential to the success of the organization. Programs set forth the goals to be achieved, and operational manuals form the basis for a reasonable degree of continuity of operation and represent the action taken by the manager to accomplish his last function. Further action is required whenever the decision is made to revise the program because of changes in the original decisions.

The manager must, of necessity, exert all his influence through his contacts with other people—his human relations. The "task" is a set of impersonal expectations; it can be accomplished only through the hands and brains of individuals. As the manager discharges his functions, he must consider the values inherent in the roles he plays, the resources at his disposal, and the techniques he uses in his dealings with other people. Since material and methodological resources are inanimate, the greatest concern must be reserved for the human resources of the organization, and the manager inevitably spends a considerable part of his total effort in attempting to understand the sense of values held by those with whom he must work. It is frequently easier to operate within a framework which recognizes that different people hold to different values than it is to collide head-on in a usually vain effort to make others revise their feelings in accord with the manager's ideas. This is not meant to imply that managers should bow to the whims of subordinates, but, rather, that they should make every effort to utilize the largest possible segment of the value-structure of each member of the organization in furthering the over-all objective.

William Whyte makes the point, in *The Organization Man*, that our ethical values and, more specifically, those of managers have undergone a change. Individualism is no longer the primary ethic of the business world. To a greater and greater extent, the social ethic of groupism has replaced individualism, and many of us—and a majority of business organizations—set far greater store by conformity than we do by nonconformity. Probably the single most important exception to this statement is to be found in the field of industrial research. However, much of the research and, particularly, the development work is carried out with specific objectives to which researchers must conform. Only a small minority are able to apply their own sets of values freely in their work. Necessary though conformity is, especially in the operation of a large public utility, I think it is unfortunate for the individual and that it underlies the situation against which Jacques Barzun argues in *The House of Intellect.* Along with the "Cult of Science" which emphasizes conformity, standardization, and specialization, we have the "Cult of Art," which too often heaps praise and popularity on free expression, cubism, and other forms of nonrationality. The third member of Barzun's triumvirate of villainy is the "Cult of Philanthropy," which he charges with supporting the lazy, the incompetent, and the stupid practitioners of "art" at the expense of the talented and hard-working intellectual whose work, while less flamboyant, is nevertheless more valuable to mankind. All of which is by way of saying that today's manager needs a great deal of ability in assessing the value-judgements of his subordinates and his supervisors and in bending each sufficiently to fit the other and get the job done.

People work in an enforced association. Our social mores being what they are, it is not easy for a man—particularly one at the managerial level—who is unhappy in his job to burn his bridges and march boldly forth in search of an equally good (financially speaking) connection elsewhere. The man who is "between jobs" is often suspect in his set and in his family. Once he has worked his way up, he is usually forced to stay and make the best of his associations. Granting this and the fact that most of his reponsibilities must be discharged by subordinates, it behooves him to guide, teach, discipline, and direct his aides by every means at his disposal, to the end of meeting his group's objectives promptly, satisfactorily, and inexpensively. The way in which his subordinates accomplish their segments of the total task, the degree to which they cooperate and assist each other in reaching the common objective, reflect the personality of the manager who directs them. In a very real sense the tools are the image of the user.

In this matter of human relations the manager may find some guideposts useful. The manager's functions have been compared to those of any biological entity—outside contacts, internal management, learning and planning, and production. The organization or sub-organization over which he presides may also be likened to a biological entity, with the added impact that it actually *is* a collection of genuine biological entities whose actions and reactions, while not necessarily equal and opposite, are the composite product of many ingredients: cultural, educational, and experiential background; hopes and expectations; physical health. The manager will find that he needs in his kit of tools a well-sharpened ability to look upon his problems as sociological and psychological situations, as well as to view their technological complexities. This might be termed the clinical approach and should be assiduously cultivated by the manager who wishes to achieve maximum success.

This he may do, in part, by accepting people as they are and trying to understand them. By so doing, he is in a better position to assign responsibility commensurate with ability, to reward work well done, and to admonish where necessary. He is less likely to use the tool for a purpose for which it was not designed or to blame the computer which was unable to assimilate the data fed to it. The manager using the clinical approach also recognizes that his own set of values and his outlook are not necessarily identical with those of the people with whom he comes in contact, but he sees no necessity for changing his own viewpoint merely to conform. Nor does he feel that the other person must agree with him on pain of being labeled an imbecile or a radical.

The clinically oriented manager is able to understand the feelings underlying the act or statement of his associate. This is extremely important in supervisory work because people are so often unable or unwilling to put into words the true reasons for acts they have performed or positions they have taken. Illogical behavior often becomes much clearer when we find out the real cause. Another factor of which we often lose sight is that our own behavior, attitude, or tone of voice has deep impact on the reactions of colleagues and subordinates. One of my graduate students some years ago, an Air Force colonel, produced an excellent analysis of this aspect of human relations under the title *Know Thyself*. While amateur psychiatry is likely to produce as lamentable results as other untutored efforts, it requires relatively little insight to recognize the effect on others of our more overt behavior and to take some self-corrective action.

Another evidence of the clinical approach is an understanding of the social system of the organization. In all companies there are examples of the grapevine, pressures on workers not to be too energetic, status customs, cliques among various groups, and traditions which are more rigid than formal policies. The clinically oriented manager is less interested in deciding whether this social structure is good or bad than he is in finding out the effect of each segment of it on the operation of the organization. The hierarchy of authority is one very important aspect of the organization's social structure and the clinical approach includes a realistic estimate of the situation as it affects the behavior of people at different levels. Prestige and status vary with organizational level and their outward symbols are closely watched by all the interested parties.

The manager who is experienced in the use of the clinical approach will find it possible to forecast, with a fair degree of accuracy, how the organization will react to his actions. He can thereby avoid moves or methods of approach which are likely to negate his plans and can act in a manner most likely to be effective. He can do this if he has built up and experience-tested a fund of knowledge of social phenomena against which he can compare proposed moves. Obviously, he must be alert to all the possibilities for unique factors in a given situation and flexible in modifying his self-developed principles in the light of current experience.

All these aspects of the clinical approach have been presented as somewhat discreet, though interrelated ideas. The experienced and expert manager probably applies them intuitively, but the person who aspires to improve his performance may well give conscious thought to their use. They are deceptively simple when stated, but, like so many things about the human animal, they are seldom effective in the same way or to the same degree with different people. Judiciously used, they can help the manager to improve the quality and effectiveness of his most frequently used tool—his subordinates.

ORGANIZATIONAL FUNCTIONS
by Robert Teviot Livingston

AN INDUSTRIAL ENTERPRISE, regardless of the money, machines, materials, and most of the rest of the M's, is basically a human association and may, indeed, be considered a macro-biological entity. Different biological entities exhibit certain universal characteristics, even though they may have different appearances or structures. If, therefore, the associations may be compared to biological entities, they, too, will exhibit universal characteristics, have universal wants, and will develop means of satisfying those wants in the environments in which they find themselves. Let me indicate some of these universal functions in terms which may lend themselves conveniently to consideration in respect to a real association.

THE BASIS OF FUNCTIONALIZATION

Work division and functionalization are natural phenomena. As any association grows, the necessity for specialization and work division becomes greater. This is an obvious requirement due to size and equally obvious as the result of diversity of activity or coverage of the organization's field. Furthermore, it takes advantage of the increase in skill and ability which people gain through practice. There is, however, a cost which must also be recognized—the cost of coordination and the necessity for communication and control. In a small beginning opera-

Mr. Livingston is Professor of Industrial Engineering, Columbia University, and Director of the Utility Management Workshop.

tion, the basis for work division is usually obvious. One person specializes in one field because he is good in that field, was trained in that field, and wants to specialize in that field. Also, each person will naturally attempt to avoid doing what he dislikes doing, although the outside world forces some specialization on us, somewhat against our wills.

In setting up a rational basis for specialization and work division, we might think once more in terms of a biological entity; obvious functions to be considered are (a) food supply; (b) self preservation, the escape from a predator or from offensive weapons (self-maintenance); (c) reproduction, which is a special form of self-preservation (preservation of the species); and (d) adaptation to changed and changing conditions.

A relatively recent article in *Science* gives the following list of five purposes of a social unit:

1. to perpetuate the association
2. to enrich the association
3. to describe the duties and the rights of the individuals
4. to safeguard the rights of the individuals
5. to regulate the interactions of the individuals with the association

Of these, all but the fourth should apply directly to an economic enterprise. There are other lists, but the following group of functions is proposed as most useful for purposes of analysis:

1. to deal outside the association
2. to produce something for which society will reward the association
3. to control and regulate internal affairs
4. to plan and look ahead

Although all of these functions are found in a real company, they vary between concerns and often have quite different names; also, companies are seldom so organized that one department can be identified exclusively with one of these functions. This is to be expected, and it is important to realize that, no matter how a concern is organized, each part of the organization and each sub-unit discharges each of these functions to some extent. For example, it is obvious that, theoretically, each organized entity is expected to contribute something of value to the association of which it is a part; that is the reason why it was organized. The manager of every unit is responsible for controlling and regulating the internal affairs of "his" unit. One of the prices that is paid for the gain due to specialization is the need to coordinate the specialized activities. When this coordination of effort is looked at from within the particular unit considered, it is seen as "dealing with the outside world." While formal planning may be organized as a department, the manager of which is expected to devote his time and effort to looking ahead, this function is also a duty (and a wise precaution) for the manager of every unit.

Before deciding finally on the organizational structure of the association it may be well to give consideration to the classifications into which the various segments may be fitted. Any sub-unit of the organization may be designated (according to its function and special mission) as (1) management, (2) staff, (3) line, or (4) service. The function of "management" is to set the broad objectives of the association, to formulate basic policies for meeting their objectives, to select persons to carry out the policies, to coordinate all the association's diverse activities, and, finally, to monitor the effectiveness of operations and the degree of success which the association enjoys. "Staff" functions are entirely advisory; staff personnel are technical specialists who work out solutions to problems arising in their fields of competence and advise management in ways of applying these solutions. "Line" includes the direct producers and those members of the association who direct them and form the link between managerial control and physical production. "Service" encompasses the multitudinous array of functions which, although not directly associated with the production of goods and services, are, nevertheless, considered essential to the smooth operation of the enterprise. We should bear this classification in mind as we consider the functions of the association under the headings I have proposed.

DEALING OUTSIDE THE ASSOCIATION

Every enterprise of whatever nature is living in a world and is a citizen of that world with special privileges and prerogatives. These are over and above the rights of an individual. We may begin with the basic right to be and the secondary right to do. Both of these flow from the people and form the subject of the basic negotiation with the world. This world grants special rights and privileges to special people and groups of people, often organized as corporations, because it is to the world's advantage to do so. The relationships and interactions which flow from this fact are considered as "trading with the world." The design of an organized enterprise creates units or domains, and the total goal of the enterprise is attained by the coordinated interaction of these units. The same is true of sub-units throughout the organization. It is every manager's duty to coordinate the efforts of the units which are within his domain, part of his division, department, section, or unit. When considered from the point of view of the unit itself—"from the inside looking out"—many of the relationships may be considered "dealing with the world."

Were the term "public relations" not used to designate a particular profession, it would be a better description than the one used above. However, in the broad rather than the narrow sense, it will be used hereafter to include those relations with all publics, and those interactions which are not directly associated with production, internal management, and providing

for the future. This category could also be called "responding
to external stimuli."

In considering the problem in the abstract, it is important
to keep in mind that the "world" differs with the level of the
unit in the organization. "Dealing with the world" encompasses
all relationships outside the particular bordered space being
considered at any time. The unit manager represents his group
in meeting the demands made upon it by different segments
of the "world" and makes bargains with the world for that
group. Depending on the organizational level of the unit, a
list of public relations (trading with the world) might include
some or all of the following:

1. Customer relations
   a. selling the product
   b. advertising the product
   c. product service
   d. appearance and other contacts of employees
2. Labor relations and negotiations
3. Investor relations
   a. obtaining the funds
   b. advertising and publicity
   c. annual reports and meetings
4. Government relations
   a. charter, franchise, and similar corporate affairs
   b. rates, service and similar matters
5. Other public relations
   a. with vendors and service companies
   b. with others in the same or allied business
   c. in obtaining needed information
   d. professional activities and appearances of employees
      and officers

In the final analysis, all relations are public relations; to a
company all relations are important. It has to live in a climate
and an environment. Making that climate or environment as

favorable as possible is part of that process of dealing with the world. Many of these activities are part of a person's specified job (selling, purchasing, finance, legal, advertising, service, and customer complaints). There are others which are incidental, such as meter reading, collecting, establishment of service. The definition of these relations will be less specific the higher we go in the organization.

The question arises as to the frequency of each kind of relationship. Where contacts are so frequent as to become routine it is probable that they should be moved down in the organization and eventually become "programmed" and, if possible, attached or attributed to one of the routine functions or operations. However, it will always be necessary to consider carefully the characteristics of those public relations which must always be handled individually and on a non-routine basis.

PRODUCTION

There is a basic assumption that any unit, be it biological or economic, will persist only if it performs some function that society (in the broadest sense) finds useful. The "purpose of an enterprise" is to render a service, or supply a product, which society believes desirable and from which all the costs incurred may be recovered—plus a profit.

"Production" is the function of turning out that which the bargain with the world calls for; this is the basic, overt purpose of the enterprise. This is a function which is immediate—usually reasonably well specified in advance, in kind and amount. There also is the question of the supplier meeting the demand and the price for failure to meet the demand.

In almost every case the operation can be broken down into two subdivisions: production and distribution. Production is usually a fairly obvious classification, but distribution may be very complicated. Basically it includes sales and customer services as well as physical distribution.

INTERNAL MANAGEMENT

In order to understand internal management, it is important to understand the total management problem for what it is. Internal management depends upon the unit being considered. Let me refer to the fourfold classification which I mentioned earlier and which it is useful to set up as an array illustrating the various interrelations which can exist.

	General manage-ment	Staff	Line	Service
General management				
Staff				
Line				
Service				

Figure 1. Interrelations Array

This permits us to consider the interactions which every unit will have, the internal responses which follow, and the problems which will arise. In every unit there can be identified these four items; the larger and more complex the unit, the sharper will be the lines of differentiation between them. They are all tools of internal management, subject to coordination and control, and the efficiency of the coordination is an index of the effectiveness of the unit manager.

It may be of value at this point to discuss "service" in some detail. In broad compass, a service function may be useful to all other organs, including both line and staff; it may even transcend unit boundaries and apply to many nonhomogeneous units, as, for example, with accounting or employee relations. The question then arises as to the proper location of authority over the service. The unit manager may well find himself in the position of not being able to exercise direct control over a function which is essential to the success of his efforts at internal management. It is wise to find where one stands in these matters while there is yet time to adapt to the situation and plan accordingly.

PLANNING AND LOOKING AHEAD

As Peter Drucker has it, the basic concern of American industry today is provision for the future. It is more or less assumed that present operation is a separate problem which will, in some manner, be successfully pursued. In the broadest sense, planning ahead means a consideration of all present activities in terms of conditions in the future. Returning to our original consideration of a biological entity, a certain portion of each of the categories may be considered in an industrial organization as providing for the future. In the world of competition, provision for the future is part of self-defense, as it also is part of reproduction and learning and adaptation. The success of all of these depends to some extent upon the amount, the character, and the success of that consideration which management gives to the matter. However, in order to organize our thinking, I shall enumerate three aspects:

1. Planning   meeting the future
   a. Forecasting   estimating the probabilities
   b. Design   preparation of plans for realization
2. Research   searching for new or better means
3. Realization   preparing for operation
   a. Engineering   fitting the means to the circumstance
   b. Construction   providing the means

Between the first two and the last there is a dynamic decision. That decision then leads to another action, which is the procurement or production of the resources which are required. Until this is done and the new thing is in working order, it is not an operating function.

Planning is dealing with the future. On the one hand, we estimate the probability of the occurrence of events in the future, then the time and intensity of occurrence; on the other hand, we search for alternative methods and means of pursuing goals. In its simplest form, it is design; design may require technological forecasting (estimating the probability of the occurrence of future technological events) and research (the search for new, different and better ways of doing old things, the discovery of new things to do, or new products to produce).

You will note that planning included both forecasting and design, while engineering was shown as a part of realization. In actual companies, design and engineering are usually the same. Herewith, for the purpose of this study, these two are separated. Properly, planning would include (a) the forecasting of what will probably occur if there is no important difference between the future and the past both within and without (it is not a static conception but rather it considers that both internally and externally there has been a steady state; (b) an evaluation of what these forecasts will mean according to several usually unexpressed criteria, in terms of "desirable" or "undesirable"; (c) an assumption that management will make certain decisions which will be implemented at the proper time. These decisions will concern all the routine matters, such as financing and the like, but will be particularly directed toward "when required" and the amount of freedom of choice to be allowed. Also, certain decisions will be made as to potential emergencies.

In forecasting the future, certain complex quantities such as sales, investment, and net revenue are usually predicted. Forecasting would be much more soundly based if more attention were given to basic phenomena, such as prediction of the future environment, and prediction of the future state of technology. These two kinds of predictions are not independent, although they are not often consciously considered together. For example, an unfavorable event which can not be handled with the present state of the technology may be handled quite easily if there is a constant advance in technology. In most cases, technology advances by an increase in efficiency, an approach to some theoretical maxium, usually asymptotic. By extrapolation it may be seen that the present trend of the technology cannot possibly handle the future state of the requirements, and this indicates that research is needed—not bread and butter research, but new research directed towards a breakthrough. It is probable that a study of certain phenomena in basic terms would show where such breakthroughs could occur; when the limit of one material is reached, new materials with different weight-strength relations, for example, can completely change design.

In order that management may make plans, it must have estimates as to the occurrence or nonoccurrence of events, the magnitude of certain quantities associated with them, and the time of occurrence of the events. We are interested because we wish to increase the probability of occurrences of desirable events and decrease the probability of occurrence and the magnitude of unfavorable events.

Research may be thought of in three categories:

1. Routine research—trouble-shooting; improvement and adaptation within existing circumstances, or with minor changes
2. Defensive research—effecting relatively large changes which will supersede or render obsolete existing equipment or services, or which will call for additions to present equipment
3. Offensive research

Obviously, these are not clear-cut. It would seem that the first is largely a matter of immediacy and usually is within the scope and competence of the operating force. If work is to be done in this area, the research function should concern itself with the "why" and not the immediate "how." Research is primarily concerned with new fields or new ideas. However, because of rapid technological progress, any research department is likely to become involved in all three categories. This may be very good for research as a function, for it is in the first two fields that it can work easily, demonstrating its immediate value in dollars and cents. As part of its plan for self-preservation, every research department should have a group which is continuously in contact with engineering and operations. Here is a source of research projects which should be very easy to sell at budget time.

SUMMARY

The function of looking ahead and planning for the future has been almost exclusively the responsibility of the top executive. For the organization as a whole, it will probably remain so. However, within each sub-unit, this function must take its place along with internal management, production, and external dealings as the responsibility of *every* manager. And we might well give careful thought to a collateral problem. While the manager is estimating the probability of occurrence of different events and setting up plans and objectives for the future, he must estimate the probability of acceptance of his program by the subordinates who will have to implement it. Herein may lie one of his toughest problems.

Part Three

THE MANAGER AND HUMAN
RELATIONS

INTRODUCTION

WHENEVER a group of people combine their efforts in an enterprise, the functioning of the organization is deeply affected by the interpersonal relations of the members of the group. A further complicating factor in the situation is that there are relationships between the organization and other parts of its social milieu and between its people and outsiders which have an influence on operations quite aside from—and often in conflict with—the internal situation.

As our great public utility concerns and manufacturing plants have increased in size and complexity, the problems posed by people have increased even faster. The manager who, today, must direct and control twice or three times as many persons as his predecessor of a generation ago must also face dealings with regulatory bodies, civic organizations, customers, suppliers, stockholders, and others. He must coordinate all these relationships smoothly and efficiently if his organization or subunit is to prosper. His administrative skills must include an ample measure of good human relations.

Human beings operate the machines, process the raw materials, sell the products, count the money, and plan for the future of industry. Without people there could be no industry; even automated plants employ large numbers of people to push the buttons and to see that the machines function as they are supposed to. But people are more often unpredictable and unreliable than the machines. We cannot set a dial on a human being and confidently expect that he will perform exactly as directed. He usually wants to know "why," as well as "what" and "how." When once told, he sometimes forgets and must be reinstructed. His failures are frequently the result of lack of motivation, rather than lack of ability; he is sometimes even willfully stubborn, or he may deliberately withhold his services. How, then, can we induce him to perform the task we have laid out for him?

It is the manager's responsibility to answer that question through appreciation and understanding of the interpersonal relations which control the functioning of our socio-industrial complex. Formal organization is vital to successful operation, but the successful manager also recognizes fully the existence of informal organizations—cliques and group interests of all kinds—which criss-cross the formal lines. He utilizes as many of these as are positive in their effect and attempts to minimize those which are negative. Above all, the successful manager is expert at evaluating and utilizing to best advantage the characteristics, traits, hopes, ambitions, fears, likes, and dislikes of his colleagues and subordinates to promote the achievement of the goals of his enterprise.

THE PAPERS

Robert T. Livingston traces modern industrial human relations techniques in their development from the behavioral sciences. He then builds his map with interactions and situations. Through the use of arrays he develops a series of interrelationships which can then be analyzed in detail. Finally, he applies this same technique to the development of a situational needs array. F. O. Rouse's thesis is that people often behave differently as individuals and as members of groups. He cites numerous examples from nonindustrial life and then points out similar situations that frequently confront managers.

John P. Foley, Jr., approaches managerial human relations from the viewpoint of the psychologist. The manager must deal with different "publics," each of which involves human relations; he starts by "doing business with himself" and goes on to expand his contacts to ever larger groups of individuals. Each of us lives and behaves as a member of a social matrix, the other members of which (like ourselves) are likely to react to stimuli with somewhat less than perfect reliability. It is one of the principal tasks of management to appraise individuals in terms of probable behavior as the basis for employment and for the utilization of their talents.

Dr. Melvin Thorner analyzes the reactions of managers at various levels to different stimuli and, also, the trend of changes in their reactions with the passage of time. He also gives attention to environmental influences on managers and their decisions. The corporation's personality is a definite image of the personalities of its managers. Goodwin Watson devotes his paper to the roles played by managers. They have definite ideas as to what their roles are and should be; but it is important, at times, to find out what subordinates, colleagues, supervisors, and outsiders think on these matters. Watson argues that many of today's emotional distortions and human relations conflicts stem principally from misunderstandings of role definition.

The Red Group of public utility managers set up a procedure for analyzing human relations problems and used it to study several typical cases drawn from the experience of the group members. In their report they summarize the principles of supervisory conduct which their analyses indicated had particular human relations significance.

A MAP FOR THE STUDY OF HUMAN RELATIONS

by Robert Teviot Livingston

IN THE FINAL ANALYSIS, all the really important managerial relations are human relations. It is true that the manager has to make decisions, but someone else can do, and usually does, all the preparation for decision. In any situation where a manager is needed, someone else must carry the decision into effect. There is a job of the manager which can be rather precisely described in different industries and at different levels, but, no matter how much these jobs may differ in terms of the physical resources dealt with or the different kinds of responsibilities they have, they have one common, general aspect: they are dependent upon other people. They rely on other people for information and they use other people to effect their purposes and they must consider other people's values.

It is conceivable that a manager might be in utter ignorance of the details of the process he is managing, if he were sufficiently skilled in human relations to have complete and warranted confidence in those who serve him in both staff and line capacities and those for whom he works. However, such skill in human relations is not only rare but has yet to be set down in a code of procedures or a book of rules. Indeed, at the

Address presented at the Public Utility Executive Program, University of Michigan, Ann Arbor, August–September 1958. Mr. Livingston is Professor of Industrial Engineering, Columbia University, and Director of the Utility Management Workshop.

present time, the state of knowledge in this field is not sufficiently great, universally agreed upon, or adequately organized. Therefore, we must still operate in a state of partial knowledge. It is the purpose of this paper to organize the thinking in this field, at least to the point of classification. Classification can be at least the start of understanding; greater understanding of any phenomenon is, per se, a good thing. This is the fundamental and most important area of human life and, therefore, it is even more important to extend understanding in this area than any other. The basic classification has to do with the interrelationships between people and will deal with variation in numbers involved, in situations observed, and in potential, also with interactions between and among people variously situated.

Human relations is a very popular phrase today in the managerial vocabulary. People often use words because it is easier to place a name on the subject, about which not much is known, than it is really to study it. Human relations obviously has to do with people. The behavioral scientists have been studying people in a formal, if not scientific, way as long as there have been behavioral sciences. Therefore, the implication is obvious: if you want to learn about human relations, go to the behavioral scientists. It is a good idea, but it does not always work; the behavioral scientists, while interested in human behavior and people, are not interested in the same kinds of things which interest the manager, and their findings and theories, no matter how well substantiated by the behavior of rats, pigeons, children, or even college students, do not, of themselves, solve our problem. A theory may *help* you solve your problem, but *solve* it? No.

There are many varieties of behavioral scientists, each studying some particular aspect of that complex nexus which is human behavior. Quite naturally, each feels that his particular area of interest is of maximum importance, but, to the layman, it is often very difficult to estimate which phenomena interest a given individual by the title he carries. In contradistinction to the engineering field, which classifies itself in terms of applied sciences, the behavioral scientists seem to categorize on what is perhaps a more basic level from the point of view of phenomena.

Referring the fields to the classification of groups, which are here thought of as organisms, and associating with both of them the kinds of relation about which the manager may find useful information, there may be set up the following table on hierarchy of theory:

The Organism	*The Field*	*The Relations*
The individual	Biology Physiology Psychology	Personal behavior Interactions
The small group	Psychology Psychiatry Sociology	Direct (usually face-to-face) Interpersonal relations
Groups of groups, largely homogeneous	Sociology Anthropology Management engineering	Intergroup relations without differentiation
The association, non-homogeneous	Anthropology Economics	Internal vs. external values
The social matrix	Anthropology History	Mores, folkways, historical and cultural values

Obviously these are all interrelated and may be thought of as all looking at the same object—man—but from different points of view, for different purposes, and when he is doing different things. Actually, as far as the individual is concerned, the manager will derive the greatest use from psychology.

Interactions. As a basic approach, human relations will be looked on as interactions. However, an interaction may be directed; indeed, it is the job of the manager to make decisions which will direct and change a potential. The potential of the situation which exists before the interaction itself will first be considered. The second point to be explored is the notion of groups and how they behave or interact. A group is a collection of particles of different characteristics bound together in some manner, physically or otherwise, for an identifiable period of time. These particles are in some ways different, have different characteristics, and do not behave identically, either among themselves or at all times. However, they are also in some manner similar and are, in some externally identifiable manner, bound together into a unit which in turn has an observable behavior. These particles are human beings.

It is an overworked truism that a manager *gets things done through men*. It naturally follows that a manager should be very much aware of human relations and should be skilled in their practice. Getting things done through people involves two kinds of relationship: (a) the provision for getting the things done and (b) actually getting the things done. In considering the arrays previously presented we may consider four factors:

$$H = \text{People}$$
$$P = \text{Processes}$$
$$M = \text{Materials}$$
$$I = \text{Information}$$

There is a whole class of interactions, namely those dealing with P, M, and I, which have to be considered. But, once considered and taken care of, they may be dismissed until a change becomes necessary. These interactions, however, are only potential input; some individual does something about them. It is true, of course, that the manager can and does do some things himself, but he can perform, personally, very little; and so, in the final analysis, he must work through others. Therefore, the action of the manager must always enter the system through the *H* element of the input. He makes decisions but, equally important, he must implement these. He may decide what is to be done but, in the great majority of cases, someone else must act to produce the desired result. The goal the manager has envisaged must be attained through the sum total of the hundreds (or thousands) of acts by others which he sets in motion. (Elsewhere this is spoken of as the sequential decision process.) The manager's acts are by no means unimportant, but they involve translating his dreams into reality through the agency of other people. It is not hard, therefore, to see how essential an understanding of human relations is to the manager. If a good job is well done by people working together, they are likely to feel good. However, it is a false hypothesis to think that "feeling good" will necessarily cause a job to be well done. The *accomplishment* of the task is the *first* thing and not the side issue. The studied effort to make people feel good is the side issue and not the first thing; it is the means to an end, and the end is production. In other kinds of association the "feeling good" may be the first thing and only if people "feel good" will there be production.

First, it should be clear that this is an attempt to state the phenomenon in recognizable form, to describe it and, if possible, to enumerate the important variables which are involved. It is not pretended that the *results* of human relations situations are not important, but it is set forth that the first point in obtaining results is to attempt to state the important classes of situations and the factors involved. When this is done, it is believed that a study of the interactions which follow the situation may be more fruitful than merely to observe results and to attempt casually to impute cause. This means considering the situations as potential, rather than dynamic, a consideration of what can be expected to happen if no deliberate change is inserted in the situation.

The Situation. As has been set forth elsewhere, one way of beginning a study of human relations is to consider an operation as a dynamic set of interactions and to realize that it is difficult to observe it while in action. In an operation, which moves in a time stream, we can consider an instant, a cross-section in time; this we will call a *situation*.

It is also important to avoid value considerations as far as possible. Thus, rather than saying how a person *ought* to behave or feel, we will consider (a) what *is*—the potential or what was done—the actions observed; (b) what is or was *possible*—apparently. We can observe the former; in the latter we must estimate, but the more we know about the arrangement and the physical conditions the better will be our estimate.

The following elements are characteristic:
1. The situation
2. The personalities involved
3. The purposes

In this discussion we shall attempt to approximate the situation which exists in any physical experiment. As for the individual personalities involved, we shall not consider them in specific detail. That is where the manager himself is responsible in a real situation. We shall assume that the individuals involved have normal personalities (whatever that may mean), that they have the usual and expected drives, desires, dislikes, etc. They are not robots or morons; neither are they overly neurotic, frustrated, or aggressive. In a word, we shall try to state the general and usual situation. In an actual operating situation these personalities may assume overwhelming importance.

As far as purposes are concerned, we must recognize that there are several levels of purposes and remember that each individual has a nexus of personal purposes and goals, and that different people have different sets and no one knows the other person's in detail. Indeed, he does not always know or recognize his own. We shall also recognize that an interaction, any interaction, is in part at least a goal-seeking project of an individual. Further, we postulate that there is a combined or group goal which somehow arises from the needs of each and all of the individuals and that this combined goal is not identical with any one of the goals of any one of the participants. We shall further postulate that each person is attempting, whether successfully or not, to maximize his personal satisfaction, and that there is an implicit recognition that, under certain rather undefined circumstances, the combined goal will conflict to some extent with the individual goals and that there must be some degree of compromise. Actually, for most people most of the time, there is no serious conflict. Having accepted a combined goal, a set of expectations is always accepted and there is no great trouble. Therefore, we shall assume that the basic purpose of the group is pursuit of the group goal but with the minimum cost, however figured, to the participants.

With these two postulates we shall attempt to study the situation in its general aspects, those which are common to the greatest number of situations. We can start by defining what is meant by the term "situation."

A situation may be described in certain dimensions:

1. It is an instant section of a continuous process which may be identified in time/space and, relationally, has a history.

2. It contains physical components and human individuals in an internal configuration both spatially and purposefully arranged.

3. It has a specified, however unspecific, reason for existence. In the industrial situation, it was created following a decision.

4. It may be considered to be the point at which a decision will be made to take some action which has the intent to change or realize the potential.

5. It has a potential, a probable result of the most probable interactions which will occur.

For the practice of management and human relations the last point is of great importance.

THE HUMAN RELATIONS MAP

Human relations, like any of the other phenomena in which the manager is interested, may be located in the operation as a concept and may be specified in terms of a situation. Management has two broad classes of possible actions to affect the operation and, hence, the output: (a) to change and control the physical system, and (b) to manipulate the input.

Input, including managerial action, has been classified into four broad classes which are arrayed in Figure I.

	H	I	M	F
Human effort	H/H 11	I/H 21	M/H 31	P/H 41
Information	H/I 12	I/I 22	M/I 32	P/I 42
Materials	H/M 13	I/M 23	M/M 33	P/M 43
Physical process	H/P 14	I/P 24	M/P 34	P/P 44

Figure 1. The Basic Input Array

This indicates the kind of interrelations of which the manager must be aware and, in consequence, the characteristics and behaviors of the inputs in which he would be interested. Here *H* stands for human effort of any kind, in which we are primarily interested; *P* stands for the physical process, *M* for the materials which are operated on, and *I* for information. By information is meant books, drawings, specifications, policy statements, operating directions, and all the things that a person must use in performing his function. The combination of *M* and *P* forms the process, but the process requires the introduction of a human being in order to make it operate; the human being needs information in order to make the operation useful.

Interrelationships. Management is the provision for, and intelligent use of, the interrelationships between and among these resources which are available to the managers. Let us assume that we are interested in looking at the different kinds of interrelations with a view to answering the question "What are human relations?" and the further question, "What kinds of human relations are we interested in, and what do we know about them?"—leading to the query as to what the manager can do about them.

With four kinds of things, there are ten possible kinds of relationships (16 if direction is taken into account) and, in these ten, people are directly involved four times. The other interrelations, in which human beings are not directly concerned, are still human relations, but of a different class. Every machine and material and memory are products of men and, thus, the product of some kind of human relations in the past. For the purpose of this memorandum, only those interrelations which include people directly will be considered. The other six, which we shall not discuss here, have the following characteristics:

1. Material vs. Material = design and construction of product (33)
2. Material vs. Process = design and operation of process (34)
3. Material vs. Information = specifications, drawings, and the like (32)
4. Process vs. Process = coordination of sub-processes to form a process (44)

5. Process vs. Information = operational direction (42)
6. Information vs. Information = unorganized knowledge may, potentially, become intelligence by this interaction (22)

Note that all these are, of themselves, static; until a person is involved, no result obtains.

The other four interrelations, which involve people directly, also have distinct characteristics:

1. Human vs. Human = personal relationships (11)
2. Human vs. Material = health problems and the like (13)
3. Human vs. Process = fatigue and Men/Machine Systems (14)
4. Human vs. Information = memory, directions, designs factors and the like (12)

An array such as is shown in Figure 1 has one particularly valuable and useful property; any *box* (which is a class) can be expanded into subclasses for more detailed study.

All of these are human relations but, for the present purpose, we shall concern ourselves with the first, *11* in the upper left corner of the array. There are two aspects of these relationships: (a) actual and recorded (what has happened), and (b) potential (what could happen). It may be said that the *real* job of management is to provide for the second type. In other words, while it is very important to "put out fires" when they occur, crises or "fires" will occur less often if the manager has used enough forethought; perhaps that is the real mark of a good manager. This array is one of the take-off points for the modern mathematical theoretician in management because it can be manipulated mathematically; all possible classes or combinations of interactions can be set forth and the kinds of decisions which are made can be studied in an objective manner to maximize or minimize whatever is desired under any given set of premises. This, however interesting, is not my present purpose.

In the next section we shall study human relations by expanding the introspective square *11*. We shall consider the effect of number, magnitude, and structure of the human element. It is important to remember that human beings are purposive and adaptive and, no matter whether we are considering the individual as an individual, or a large group such as a culture, we must recognize that there are needs (objective, overt, and less than overt), purposes, goals and ideals. While it is never possible to know in the strict sense precisely what these are, we cannot neglect considering them. We can divide them into two categories: immediate, general, and specifically recognized, and those which are always in the future. A goal recognized is reconstrued—an ideal remains unattainable, something to be striven for. In a later section we discuss these needs. For the present we shall conceive of a two-dimensional area moving in time and, thereby, in its search for ideals, creating history. The two divisions are presented as (a) interrelational dynamics; and (b) situation needs.

THE BASIC HUMAN RELATIONS ARRAY

We are concerned with a study of human relations. Obviously there are many kinds of human relations, and the natural way to attempt to study them is to set them along some kind of continuum which will not only differentiate one from another in some familiar and significant manner, but also, if possible, in some metrical manner. Thus it would be desirable if we could start at point O where there was none of this quality called human relations and build up to the greatest possible amount of human relations.

There are a number of ways of doing this; a number of different scales possible. Among the more attractive are: (a) by number of people involved and considered from O to the whole world; (b) by frequency (or duration) of interaction;

(c) by directedness to an idealized individual as a center, or toward a goal; (d) by importance, according to some externally applied criterion or by any other desired characteristic.

In the basic array presented in Figure 1, the upper left hand corner showed the *H/H* interaction which we have called introspection, but it is much more than introspection in the usual sense and, in certain ways, it is the most difficult locus on the whole array, as well as the most important. It is the most difficult because it cannot be observed objectively; it is the most important because it enters into every other interaction on the array and enters as many times as there are people involved, multiplied by the number of sub-acts making up the interaction. This difficulty exists because an individual is not a set, constant system but rather a constantly changing one, and the change is, in part at least, occasioned by the acts (stimuli) of the other members involved in the interaction.

Potentials. Human relations is merely the name of a phenomenon which is going on all the time. Naming a phenomenon does not explain what it consists of, nor does naming it directly or immediately assist a person in practicing it. Naming is useful to identify the phenomenon and, when once identified, it is then possible to describe what is included as the identified phenomenon. The most useful first step in a description is to classify and name the relationships which exist in some useful manner. Usefulness will obviously be related to the purpose of the discourse. For our purpose we are interested in describing them for the quite natural engineering purpose of improving the operation. This last statement is the key to this presentation. Human relations, while important, are not our concern here until and unless they are changed from potentials to reality, from static situations to dynamic interrelations. It is in the dynamic interrelations that the manager is interested and for which he is responsible, but a deep understanding of the dynamics can only come from a pre-understanding of the potentialities. In the presentation which follows, the static situations are considered, but always with the understanding that the potentialities are only of interest in the light of their realization. We shall not attempt to discuss the dynamics in detail; however, they will be classified and their potentials will be discussed. The potentials are the starting point, if for no other reason than that this is what the manager has to deal with. His action changes the potential to some new realization.

The Human Relations Array. For the purpose of this discussion we have assumed a scale which corresponds to (a) in the list above, but the scale has not at this point been quantified, for a variety of reasons. By not doing so we can merely name certain categories which, while they may overlap, nevertheless have areas of substantial uniqueness. It is likely that some of the classification systems not specificed may, in some manner and to some degree, be related to the scale. For example:

Directedness. Potentially the directedness is negatively related to number; thus, there is a greater possibility for specific and identifiable interactions between two people than among two million people.

Frequency should be related, although not arithmetically, to number available to interact.

Because we are concerned with interactions, we shall make a two-dimensional chart, called an *array* or, if manipulated mathematically, a *matrix* in which the number of people are the two axes or directions. By drawing lines parallel to each axis, a series of boxes is delineated. The obvious thing is to take the situation from 1 to *n* people and record what is known about groups of each size—there are certain phenomena which flow simply from the number of people involved. Let us use the following categories in Figure 2.

1. The Individual
2. The Diad—interaction with another (any other) person
3. The Group—small groups—the *in* group (your own); all other groups—the *out* group (any other)

4. Groups of Groups—the association or company, the industry, groups of companies

5. The Culture or Social Matrix—a dynamic society or group of interacting institutions or companies such as society

These boxes represent potential interactions or classes of human relations situations. Thus, for example, there will be a box where column *I* intersects row *D* and the members are *I/D 12*. As a convention, and for identification, the first number is considered as the originator. Thus we can conveniently locate any interactive potential. It is apparent that the division, here made into five major categories, is a conventional one and that the boundaries between categories are established largely by the point of view of the person who is considering the problem: in the first case *I* is the person considering the problem. Thus any person will of necessity consider the potential human relations in respect to himself.

	I	D	G	A	C
Individual	11	21	31	41	51
Diad	12	22	32	42	52
Group	13	23	33	43	53
Association	14	24	34	44	54
Culture	15	25	35	45	55

Figure 2. The Human Relations Array

Individual Interactions. The first column of Figure 2 lists the classes of human relations in respect to a given individual. Thus we have *his* relations (the *from* actions) or communications:

with himself—called introspection (11)
with another person (12)

with a group (13)

with the association, or company (14)

with the culture, society, or social matrix (15)

The first case is a matter of knowing himself; the second comprehends his behavior with a single other person; the third identifies a given individual's reaction to a group; the fourth calls attention to the fact that he has relations with the association or company to which he belongs outside of the immediacies of his job; and the final one reports the fact that he is a member of society.

Similarly, if we go across the first row we view all the human relations which impinge upon the individual. Thus we have:

from himself—here he talks back to himself (11)

from another person (21)

from groups (31)

from the whole association or company (41)

from society or the culture (51)

The last column and row represent the culture, that which has been handed on from past generations to the present and which is constantly affecting and controlling people's behavior. It includes all of the customs, mores, usages, biases, and social pressures which we all meet. This acts very strongly on each individual, on the various groups, and on the association.

A given individual's behavior is not constant, even within these categories. There will be variations of behavior according to (a) the "state" of individuals; (b) the number of people in the group; (c) the different personalities; (d) the purpose or goals—individual $\neq$ group, immediate $\neq$ long term; (e) the expected duration of the contact; (f) the particular situation. And, of course, many other things.

The Individual's Focus. The individual enters consideration from many points of view. Luckily, we are considering managerial human relations, so we can order our thinking into six main categories or roles:

his role as an individual in a position as "the manager"

his role as the representative of the group

his role as a leader of his group

his role as a member of all of the associated groups

his role as a member of the company

his role in society (this is a complex of roles which are grouped together here in convenient form)

These six represent only one convenient method of categorization. Of course these are really all rolled into one role, but it is convenient to look at them separately.

The Diad. While people are individuals and, in a certain way, alone and isolated, yet in real life most of our overt acts are "two-by-two" acts, so it is important to understand the possibilities of this two-by-two interaction. No matter who we are or what position we occupy, most of the human relations we have are with one other person; certainly most of our unpremeditated and casual relationships fall in this class. In other cases we often have time to consider and to play a role but it is the face-to-face relationships which are by far the most frequent and perhaps the most important, so it is both logical and proper to move from individual introspection to the interrelations of individuals, which is the second basic of human relations.

This is the first which is obvious and subject to observation. The group of two is known in the technical literature as a diad, and, because it is so basic, it is important to understand it. In real life a majority of human relations are diads. The actor may be a representative of one group, as may be the (anticipated) reactor, but what actually happens and can be observed is what *A* does to *B* and occasionally what *B*'s response is.

In order to understand interactive behavior, it is useful to make two assumptions: (a) people behave logically, and (b) life is a game. This will perhaps take a little preliminary explanation. According to the theory of self-consistency, everybody behaves in what he believes is a self-consistent manner. That is to say he behaves, down to the smallest detail of the way he thinks or feels, as the person he thinks he is would behave. And that means he behaves in a logical manner, in a manner he thinks is logical. The trouble is that, when we observe him, we are not in possession of all the necessary data. We do not know who he thinks he is, we do not know the values which the person holds. What do we do then? We build up an imaginary situation involving him which we then interpret in terms of our own values. Of course, we may be a bit sophisticated and say to ourselves, "He is different from me," and then try to guess—often wrongly—about the other person's behavior and do the wrong thing! There are a number of old adages we often forget, and one of them is particularly important here. It says "Don't judge others by yourself"; yet we do it every day.

The second point also needs a bit of explanation: "Life is real, life is earnest," is true, but, nonetheless, it is a game. People are competing and striving to excel. Although we may not like the words, it is useful to think of the basic interaction as a game, a game with two players, with rules, with cards, with odds, with a pay-off, a game in which skill is very important. To play a game one should know the rules, the cards and their probable distribution. This is a matter of common sense. If one plays bridge, in the long run the more skilled players will win, but, in order to play at all, one must know the rules. Your goal may be to win, but the first question is how do you win and with what cards. Your opponent in a game, the other member of the diad of real life, also has to play according to the rules, and he has only certain cards to play. We may not know the cards he holds, but, in bridge at least, we know that he does not hold any jokers. When we are dealing with another person in an organization, we should recognize that there are only certain cards he can hold, only certain bets he can make, only certain cards he can play.

The odds and the pay-off are also very important. What can the other person do which will profit us, and how valuable is it to us to have him do it? We may be able to figure out fairly accurately what the odds of getting someone else to agree with us are, for example, but does this agreement mean anything significant? In other words, can he do anything about it and for us?

We are apt to think of games as being "for fun," even if the money stakes are high. In the game of human relations in management we are often playing for very high stakes, and the trouble is that it is often difficult to know when the game is going to change from fun to deadly seriousness; when the pay-off is suddenly going to change greatly. This is what we meant by the importance of understanding the occasion. There are rules which are more or less adhered to, and for breaking them a penalty of one kind or another is imposed. There is a price for playing the game (also for abstaining), there is a winning player and a loser, and the skillful player wins more often than the unskilled player. More important, the person who knows the rules knows better how to play; and, most important of all, the person who knows not only the rules but also the strategies available to the other players and their mode of playing has a great advantage. So we say, life is not only a game, but also a gambling game. However, there is one last thing to remember: there are times when people break the rules.

It is useful to consider what is going on when any two people are together. One classification of such occasions would be:

1. Planned interview
    a. with a known purpose and considerable knowledge of the other participant
    b. with a known purpose but little knowledge of the other participant
    c. without a known purpose, and either with or without knowledge of the other participant

    2. Meeting unplanned but recognized
       a. with significant purpose
       b. with non-mutual purpose but with individual purpose
         (luncheon at a club for example)
       c. casual and accidental

What is useful in such a classification? Perhaps the following will be helpful:

    1. What are the consequences (importance)—rewards and penalties?
       a. immediate vs. potential
       b. primary vs. secondary
       c. opportunity to retreat
    2. What is your "state" of knowledge
       a. about the other person—real and role
       b. about the situation:
       immediate
       subject of conversation
    3. How much "control" do you have
       a. by position, status, or role
       b. by personality, ability
    4. Permanence, duration, and freedom to escape

It is apparent that this merely presents a sort of check list for planning your interrelations with other people. It is, however, a useful fact to remember that, whether consciously or not, whether or not we admit it to ourselves, when we are with another person, even casually, we are in one way or another trying to do something to him; it may even be as simple as trying to get him to leave us alone. However, in industrial life, we may assume that there are two situations:

    1. Organizationally directed interrelations
       a. the designed work place interaction
       b. meetings originated by another to serve his purpose
       c. meetings originated by you to serve your purpose
    2. Nonorganizationally directed interrelations

    a. personal problems which either person may wish to
       have help in solving—this may be subconscious
    b. casual meetings

Obviously, any given situation may well be a mixture of the
foregoing.

Group Behavior. If we refer to the basic human relations
array, we can make an interaction for the group in a similar
manner to that for the individual; the group interacts with
individuals, with other groups within the association, and with
the culture. Also, the group is affected by people within and
without the group, by other groups, by the association as a
whole, and by the culture. The behavior of an individual
within a group is different when he is not in the group. We
can make certain generalizations about the variations of an
individual's behavior:

1. Given a constant exterior situation (same people in the
same place, etc.) it will vary with his "state."

2. Given a constant state, time, and place, it will vary with
the personality of the other person involved.

3. Given a constant state, time, and place and one personality it will vary with the number of people involved.

4. Given all the above, it will vary with other matters such
as familiarity of group members and homogeneity.

For the purposes of this discussion it is valuable to identify
three main categories of groups to which the people belong:
(1) in-group groups, (2) tangential groups, and (3) out-
group groups. Of course there are subclassifications and other
methods of looking at the question. Thus: (a) formal vs.
informal groups; (b) production-centered vs. non-production-
centered groups; (c) Professional vs. social groups; (d) Action
groups, and the like.

In considering the in-groups, it must not be forgotten that
position in hierarchy is a factor which causes groups to form
with different interests than the formal groups shown on the

organization chart. While company executives like to think, or at least talk about "one big family," yet even where this is so there are within the company smaller groups which may be more significant to the member than the large group. Thus, to the vice-president in charge of operations the whole operating department is "his group" but, to the members of the operating department, there will be several much smaller groups which to them are far more significant than the department.

Personalization. We have so far spoken of the group as an isolated phenomenon, which it is not. Everybody belongs to a number of different groups, each serving a particular function in his life, satisfying a particular need. For convenience of discussion, it is useful to personalize a group and view all groups from the point of view of this group as a focus. In real life, the focal group will of course change as the individual upon whom we are focusing changes his group and his role. Just as the individual is the center of his universe, we should consider the group as an individual with character and personality and distinctive behavior as a group, even though it will be the individual members of the group whose behavior is being observed.

The potential interactions between groups can be considered in the light of the physical relations of the groups:

1. In respect to the process
    a. who feeds what to whom and how dependent as far as production is concerned
    b. whether line or staff
    c. relative obviousness (importance, cost, etc.) of the group work and who is aware of it
2. In respect to the organization
    a. level in the hierarchy—up vs. down
    b. formality of organization of the group and relation to other groups

3. Personality elements
   a. relations between "head men" of the groups to the "big boss"
   b. professional homogeneity of the group; engineers vs. accountants, etc.
   c. age and age distribution of the group

Groups interact with groups and with individuals, both within and without the group. In industrial life, the interactions of individuals, as individuals, may be quite different from their interactions as members of the group. Generally at work, everybody to a distinct degree is a group representative as much as an individual. This is why the people in certain groups sometimes appear so different from people in other groups.

Groups also react within an association—this is the means by which work is accomplished—and these group interactions are specified and become formalized in the work flow and communication pattern. Groups react with the culture and subculture. There is a large literature on group behavior. Each particular culture creates or provides for special interest groups such as service clubs, parent-teacher associations, fraternal organizations, hobby clubs, and professional societies. Each of these determines certain parts of the individual's, as well as the group's behavior. So far we have looked at:

the individual as an individual
the individual in respect to another individual
the individual as a member of a small group
the interactions of small groups

Now we shall try to carry the basic idea up higher. It may seem like trying to strain at a point to carry the notion of interaction up to the consideration of a total company. Certainly it may at first seem to be more confusing than the more usual method pursued in many books, but it is believed that by doing so a new viewpoint will be gained. For discussion we can list:

the large group

groups of groups

the association or company

the culture or social matrix

If we exclude the large groups from formal consideration, then there is seen to be a gradual rise from the relatively simple individual, to the group, to the group of groups (perhaps largely homogeneous), to the association or company, and to the culture. If we wish, we can think of groups of similar companies forming industries, and of different kinds of companies forming economic units such as "valleys" or countries or cultures. If we think seriously about the matter and realize that all of these units are made up of people, we can realize the magnitude and importance of the concept of human relations.

SITUATIONAL NEEDS

In discussing interrelational dynamics it is often impossible to set the problem clearly, because the number of people involved and their structural interrelations, while important, are not the only determinants of behavior. Needs, purposes, and/or objectives are also important determinants. What are the situational needs and how may they be classified?

The Situational Need Array. Upon the assumption that all of the categories set forth in the interrelational dynamics array may be considered entities in the sociological sense, we may borrow (and adapt) from sociology six major categories to use for the situational need array (Figure 3). These are:

1. Homeostasis—the preservation of the steady state. Here we can see the four basic lines of behavior: activity, unified direction, self-consistency, and response to external expectation. Preservation of health and resistance to change from what immediately precedes.

2. Self-preservation—against external changes, dangers, and hostilities, both real and imagined.
3. Reproduction—includes not only physical reproduction but also translation of ideas, ideals, dreams, and values into reality.
4. Learning—intended to cover adaptive behavior. Generally there will be an attempt to adapt only enough to get by, so that the previous category will be disturbed as little as possible.

	H	S	R	L	A	D
Homeostasis	11	21	31	41	51	61
Self-preservation	12	22	32	42	52	62
Reproduction	13	23	33	43	53	63
Learning	14	24	34	44	54	64
Action	15	25	35	45	55	65
Dreaming	16	26	36	46	56	66

Figure 3. The Situational Need Array

5. Action—operating, doing things, including the whole story of receipt of stimuli and response thereto, of work differentiation, and, in general, the requirement that all entities have of paying their way in one way or another.
6. Dreaming—dreams, ambition, motivating desires and imagery, the world of limited external possibilities and unlimited internal desires.

The problem here is that these universal needs vary in intensity and the situations met with give different possibilities of satisfaction. Conflicts occur in this introspective array of situational needs.

While there are 36 squares shown for our present consideration, we need not consider direction or introspection, as what we wish to look at is potenital conflict and relative values. For it is an understanding of how these are evaluated in different human relations situations which is the second step in the understanding of the dynamics of management. The next im-

	H	S	R	L	A	D	I	D	G	A	C	FUTURE →
Homeostasis	11	21	31	41	51	61	111	211	311	411	511	
Self-preservation	12	22	32	42	52	62	112	212	312	412	512	
Reproduction	13	23	33	43	53	63	113	213	313	413	513	
Learning	14	24	34	44	54	64	114	214	314	414	514	
Action	15	25	35	45	55	65	115	215	315	415	515	
Dreaming	16	26	36	46	56	66	116	216	316	416	516	

	I	D	G	A	C
Individual	11	21	31	41	51
Diad	12	22	32	42	52
Group	13	23	33	43	53
Association	14	24	34	44	54
Culture	15	25	35	45	55
	I	D	G	A	C

PRESENT →

Figure 4. The Human Relations Interaction Potential Array

portant expansion to be made in this study is to detail the interrelation between and among these categories; when do these needs conflict, when supplement, and how are they ranked.

This array is interesting, of itself, but only of philosophical interest. However, its usefulness comes in when it is combined with the previous array (see Figure 2) and especially as to the relative weight the different dynamic situations put upon the situational needs. From a study of this array, many of the problems of the manager can be better understood.

A complete analysis of the interrelation (Figure 4), which can serve as a road map locating not only the first degree interrelation but the compound or second degree interaction, is a study of itself; however, it is believed that a consideration of it will be very helpful in locating *any* problem in human relations and can serve as a basis for understanding a case and selecting a behavior pattern.

PEOPLE IN GROUPS

by F. O. Rouse

> To measure the total vectorial intrinsic and effective investment in a given group, i.e., the total group synergy, we have to take account of 1) the number of people interested; 2) the intensity or strength of the satisfaction each gains; 3) the ergic quality (vector direction . . .) of the satisfactions; and 4) the subsidiation relations of these satisfactions with respect to other groups and other purposes of the individuals concerned.

THE ABOVE EXCERPT is quoted from Raymond B. Cattell's "Concepts and Methods in the Measurement of Group Syntality," found in the book *Small Groups*, edited by Hare, Borgatta, and Bates. It is cited here only to illustrate that it is possible to study the dynamics in a group—particularly in small groups of three, four, five, or six people. It is not my intention to belabor you with such involved discussion from here on. To the contrary, I shall report to you only the results of a few research experiments in this field of the social sciences and cite several situations involving small groups of people I have known. Then I shall attempt to relate the findings of the research to the analyses of the practical cases. It is hoped that this approach will be of help to you in evaluating behavior you have observed in small groups.

Address presented at the Fifth Utility Management Workshop, August, 1956. Mr. Rouse is a management consultant.

GROUP VS. INDIVIDUAL BEHAVIOR

I first became interested in the subject of people in groups when I became aware of, and concerned about, the fact that more goes on in a meeting involving a small number of people than can be accounted for in psychology. For example, at the bargaining table with a union leader, one frequently finds that he is dealing with a man different from the one he deals with when the same man is acting the role of shop steward.

We can all recall the differences in the conduct of an associate when he is in the privacy of his own office and, later, when he is at the luncheon table with two or three officers of the company. Similar changes are noticeable when the officer attends a staff meeting or a meeting of the board of directors. Have you ever noticed the conduct of the members of a subcommittee operating first in and then outside of the full committee? And what about the small group when an outsider first joins it? Why do people act differently in these situations than they do when alone or with just one other person?

In thinking back on these experiences, and through reading the literature in the field, it is becoming clear that one needs more insight and ability in dealing with the problems of people in groups than one gains from just the study of psychology. In other words, knowledge of the individual, as such, is not enough if one is to be a truly successful manager.

In exploring these matters, it might be helpful to keep in mind some of the old saws and clichés about people. Some of these expressions may be taking on new significance in reference to managing people in small groups. Research is beginning to produce evidence of the validity of many of our instinctive feelings and commonplace expressions; and, on the other hand, it is also beginning to disprove many of the concepts frequently held by the sophisticated manager. I have in mind such ideas as: Just one big happy family; team spirit; group loyalty; pride;

human motivation; sense of dignity; personal worth; recognition; belonging; security; sense of importance; usefulness; participation; two heads are better than one; the best committee is a committee of one; and so on.

We have said that all relations are human relations—mostly between two people—and that everyone has a need for intimate association and cooperation. These observations, as reported in the history of man, are surely borne out in the normal pattern of life. The child needs intimate association in the form of love and attention; and he most certainly makes demands for cooperation from his parents, especially his mother. As he moves out into the play group, his conduct begins to form in relationship to other people. He is on the road to social adjustment or maladjustment, as the case may be. In any event, he is interacting with others. His personality and character are being developed in the process of interaction and goal-seeking. These characteristics are carried throughout life, and so we find people becoming "joiners" a little later on and, in other ways, trying to fulfill various individual needs—that is, to find or make their place in the social structure of their environment. Their success is dependent, to a considerable extent, upon their awareness of, and their ability to use, consciously or unconsciously, the principles of the dynamics of human relations in small groups.

People behave differently in groups than they do out of groups. People behave differently in small groups than they do when in large groups. This suggests that the old adage "Be yourself" is not enough. This thesis is stated by Professor Livingston when he talks about such things as the role of the manager: How successful are you in acting your role, and which role are you playing? In thinking about people in small groups, it will be helpful to keep in mind, if one can, the many possible relationships between two people. I do not know what the total number of possible relationships is among a group of, say, five peopule, but it is a great many, any way you look at it. In any event, it is all of these possibilities, among others, that we must consider in thinking about the dynamics of small groups. If being yourself is not enough, and if acting a role is important, then what are the internal and external conditions and forces at play when in the company of other people?

INTERPERSONAL RELATIONSHIPS

We all have what we call our close circle of social friends, and this pattern is found in the business situation as well. How often do you have lunch with the same two or three people rather than with others? This small group association is something that we, as individuals, search out. Among other things, it helps fill our needs for intimate association and cooperation. We feel more comfortable when among our closest friends; and, I suspect, the smaller the group, the more comfortable we feel.

Several interesting experiments have been carried out in an effort to learn what really goes on in the relationships among people in small groups. Techniques have been devised to help in the analysis of the interactions—the personality clashes, the positive and the negative forces—which are at play within a group. For example, Ethel M. Riddle conducted an experiment with a group of six poker players, players who knew each other well and who were accustomed to playing together. Prior to the experiment she gave the group practice in the wearing of rubber stethographs and in filling out individual questionnaires concerning their feelings and attitudes. After this practice the players, so it is reported, were able to lose themselves quite naturally in the game. As the game went along, they were required to note their answers to such questions as "Did you try to bluff anyone during this game?" and "Did anyone try to bluff you?" They also recorded their emotional states on a scale ranging from "elated" to "gloomy." The stethograph recorded the bodily states, ranging from "maximum excitement" to "maximum physical retardation." There were three variables to be considered: the effects on the player of (1) his own hand, (2) his desire to win, (3) his own bet. From the data collected, various correlations were determined:

One player had a stronger desire to bluff than to win.

Other players had a stronger desire to beat the one they believed to be the biggest bluffer than simply to win the pot.

The player most anxious to win was always low in his willingness to risk his money. Incidentally, he was the man who could least afford to lose and, also, this was visibly evidenced by his low stack of chips.

This same anxious person was the most suspicious. He reported his feeling of being bluffed much more often than did the others.

One player had the same desire to win over all of his opponents, while others varied greatly in terms of the opponent they were trying to beat at the moment.

The biggest bluffer turned out to be the player who stimulated everyone else to try to beat him; but, oddly enough, most of the players did not report that they believed he was bluffing.

Of course this is only poker, a game, but perhaps some of this may suggest the thesis that these and related acts may be found in the business situation as well. From these illustrations it is seen that more goes on—more forces are in evidence—in a group of poker players than simply that of a desire on the part of each man to win the money. At least two major things are clear. One, the reason for coming together—the group goal or objective—is an announced one: to play poker and to win money. Then there is the second major reason—the goals of the respective individuals: these vary in terms of the others in the game and in terms of the particular circumstances of the moment of play. Incidentally, there are other reasons why men play poker and some of them may be important. Some men want to get away from a nagging wife or an unpleasant home, or they may just want to get out with the boys. This latter desire may have some overtone of the occasional wish to return to the childhood gang.

THE GANG ANALOGY

A nice illustration of the several goals in a small group—the group gang and the goals of the various members—is the one about the three little boys who joined together to build a lemonade stand. Their group objective was to build the stand. Their individual goals were vastly different. One boy wanted the money he could earn from selling lemonade to buy himself a baseball glove. The second boy wanted to build the stand so that he could use the new set of carpenter's tools he had just received as a gift. The third little boy wanted to help because this venture was one of the few times the other two boys would let him join them in any of their activities.

Perhaps, at this point, we should attempt a tentative definition of a group. Actually, in the context of our discussion, we are concerned with two kinds of groups: one informal, the other formal. It may be said, at this point, that a group begins to form when there is some interaction, when there is some expectation that it will meet more than once, and when it is felt to have some common interest or concern as a group.

One of the most interesting sources of information about groups, and one with considerable authority behind it, is Thrasher's study on the formation, characteristics, and activities of gangs.[1] This enterprising individual has reported on 1,313 gangs. That should be sufficient evidence to convince almost anyone! He reports that the necessities of maintaining face-to-

[1] Frederic M. Thrasher, *The Gang* (University of Chicago Press, Chicago, 1927, 1936).

face relationships set definite limits on the magnitude to which the gang can grow. Ordinarily, if all members are present, it must be possible for all to hear what is said by any one of the group.

The formation of a gang, or a group, starts with the so-called "intimate" relationships between two boys. Generally, there is a subordination of one boy to the other—hero worship, for example—or the abilities of one may supplement the abilities of the other. Additional members may be admitted to this kind of "two-boy gang" and, eventually, there develops a semiformal organization of some size. As soon as a third person has been introduced into the group, however, complications and friction may start—indeed, they usually do. It is the coming of conflict that brings about a certain amount of leadership and consequent subordination and discipline of members. As activities develop, the positions of members become defined and the social roles become more sharply differentiated. As a result there arises a more or less efficient and harmonious organization of people. As elsewhere, a sort of social stratification normally results among the membership. There are usually three, more or less well-defined, classes of members: the "inner circle," which includes the leader and his lieutenants, who are usually his most intimate pals; the rank and file, who constitution members of the gang in good standing; and the "fringers," who are, in effect, hangers-on and are not considered regular members—they are, for example, the ones who are likely to disappear entirely in case of trouble. Thrasher tells us that the gang may be conceived of as a "unity of interacting personalities involved in a struggle for recognition." This struggle takes the form of both conflict and competition. It operates to locate each individual with reference to the others and also with the leader, who is playing the central and guiding role. It is in these roles that personality is developed in the individual, and usually this development is in the personality pattern of the gang. The boys believe that any standing in the group is better than none, and that there is always the possibility of improving one's status. In striving to reach the role the individual hopes he will take in the group, he may assume a tough pose, commit feats of daring or of vandalism, or become a criminal. Thus, the conception of his essential role in the gang helps to explain him as an individual. Other things being equal, a big, strong boy has a better chance than a "shrimp." Traits of character, as well as physical differences are significant in these selection processes, and include beliefs, sentiments, habits, special skills, and so on. Besides leadership there are other social functions, and they also are determined by individual qualities in the process of struggle and activity. One boy may become the "brains" of the outfit; another the "funny boy" or the "show off."

This brief description of the "gang" has been used because it clearly describes the processes of force that exist in a group —the struggle for recognition, intimacy, status, and many of the other satisfactions an individual seeks to fulfill in terms of his needs for association with others.

Studies similar to these on gangs have been made of age groups at other levels—the fraternity, for example—and a few at the work place in industry. We shall not spend further time in reviewing them here, beyond saying that the growing body of knowledge about people in groups is becoming impressive and worthy of one's attention.

GROUP FORMATION AND MANAGEMENT

Most groups have a more or less identifiable personality. For example: people tend to move into groups in which, in their judgment, the members hold opinions and have abilities which are close to their own. This seems to be based upon the drive in each of us to evaluate, by comparison, our own opinions and

abilities—we want to compare ourselves with others. Therefore, it would hold that a person is less attracted to a group
where the members are very divergent from him in their
abilities and opinions. If this selectivity is a fundamental fact,
then we have a useful point for observation in the selection
of people for higher positions in our organization. But, for that
matter, we have all used for a long time the expressions: "You
can't make a silk purse out of a sow's ear"; "How will he fit
in?"; and "Look at the company he keeps."

Perhaps one place in which we can use this information with
renewed care is in the formation of work groups and committees. Why put a person with radically divergent opinions and
abilities into a group if it will be likely to make trouble or
cause problems for us. (There are times, of course, when we
intentionally do this.) One student in this field has stated that,
when the selective tendencies of individuals to join some
groups and to leave others over differences in opinion and
ability are coupled with observations on the effectiveness of
the "influence process" and "the intensity of competitive activity" (all of which arise when there is discrepancy in a
group), one can be guaranteed that he will find relative
similarity in the opinions and abilities among persons who
tend to associate with one another.

A sense of group personality is characteristic and is highly
essential to the cohesiveness of the group. This sense of identity
is part of the bond that unites and holds people in a group.
Some of the tests for group cohesiveness are that the members
all work together, everyone takes responsibility for group tasks,
there is a willingness to endure criticism and pain, and there
is a will to defend the group against attack. The simplest test
of all is to observe a group at work and to note the use of "we"
and "I" during their discussions.

We have mentioned discrepancies, internal conflict, competition, influence, and disturbing elements in a group. These

arise, for example, when there are differences of opinion and ability among the members of the group. Therefore, in any group there will always be problems among the members of the group. The intensity of these disruptive influences can be measured to some degree by observing the intensity and the character of competition which develops. For example, is Jim opposing Bill's idea because he has an honest difference of opinion—a different point of view from Bill's? Is he opposing the idea because Bill represents a threat to his position in the group? Or, perhaps, does Bill represent a natural rival for higher stakes—say, promotion in the company—and is Jim, therefore, taking advantage of the opportunity to discredit his opponent? Or is it as simple a matter as Bill's proposal bringing about an additional work load which Jim, who is lazy, does not want to undertake?

Acts of internal hostility and friendliness affect a group as a whole; they also affect the individual members. These acts help to establish the emotional climate and the equilibrium or stability of a group. The intensity and frequency of interactions, the level of friendliness, the amount of internal activity, and the amount and nature of activity imposed upon a group by the external environment, all have their bearing on group solidarity.

The motivational force in a group influences the group activity itself; and, of more importance, group activity influences the motivational force within the group. Now let us try to make sense out of the jargon. To me, it means this: in forming a small work group, select people with fairly similar opinions and abilities—people who will get along well together; place them in a situation that will require frequent contact with each other; and, finally, stimulate them to action. This should help to produce an effective work force. The key point is to get the individuals involved, get them active—action begets action, action begets motivation, and motivation begets action.

In forming a group, and in managing a group, there are several other important factors to be taken into consideration. For effective group work, the size of the group is important. The number of people involved tends to alter a person's behavior; but, if a group is too large, these advantages and the opportunities for the individual to find satisfactions are diminished. A useful small group is one in which all the members can hear what is being said by any of the other members; one in which there is time and opportunity for each member to have his say; one in which the influence process can work, i.e., the majority opinions have a chance to affect the views and the behavior of the minority; and, finally, one in which the objectives and the aims of the individuals can, in some way, be related to the group objective.

LEADERSHIP

There are many things a leader can do to help a group in action. For example, our manuals on conference leadership tell us a number of do's and don'ts in stimulating a group to action, in helping the group to make progress in its discussion, in building up participation, in giving personal satisfaction to the individual members, in developing group spirit and teamwork, and possibly, even, in bringing about "one big happy family." For example, did you know (and I am borrowing from Thrasher):

That you can control "Mr. Know-It-All, the person who wants to impose his opinion on everyone else," by encouraging "other members to comment on his remarks freely; by letting the rest of the group take care of him; by building up the confidence of the group in themselves so that they will not be imposed on by this type of member."

That you can control "the person who wants to argue—this type is always trying to cross up the leader—he will quibble over the most trivial detail and loves to get the other fellow's goat. The first rule here is to keep cool . . . give him enough rope to make some absurd, foolish, or far-fetched statements . . ." and then, "get the opinion of the majority."

That you can change the opinion of "the person who thinks you are telling him how to run his job and resents it. . . . Get him to feel that his experience can be valuable to others, that the purpose of the conference is to exchange ideas and to pool experiences."

That you can handle "the individual who wants to do all the talking. . . . Establish a rule that no member should speak too long on any question until everyone has had a chance to talk. Don't look at him when you are presenting a question. Fail to recognize him. This makes it difficult for him to get the floor."

That you can help "the shy individual. . . . Call on him by name to give an opinion; but ask him an easy question he is sure to answer well, and then praise him. Find something for him to do to help you in the conferences; for example, to hang up charts, assist in a demonstration, or make a report."

These statements may not be quite as humorously intended as they sound here. Rensis Likert, director of the Institute for Social Research at the University of Michigan, states:

Books on management and administration tend to deal with the relationship between superior and subordinates, between supervisors and employees, as *individuals*. Research on management similarly has tended to focus on the relationship between the superior and the subordinates as individuals. We are encountering increasing evidence, however, that the superior's skill in supervising his subordinates *as a group* is an important variable affecting his success: the greater his skill in using group methods of supervision, the greater are the productivity and job satisfaction of the work group.[2]

[2] Rensis Likert, *Motivation: The Core of Management*, American Management Assn., Personnel Series 155 (1953), pp. 9–10.

Let us quickly get to the nub of all this research, study, and importance assigned to knowing about how people tend to behave in small groups. For me, it is simply this: when a group as a whole has made a decision, the individual members seem to take on that decision. Why? Because the forces (the dynamics) in the group tend to overcome the resistance-to-change found in each individual.

THE PSYCHOLOGY OF
HUMAN RELATIONS AND
MANAGEMENT

by John P. Foley, Jr.

THE GENERAL TOPIC which I have been asked to discuss is that of human relations, from a psychological point of view. This is really a sort of redundancy. For we usually think of psychology as being the scientific study of behavior—behavior of human organisms as well as animals. Hence it is not unusual to find a psychologist called upon to talk about human relations. I would like to focus my remarks, as much as possible, upon human relations within the business or industrial setting—particularly as that setting is found in the modern company with its hierarchical structure and with its established management function.

As long as men are associated in an industrial enterprise, with certain common goals, there will inevitably be a managerial function. This is not surprising; as a matter of fact, if you throw together any large number of organisms—whether they be humans or animals—inevitably over a period of time, out of that initial complex, there will occur a certain differentiation of function. For example, many years ago psychologists were interested in what they called the pecking hierarchy in chickens. Studies were done in Germany and in this country,

Address presented at the Fifth Utility Management Workshop, August, 1956. Mr. Foley is President of John P. Foley & Co., Inc.

all of which indicated that, when chickens were together, whether in barnyard or laboratory, sooner or later there emerged from this association a sort of pecking hierarchy. In other words, certain animals in the group tend to take precedence over other animals; they come to dominate the latter. Other animals, either because of physical size or for so-called personality reasons, assume a more submissive role in this interpersonal situation.

THE APPROACHES TO MANAGEMENT

Now, if we find this sort of differentiation occurring in the animal world, there is little wonder that we find it in human culture as well. It is true, of course, that the role of the manager in modern business or industry is constantly in a state of flux. Perhaps for this reason it becomes all the more important for us periodically to take a good look at the manager's role.

A number of so-called "schools of management" have arisen, each of which emphasizes a certain approach to management problems and brings certain theories and techniques to bear on such problems. In the final analysis, however, these particular "schools" or viewpoints are not contradictory; rather, they are mutually supplementary. The more we know about the different approaches to management, the better picture we have of this job of managing people.

I like to look at the management function as one which has evolved naturally. It has evolved from what was originally a sort of homogeneous type of activity in which every man was pretty much the owner of what he did. He was also the worker or producer; he was the manager (although this distinct function had not yet evolved); and he was the consumer or customer. For example, in this country we need not go back too many years to arrive at the time when each man produced his own food, and he produced shoes and clothing for his family.

In a very simple culture of that sort, we do not have the separate functional groups or "publics" differentiated at all. Rather, the owner was the producer; he was the consumer; and he was the manager. Later, of course, we find occurring over a period of years a progressive evolution or differentiation of these separate functions. Today, in our present complex society, we can separately distinguish among each of these various functional groups. Hence a person currently performs as a manager, carrying out activities which at one time, historically, were also the activities of the person who functioned as the worker, the consumer, and so on.

THE MANAGER'S VIEWPOINTS

So, today, we speak of the manager as having to deal with a number of different "publics." He must deal with stockholders, with employees, with suppliers or subcontractors, and with customers. Moreover, he has certain relationships with his community. And today, more than ever before, he has important relationships with government—the government here being a sort of backdrop against which the business enterprise is operated; certainly there are many laws and regulations which every business must take into account. All of these publics are people, and the manager's role in his dealings with each of these publics is essentially a human relations role.

Looking at his job from another, slightly different point of view, we can say that the manager has to deal with six M's. He has to deal with *materials;* he has to deal with *methods* or procedures; he has to deal with *machines* or equipment; he certainly has to deal with *memories,* by which I mean policies, directives, memos, specifications, and other types of recorded information; he has to deal with *money;* and finally, perhaps most important of all, he has to deal with *men.*

In one of the companies for which I have done a good bit of

consulting work they issue each year an annual report to their stockholders, like all other corporations. I have been very much interested in the fact that, for the last few years, their annual report has carried the title, "Financial and Human Resources of X Corporation." This is the formal title on the front page of the report. Now, when any company gets to the point of entitling its annual report, "Financial and Human Resources of X Corporation," I think we have a very clear-cut recognition by the company of the importance of its human resources. In fact, a couple of years ago the president of this company made the following comment to me: "You know, every year, in our report to our stockholders, we list our so-called assets and liabilities. From a traditional accounting point of view, this listing of assets and liabilities is undoubtedly as accurate as we can make it. But I shudder when I realize that in such listing of assets we do not attribute even one dollar of value to the chief assets of this corporation—the people who make up the backbone of the organization." As a matter of fact, one would not have to go back too many years to see ample evidence of the basis for this statement, because one could have bought this company's stock for a few dollars a share, whereas today it has a reasonably good price tag on it.

HUMAN INTERACTIONS

If one were to read the writings of the economic and business philosophers who are interested in management, he would encounter the frequently quoted statement that "every manager has essentially four types of administrative function to perform. First, he must be able to *plan;* secondly, he must *delegate;* thirdly he must *coordinate or integrate;* and fourthly he must *control, measure or "check up on."* Again, when we look at these functions or managerial activities, we are impressed with the fact that each of these involves interactions with people.

So here again, we are confronted with the human relations problem. In fact, management is usually defined as "getting things done through people." In other words, the manager must be able to predict and control the behavior of others. My fundamental thesis is that, in order to be able to do this well, the manager should—rather *must*—have an understanding of himself and of those around him.

Human interactions in an industrial or business setting can be roughly classified under five headings. *First,* we can speak of interactions within the individual. Figuratively speaking, we can think of the manager as "interacting within himself." May I suggest very briefly some of the things that are involved here. All of us are fully aware of the fact that each individual is a unit; he is a whole, a *Gestalt,* a responding organism. Ordinarily we are dealing with the responses of John Smith or Bill Jones, not any "parts" of him, because we do not respond as "parts." We respond as a unit. Nevertheless, we often "do business with ourselves," so to speak.

We have, for example, a self-concept. This is something we have built up over a period of years. True, it changes within certain limits, from time to time, as a result of various experiences we undergo. Nevertheless, there is always a "common denominator" on which any future changes are superimposed. We also have a body-image. It is amazing in how many activities of everyday life this image plays a vital role. For example, in learning to drive a car, the new driver and the car are not one. I am sure each of you had such an experience when you first were learning to drive. As you steer down the road, the fender is out *there,* and you are in *here,* and your job, as you see it, is to keep that fender from touching other fenders that come near, in the process of steering the car. However, after a period of driving this car, more and more the car becomes a part of you, so that eventually, it is *you* who are *steering yourself* down the street, and your main concern is that you will not hit the curb or the car which is parked next to it.

In the same way we might say that each of us builds up a concept of himself. This concept plays an important role in the way we behave each day. In this sense we are playing a role. We also have certain goals or aspirations. We have certain quality standards. We have certain inner security or lack of it. And all of these things constitute our own perception of ourself and, in turn, influence our reactions in everyday situations in a very real sense. These examples will illustrate what I mean by "interactions within the individual."

Second, we have what might be called "person-to-person interactions." Typical examples are found in situations where a manager is reacting to his subordinate, or the subordinate to the manager, or one manager is interacting with another manager, or one worker with another worker, and so on. Quite often the result of such a mutual interaction will be somewhat greater than the sum of the individual actions involved.

Third, we have "small group interactions." Here we might illustrate what we are talking about by citing committee behavior, the activities of a task force or team, the activities of relatively small units within a corporate set-up, interactions among families, and so on.

Fourth, come "large group interactions," as illustrated by the activities of a department or division of a company, or by the activities of the financial function, the industrial relations function, or the research and development function, or as illustrated by staff-versus-line functions within the corporate sphere.

Finally, there is an even larger type of interaction which we might call "associations." Here, of course, we may be dealing with one company versus another in the so-called competitive situation. Or we might even be dealing with states, countries, cultures, or other large groupings.

SOCIAL BEHAVIOR

Now, it is important for us to recognize that no individual ever behaves in a vacuum; rather, he is born and he lives, breathes, and dies in a social matrix. Perhaps the most effective way of illustrating this point would be for each of us to make a detailed record of everything we do from the time we get up in the morning until we go to bed at night. For example, if you are awakened by the alarm clock, you would note "alarm clock rings." Then you brush your teeth, wash with soap, shave with a razor, and so on, noting every response you make in a very detailed record. Having completed the day's activities, you can look at the detailed list of activities from the point of view of the degree to which they are social in character. I think you will find that there will be very few activities on the list which are not, indirectly or directly, influenced by your membership in society. And the minute we start talking about society, we are talking about relationships with other people. We are immediately becoming concerned with social or human relations problems.

From a psychological point of view, our behavior is social in two different senses. Or, to put it another way, we might say that we can conceptualize our behavior from two different viewpoints: first, our behavior is social in the sense that we are usually responding to other people; second, our response is conditioned (or influenced) by our membership in a number of social groups.

The social psychologist Kantor years ago defined a social group as "a group of people who share a certain type of behavior." In other words, a social group is one which exhibits behavior in common. We all share all sorts of behavior equipment. For example, the way we dress, the food we eat, the way we process that food(the way we cook it or do not cook it), the language we use, our sleeping habits, our relations, family and other—all of our social customs or mores are of this sort. We can thus define a social group in terms of a number of people who share one or more forms of behavior. In this sense the largest proportion of our behavior is social. It is social in the sense that each of us is a member of a large number of different groups, groups with whom we share behavior. For example, there are family groups, community or neighborhood groups, urban versus rural groups, occupational groups, all sorts of subgroupings within the corporate structure, fraternal groups, avocational groups, religious groups—more groups than one can even begin to classify. The important point here is that our present behavior can in large part be explained in terms of a knowledge of the groups to which we belong. Each group represents a frame of reference within which our particular behavior becomes meaningful.

A number of years ago I had a graduate student who carried out the following experiment; I mention it because it illustrates the way our behavior becomes patterned on the basis of our membership in different groups. This particular student was interested in the so-called free association experiment. For example, when most people are suddenly confronted with the word stimulus "table" they will respond by saying "chair." For many years psychiatrists and clinical psychologists have used this type of technique for a variety of purposes. There are available tabulations of the most expected frequency of response to a standard set of stimulus words. To some words you get a large percentage of what we might call "common" responses; people agree among themselves in their "free associations" to these words. Other stimulus words give rise to more widely divergent responses.

In this particular study there were a number of words from one of the standard stimulus lists. To this group of standard words, which have been frequently studied and response-tabulated, my student added another group of words which he himself chose. He chose words which were purposely ambiguous in meaning, but which had definite meanings in certain occupational fields such as law and medicine. For example, the word "carrier," or the word "chamber," or the word "instruments." This entire group of stimulus words was then given to students in different years of law school, students in different years of medical school, and students who were taking liberal arts courses and whose curriculum was not so specifically oriented. To each stimulus word the subject was to record his first and most immediate verbal response. The responses to stimulus words given by the subjects in all experimental groups were tabulated.

In essence, this is what was found. In the case of the neutral words, there were no differences whatever in associations. However, in the case of the ambiguous "critical" words, it was found that the medical students, as might be expected, gave a reliably larger percentage of medical responses to these words, whereas the law students gave a larger percentage of legal responses, and the liberal arts students gave a larger percentage of responses which were predominantly neutral—neither legal nor medical in nature. Moreover, the percentage of medical responses given by medical students increased as a function of the length of time spent in medical school, with the seniors giving a larger percentage of medical responses than freshmen. The same was true of the law school students.

Now, what is the import of this experiment for our present topic of interest? The implication is this: here we have a clearcut illustration of a type of verbal learning—perceptual conditioning, if you will—which was occurring as a result of time spent in learning to become a lawyer or a doctor. Later on, when the student gets out of law school, he is a lawyer and his perception of words will be influenced to a very real extent by his training. Each of us exhibits this verbal conditioning. And each of us makes use of this concept every day in guiding our relationships with other people. As a matter of fact, it could be argued that, to a very real extent, the individuality of a person is the result of the rather unique combination of group memberships which apply in his particular case. In other words, no two people in this room are members of exactly the same group—and no two of us are alike for this very reason.

THE S → R SCHEMA

We often refer, diagrammatically, to the subject matter of psychology—the science of human behavior—in this way. We say that psychology is a study of the responses of organisms, or individuals, to different forms of stimulation. We have what has been called the $S \rightarrow R$ schema, or paradigm, or diagram. Another way of writing this schema is to say that the response of the individual is a function of certain stimulating conditions: $R = f(s)$. But this alone does not tell the whole story because, in order to be able to differentiate various responses, we have to be more specific about what we mean by stimulus. For this reason we might put a little subscript w on the S, or stimulus, in order to refer to the fact that we never respond in a vacuum but, rather, any stimulus which impinges on one of our sense organs is perceived in a certain way, and the way in which it is perceived is in turn a function of our previous stimulation. This subscript w is an abbreviation of the word "world," which refers to the sum total of the previous stimulation we have received. We thus have the schema, $R = f(S_w)$.

Psychologically, we might say that from the moment of conception the individual encounters an ever widening arc of stimulation as he grows older, and during this time he is constantly building what we might call a "reactional biography." He acquires certain behavior equipment, most of which is social in the sense of the previously discussed meaning. The individual grows up in a particular culture and group of subcultures, or social groups. Most of his reactions are with other people, and most of them occur under social auspices, in this meaning of the term. Hence, his reactional biography is definitely social in nature.

This $S \rightarrow R$ formula is simply the application to the area of behavior, of the cause-and-effect concept which you find in any experimental science. In any experimental science, what you are trying to do is to envisage, or subsume, a large number of diverse phenomena in terms of a limited number of cause-and-effect relationships, or principles. This is what a psychologist is trying to do when he applies the $S \rightarrow R$ schema to behavior.

VARIABILITY IN HUMAN BEHAVIOR

To a very real extent, human relations problems can be structured in terms of certain other problems, such as the problem of communication. Or, we can think of them primarily as constituting problems in semantics. For example, when two people interact and one says something, we have to distinguish between what A actually said, what A thought he said, what A intended to say, what B thought A said (or what he understood A to say), and what B thought A intended to say or should have said. We could add to this list almost indefinitely, I am sure. But the point I want to make is this: when A says something to B, there are certainly a number of different angles to this simple interaction, when you look specifically at the behavior of A and B. There are many ways in which one can approach such a relatively simple situation. So the problem of communication is certainly a very fundamental problem in so far as human relations are concerned. Little wonder that it presents such difficulties in most industrial (and other) situations.

Now, if we look analytically at the behavior of individuals, we find that there are at least two kinds of variability in behavior which I think it makes sense for us to distinguish. First, there is variability within the individual; second, there is variability within the group, or from one individual to another. I would like to comment briefly on these two kinds of variability in behavior; both are basic to human relations and both have implications for selection, placement, training, rating, management development, and the like.

First, let us consider variability within the individual—we might refer to this as intra-individual variability. If we were to select any one individual, irrespective of his job in the company, and look at him analytically to get an accurate measure of his psychological make-up in terms of his behavior equipment, we would find that he varies widely in respect to his abilities, his interests, his personality characteristics, his drives or motivations, and so on down the line. For example, each of us is more able along some lines than others. We vary in our abilities, aptitudes, and skills. If we could measure accurately a given individual's degrees of competency along a number of different lines, and if we were to plot these different competencies or abilities in the form of a frequency graph, we would get a normal curve or some sort of bell-shaped distribution curve. In other words, in any one individual case, there would be certain abilities in which the individual would rate very high and other abilities in which he would rate very low; and in the vast number of abilities he would be mediocre, or about average. Such findings illustrate variation within the individual—intra-individual variability.

Second, we have variability from person to person, or variability between people—inter-individual variability; this is the well-known fact of individual differences. Thus, if we could get an accurate measure of how well everybody in this room rates on a certain ability factor, and if we were to plot all of our scores on that factor in the form of a distribution curve, the resulting curve would tend to approximate the bell shape.

We would find a few people who rate low and a few people who rate high in the given ability factor, whereas most people would rate somewhere in the middle. The larger our group and the less highly atypical or less selective, the more closely would the resulting curve approximate the normal bell-shaped distribution.

These two types of variability are encountered every day by every manager. And the manager's understanding of them, as well as his understanding of just what the particular pattern is in the case of the individual with whom he is dealing, is fundamental to almost every decision the manager makes— whether that decision relates to the placement of people, the selection of people, their rating and development, the delegation of work, or anything else.

APPRAISAL OF THE INDIVIDUAL

Psychologists have wrestled for many years with the problem of how best to classify the various behavioral characteristics presented by people. You will find that no two psychologists agree completely on the best method of classification. One encounters long lists of traits—almost like laundry lists. One finds lists of motives and drives, lists of personality characteristics, lists of ability factors, and so on down the line. I have developed a very simple and practical way of thinking about this problem of the constitution of the individual—what his psychological make-up is—for use in training interviewers and merit raters. It is, perhaps, oversimplified to some extent, but I think it does provide a rough though convenient framework within which one can make meaningful statements and decisions about people. Psychologically it makes sense, too, in terms of what we know about their make-up. Perhaps its most important advantage is that it is practical and usable.

It seems to me that there are five essential questions which we should ask about an individual. We can ask these questions if we are called upon to appraise him or are concerned with his development, if we are attempting to communicate with him—in almost any kind of practical situation. First we would ask the question: "Can he? Can he do the job under consideration?" This question immediately confronts us with the necessity for sizing up his *ability*, his *training*, and his *experience*. In other words, when we ask this question we are trying to decide whether or not he possesses the necessary information, background, and skill which are requisite for such-and-such an activity. Now, if the answer is "No," we would automatically eliminate him as far as delegating this job is concerned. As I have indicated, "Can he?" is a broad question —there are many sub-questions implied by it, just as there are in the case of each of these five major questions. But notice that, when we look at a man's work experience, when we give him psychological tests to determine his abilities, or when we look at his educational background, we are interested in drawing information relating to this first basic question—"Is he capable?" If the answer is "Yes, he's capable," we do not stop there.

Our second question is "Will he?" In other words, assuming that he has the requisite amount of ability, experience, and so on, "Is he willing to put this ability to work?" Now this second question immediately involves us in an appraisal of his motivation. In my opinion, it does not do a man any good to have training or ability if he is not motivated to apply it. Under question two one can distinguish certain sub-factors, such as initiative, willingness to work, perseverance, self-discipline, willingness to make present sacrifices for future gains, and so on. Such factors are all concerned with this fundamental question of motivation.

If the answer is favorable on the second question we would next proceed to the question—and notice that these are interlocking categories—"In the process of putting his abilities to work, will he get along satisfactorily with others?" Here, of course, we come face to face with the appraisal of personality factors, which influence the individual's success in human relations. The definition of the word "others" will, of course, differ considerably and be more important for some jobs than for others. But, no matter what the job, we still have contact with people—with co-workers, subordinates, superiors, customers, and many others.

The fourth question I like to ask is: "What about his basic character?" Here we encounter such factors as considerateness, forthrightness, sincerity, honesty, responsibility, and so on. It would be very nice if we could set up a complex regression equation and, in our appraisal of a man, simply determine his standing on each of the factors, throw the weights into an equation, and come out with a final solution. To date we have not arrived at such a solution, and I doubt very much if we ever shall, for the simple reason that these relationships are exceedingly complex. Companies have often asked me why different weights cannot be assigned to such factors, leading to a solution for the individual case. The best reasoon why such a procedure will not work is found right here in question number four. If you had a man who was unfavorable on question number four, no matter how favorably he had rated on questions two and three, you certainly would not employ him!

Finally, there is a fifth set of factors which enter into many of our managerial decisions about people. These I shall call miscellaneous factors. This fifth question, or category, is admittedly a catch-all, but, from a purely practical point of view, these miscellaneous factors can sometimes be extremely important. In any given individual case, a man's standing on one of these particular factors can entirely dissipate his effective job performance. From a realistic standpoint, therefore, we must consider miscellaneous factors in certain instances. I am thinking of such things as a marked physical disability or, perhaps, a bad marital situation, or lack of geographic mobility as illustrated by disinclination toward travel or moving from one location to another. Such miscellaneous factors are legion; in certain instances they can be crucial.

I mention these five types of factors simply because I think they provide a convenient framework within which you can often order your thinking about individuals. I did not elaborate on the third set of factors—the personality factors—as I am sure they are well-known to you. I hope you will find these five sets of factors useful.

In conclusion, let me repeat my fundamental thesis. An understanding of the make-up of people is indispensable to successful management. The more the manager knows about the make-up of the people he is managing, the better job he should be able to do.

ARE MANAGERS PEOPLE?

by Melvin W. Thorner, M.D.

THE GROWTH of industrial activity in the last hundred years has accelerated to hitherto undreamed-of levels of complexity and organization. The many smaller enterprises of half a century ago have become the somewhat fewer but much larger corporations of today. Many of the aggregational forces going into these associations have shown similar growth in more efficient technologies and organizational patterns. The basic units composing these large companies have not shown any tendency toward comparable change. The units to which I refer are people, and they have not developed any fundamental capacities not possessed by the people who were their ancestors one hundred or more years ago. Obviously, the demands upon people have changed and the individual capacity to respond to these demands is valued differently than under former circumstances. I shall consider the effects of modern industrial demands upon contemporary people who are currently called upon to exercise decision at the top levels of industrial enterprise.

As in all discussions, semantics here rears its quite ugly and malodorous head. The English language can easily consider a "manager." He "manages" affairs, i.e. he pushes them around. He may have more or less "managerial" ability and knowledge of "management." But consider the poor "executives"! Can we

Address presented at the Fifth Utility Management Workshop, August, 1956. Dr. Thorner is Professor of Psychiatry at the University of Pennsylvania.

properly say that he "executes" anything or anybody? He might have "executive" ability, but it would be awkward to say that he has knowledge of "executiveship" or "executive science." I think the awkwardness of our language on this point is not the result of mere chance, but is possibly a tacit recognition of the difficulty of being more specific; this is a sore point for many corporate presidents when they try to justify salary and bonus dispersals to their "executive" personnel. What is it that they do? To substitute the somewhat old-fashioned term "entrepreneur" hardly leaves us much better off.

DECISIONS AND MANAGEMENT—THE PERSON

Two things that "managers" and "executives" have in common are that there exists somewhere a piece of paper which gives them their title, and they receive larger checks than most of the people working for the corporation. Another common attribute is that they are members of the human race and fall within the limits of tolerance and specifications common to all other members of the human race.

The important difference between managers and non-managers is that the former are frequently called upon to make decisions which are more or less binding upon a considerable segment of the corporation. While the effects of the decisions of executives may be greater than for those made by lower echelons, the processes of making decisions are about the same for all people.

I cannot pretend to know in any satisfactory detail how the human computor works to produce decisions, but one can have recourse to a considerable body of information which demonstrates certain input-output relationships. The computor itself, i.e. the manager, is largely surrounded by "black box" mystery.

The record of the classes of decisions a man makes is as characteristic of him for any period of his life history as his face or his name. Let us look briefly at the effects of age upon decision-making, and, for convenience, let us do it backwards. Older men within a few years of their retirement on pension will make "conservative" decisions with greater statistical frequency than younger men. It is perhaps a little difficult to obtain a consensus upon what constitutes a "conservative" decision, but I mean it here to indicate a decision which is least apt to have unfortunate consequences upon the decider himself. For example, many of us are amateur political office holders. We can state with great forcefulness what it is that our president or congressman ought to do. If, by chance, we were to become congressmen, we would find that this forcefulness disappears and the correct course to follow is no longer so strikingly obvious to us. Living as an "out," our wildest and most radical ideas have very little chance of calling down disaster on our heads. As "ins" our slightest deviation can call for public retribution. The older "in" is particularly apt to be aware of this, partly because of his experience in life, and partly because he is apt to attempt to insure that his last few years on the job shall not rob him of the rewards of his lifetime application.

At the other end of the scale is the young executive. His decisional activity is less predictable on the basis of age, alone, than is true for the older man. He may pass from a secure college adolescence into his job with rosy visions untinged by the spectre of harsh retaliation for errors, or he may enter his job with the obsequiousness born of conditioned timidity, determined to do no "wrong." The "wrong" is obviously of the type defined by an African Bantu savage. When asked his opinion of right and wrong, he thoughtfully said, "I go to kill my enemy—that is right. He comes to kill me—that is wrong." The young man may have come fresh from his post-school vacation, which was spent in reading "Gamesmanship," and primed to make all the moves most calculated to win advancement.

What of the middle-aged executive who has ambition and imagination, and who has not been cowed into conservative retreat by adverse experience? Here again, age alone does not furnish many clues to the pattern of decision-making. There is a frequently recurring life circumstance which may, however, exert influence upon his decisions. In the forties or early fifties many an executive has just about realized many of his youthful goals. His house is owned, his insurance paid up, his children married and his income nearly adequate. (Absolute adequacy of income is one goal that is apparently seldom reached by anyone.) This gradual dissolution of goals may be very disturbing, and the resulting emotional disturbance may have marked effects upon his capacity for adequate decisiveness. A forty-eight-year-old man troubled with his sexual indolence, and seeking a youthful mistress with whom to reassure himself, may be less than acute in grasping the complexities of an industrial problem.

Decision patterns, as mentioned before, do have a kind of individuality. These patterns are subject to change, but the range of this individual change is usually small compared to the differences among people. Just as one does not suddenly start to speak in an unfamiliar foreign language, one does not often change his patterns of job response radically or suddenly. Thus the range of decisions made by an individual in the past furnish a statistical basis for anticipating his future class of decisions. The longer an individual lives, the more certain it is that no radically new changes will come about in his decision-making. With one committee of research engineers with a two-year history, it was possible to predict the individual votes on alternate decision problems with a high enough accuracy that the corporation president was tempted to dissolve the committee, since its decisions could often be predicted whether they met or not.

DECISIONS AND MANAGEMENT—THE ENVIRONMENT

Thus far there has been a cursory observation of the person. What of the pressures and demands of the environment and the reaction of the individual executive to them? I have a firm belief that the most important group of environmental demands (as far as influencing decisions is concerned) is the group of personal demands made upon an individual by his family and social contacts. One could call this "instinct for self preservation." It would be idle to pretend that professional or corporate demands are more influential. Into every business or research decision that is made, conscious or unconscious elements of these personal demands enter. I suspect that many formal studies on individual and group decision-making have failed to take proper account of this influence of personal upon professional activity. As a corollary, one might say that the strict logical factors which can be stated as bearing on a decision may, at times, be considerably modified or even overwhelmed by those personal needs which develop in response to familiar and social demands. These demands may take many forms and they may be overt or tacit. There is ubiquitous social structuring which follows position in the corporate echelons. The status of the husband may so effect an executive's wife that her urging for greater status (and income) may result in executive decisions made for personal aggrandizement rather than business logic. A henpecked husband may be unconsciously pushed into building up a power empire within a corporation, where the empire primarily satisfies personal rather than corporate needs. These examples might easily be multiplied, but it would serve no useful purpose to do so. It is not within the proper province of a corporation to arrange the personal affairs of its executives. It would, however, be useful to be aware of the fact that response to personal demands may bias the decisions of executives. A study of the decision-pattern regularities of executives is very helpful in this respect.

The environmental demands of the social structure of a corporation may also have great influence upon managerial decisions. Who gets carpets in the office, who gets two private secretaries, who has the largest expense accounts? These are all potent items in the power politics which exist in corporate living. There may or may not be conscious recognition of power politics, but this fact does not seem to change the facts of social structuring. Internecine jealousies and their effects do not depend upon recognition for their existence. It is not suggested that power politics in corporations is good or bad; it may be either, neither, or both. My own experience makes me feel that more good than harm to the corporation comes from it, although unquestionably both wanted and unwanted consequences ensue. Here is an area where manipulation of the social structure is both possible and justifiable. Unfortunately, no glib generalizations can be given. Each structure has its individual action characteristics and needs. In many of these situations wanted improvements may come out of planned disequilibrium.

The specifically delineated job area of an executive is the most vocal of the environmental demand groups. But every experienced executive realizes that the demands of his job do not exactly correspond with the written directive of his imputed duties. Nevertheless, he usually must attend to the stated area of his competence, all the while realizing that changes, expansions, and contractions in this area are unstated demands upon his ability to perform. A great artist must have in his performance more than his teachers could tell him. Here is another area where corporate manipulation can make for net gain. As a consultant I am constantly impressed with the number of square executives found in round corporate holes. I suspect this is because the president, or his agent, thinks of logical reasons why there should be round holes, and often meditates upon the absurdity of the preponderance of square executives. The shortage of brainpower is getting worse (because of increasing demand), and the maximization of thinking might be furthered by squaring off the holes better to fit the square executives on the payroll. The shavings left over from this operation can usually be dealt with by lesser wits. In an era of lockstep education and job specification (written by people who cannot do the job they describe) there are still some intelligent executives who have unique as well as general abilities. These abilities may in the final analysis be more useful to the corporation than the performance of duties which can be specified in advance.

Out of experience in the army and navy during the Second World War there has emerged a fact of executive life which is often neglected in theoretical considerations. It very often happened that a man who seemed relatively incompetent except for routine work in civilian life became a very competent officer with valuable managerial abilities. It also frequently happened that successful men in an executive position in civilian life made poor officers or failed to obtain a commission at all. These data, plus more recent experience, should make one distrustful of thinking of "executive ability" as if it were a unique and personal characteristic that would appear any time there was an environmental demand. It is apparently the reaction of an individual to the environmental demand that makes the good executive, and it would be unwise to assume that any individual can be adequate for any and all environmental demands. No amount of standardized testing for "executive ability" can be successful in prediction unless this "product" or "reaction" theory of executive ability is recognized.

In conclusion, I should like to state what a corporation looks like to me. It is a collection of people who organize themselves and nature, intending to secure for themselves by their mutual endeavors a means of occupation, subsistence, and material gain. To the extent that they individually and collectively achieve their ends they are successful. This viewpoint is not a contribution to economic theory, but it does represent the fact that corporations are people—and their executives are people too.

A SOCIO-PSYCHOLOGICAL APPROACH TO HUMAN RELATIONS

by Goodwin Watson

IN THIS BRIEF paper the vital importance of good human relations will be taken for granted. Exhortation is assumed to be of very limited utility. Our presentation will be directed toward one type of inquiry, which can be made in almost any shop and which is likely to bring to attention quite specific ways of improving interpersonal relations.

Probably all of you are familiar with the concept of *role*. Every social system is made up of interrelated positions; the behavior associated with any position is called its role. The role of a manager is more or less independent of the particular individual who steps into the post. Whoever he may be, he is expected or compelled, so long as he remains manager, to perform certain duties, exercise certain rights, and carry on as a manager should. We can speak with similar meaning of the role of a research chemist, a statistician, a private secretary, a supervisor, or a visitor. Here at this conference there is a role appropriate to the director, the executive secretary, a participant, a panel chairman, or a guest speaker. The thesis of this paper is that most human relations difficulties arise from divergent perceptions of interrelated roles. The broad term *role* needs now to be differentiated by the introduction of two mod-

Address presented at the Sixth Utility Management Workshop, August, 1957. Dr. Watson is Professor of Education, Teachers College, and a consulting social psychologist.

ifying variables. One is the distinction between ideal and actual role. The ideal role is what one thinks *should* be the behavior of any person who fulfills his role properly; the actual role represents what he *really* does. Since all performance falls short of perfection, there is always some discrepancy between the actual role and the ideal role. The second variable needed for this study is the role-perceiver. This may be the person in the role or others who supervise him or who work under his direction. We are interested in how the manager of research, for example, perceives his own actual role-behavior and how this compares with his own ideal. We are interested also in how his associates, higher and lower in the hierarchy, perceive his behavior and how they see it as deviant from the ideal role.

The data for exploration of points of friction in a manager's interpersonal relations in a department would come from answers by all concerned to two questions: (a) What do you think a good manager should do? (b) What does this manager actually do?

With answers from the manager himself and from his superiors and his subordinates we can derive seven significant indices.

1. The manager's awareness of his own imperfections (deviation of his own perception of actual role from ideal role).

2. Difference between the ideal role as conceived by superiors and the ideal role as conceived by the manager himself. Quite possibly the expectations differ and need clarification.

3. Differences between the actual role-behavior seen by superiors and that which the manager believes he is carrying out. Quite possibly the superiors are inadequately informed and have generalized from too limited a sample of observations. Or, the manager may be mistaken in his own impression of how he actually spends his time and performs his tasks.

4. Discrepancies between what superiors believe his ideal

and his actual role to be. These are their points of dissatisfaction with him. Differences between the ideal role as perceived by the manager and what subordinates think a manager should properly do.

5. Differences between the actual role as seen by the manager himself and as seen by subordinates. Studies have shown that most workers have a fantastic image of what their manager does to earn his salary.

6. Discrepancies between what subordinates believe his ideal and his actual roles to be; these are the points at which subordinates are consciously dissatisfied with managerial performance.

7. Comparison of the ideal-actual discrepancies as seen by the manager himself, as seen by his superiors, and as seen by his subordinates. It is probable that these differ and that sincere effort to move closer to the manager's own ideal might neglect factors which are regarded as very important by subordinates, by superiors, or both.

A study of actual and ideal roles, from the several interrelated viewpoints, will not solve all problems in human relations, but it is likely to redefine many of them. Much of what has commonly been seen as clash of personalities, temperamental incompatibility, or character defects turns out, upon analysis, to stem from different conceptions or perceptions of role. The confusion of expectations is likely to be greater at the upper levels of responsibility. It is much easier to achieve consensus of all concerned on what a good typist should do than on what an idea man or a pure scientist or an industrial executive should do. Each co-worker is most vividly aware of the particular points at which his own role in the organization must mesh with the managerial role. He is probably not aware of many other aspects of the managerial role. One way in which the manager improves his interpersonal relations is by getting a little more shared agreement on what managers do and should do. Increasing the area of agreement calls for two-way adjustment. The manager must take more account of how others perceive his role; he must also help them to get a more accurate grasp of what he sees as his role.

We have used comparative role-perception as a method for studying stresses in the manager's own interpersonal relations. The method is no less useful in analysis of human relations problems between or among departments, cliques, or individual workers. In one classic case at the Harwood Manufacturing plant, a chronic conflict developed to the point where the mechanic and the forelady were calling each other liars and both were ready to walk out. An analysis by Bavelas revealed confusion over whose role it was, or should be, to decide which repair job needed to be done first. Once this bit of role definition had been accepted by all concerned, relations became amicable. Innumerable tensions center about disputes as to whose job it should be to do what. Each participant resents any implication that he is failing to do what he should. Loyalties within a work team or among specialists may expand a personal misunderstanding into a serious schism. The individual is almost always a member of a group or groups in which other members share his perception of role. Trying to change a single member's view, while leaving the group norm out of the discussion, is usually futile. Either the group as a whole changes expectations and demands, or the individual remains faithful to the accepted group standard.

The responsibilities of a manager extend out into a community broader than his own department or corporation or line of business. He has human relations problems outside his organization as well as in it. Worker morale and consumer good will may depend upon accord between what the community expects of a manager and what he does. It is often useful, therefore, to extend the inquiry about ideal and actual roles to include opinion leaders in groups outside the particular business.

One point needs special emphasis. There is no implication in this paper that a manager can abdicate his own responsibility for role definition. To discover how others see his job may be very helpful, but not in the sense that the manager necessarily judges his performance through their eyes. We are making no plea for an other-directed management in which the executive's personal judgment would defer to polls of subordinates, superiors, associates, or the public. Our point is, rather, that inquiries into perception of ideal and actual roles will often reveal serious misconceptions which underlie chronic tension and recurrent conflict. We do not deny that there are some problems which arise from emotional distortions and perhaps, although rarely, from malevolence. Our thesis, however, is that much which has been regarded as maladjustment of feelings and incompatibility of personalities is better seen as cognitive discrepancy. One great advantage of this approach is that change is most readily introduced on the cognitive level. Most of us can not cast out devils or undo the emotional damage of a bad childhood; we can, however, straighten out misunderstandings of role definition.

Report: AN OPERATIONAL STUDY OF SUPERVISORY HUMAN RELATIONS

Fourth Utility Management Workshop, May, 1955

THE RED GROUP, after an organizational meeting and an exchange of personal experience, came to the conclusion that it should make a study of some particular phase of human relations.

In view of the importance of human relations in all supervision, it was decided to specialize in this field, using an operational study approach to the problem. A hypothesis or proposition for study and testing was selected from numerous possibilities that were suggested, and its final form was stated as follows: Skill in human relations is an essential qualification of a good supervisor.

Seven case studies were made to determine whether the group's experiences supported the proposition, and the results were overwhelmingly in the affirmative.

METHOD OF FORMULATING THE TASK

A group discussion of suitable subjects which might be explored resulted in the suggestion of three possible fields of study:

1. Some phase of employee training, especially training to change attitudes

2. Some phase of human relations, perhaps simply "getting up-to-date" on human relations

3. An exploration of the concept that the primary responsibility of an executive is to train those next below him

The subject which seemed to lend itself best to valid interpretation by the group was one dealing with human relations of supervisors, since the combined experience of the members of the group in this field amounted to 235 years.

Once the subject had been decided, the question was raised as to how the study should be conducted—what approach should be used. In this connection, the members of the group expressed a desire to utilize their background of broad experience in some way. A brief excursion into the philosophy of the scientific method occurred at this point. The following approaches were considered:

1. Use of an essentially rational approach—the so-called "arm-chair" method. The idea of beginning with certain premises and "thinking the thing through."

2. Use of an essentially *empirical* approach—the idea of obtaining data by observation and measurement and then "letting the facts speak for themselves." The method of determining the cause by studying the effects.

3. Use of an essentially pragmatic approach—an approach which stresses "the working application." The point of view is, "Does it work?" Thus, the emphasis is on results.

At length, a method related to the empirical approach was selected. This method is known as the "operational" approach, and it involves the study of actions, happenings, or "operations." The group decided to study the things that actually happened in human relations situations, in so far as this was possible.

Thus, the task the group set for itself was to make an operational study of supervisory human relations. The source of data for this study was to be the background and experiences of the group members, who averaged 26 years of experience each in the utility industry.

Since the group task was one involving human relations, it was necessary to arrive at mutually acceptable definitions of human relations and certain other terms.

It was generally agreed that human relations involve any action between people regardless of its favorable or unfavorable effect.

Several possible definitions for *human relations* were discussed:

1. Human relations is getting work done through people, or accomplishing things through people.

2. Human relations is the associating together of people.

3. Human relations is understanding people.

4. Human relations is recognizing people as unique individuals who have to be motivated to produce to the level of their capacities, in order to achieve the goals which have been established for the organization so that the end profit is realized.

5. Human relations is the interactions of people.

The first four of these definitions did not seem to suit the purposes of the group; however, the fifth one did. Actually this definition was developed and adopted because of group dissatisfaction with the others.

In order to give a complete understanding of the definition, it was considered necessary to define the term "interaction." *Interaction* means the transmitting of a communication of any sort (oral, written, gestural) from one person to another. From an operational point of view, interaction has not occurred unless the communication is received, and this is conditional on the production of some sort of a perceivable reaction on the part of the receiver.

SELECTION OF A HYPOTHESIS TO STUDY AND TEST

Following the formulation of the task and the definition of human relations, the group desired to study some specific aspect of the field. They decided to select a hypothesis that they could test from their own observations and experiences, one which would permit them to place more faith in the data to be collected and to have more confidence in the results.

Accordingly, several possible hypotheses or propositions were suggested:

1. Human relations skill can be developed through deliberate training.

2. Human relations aptitudes are inborn, the implication being that only those people with inborn aptitudes could develop human relations skills.

3. A thorough knowledge of the job to be done is more important than a knowledge of human relations.

4. Supervisors who maintain good human relations are not the best supervisors at getting out the work.

5. Good human relations significantly help the supervisor get his job done.

6. Good human relations skill is the prime qualification of a supervisor.

7. A good supervisor must be an extrovert.

Sub-groups studied these and other propositions for the purpose of establishing a hypothesis which all concerned would want to study. At length, after considerable deliberation, and considering the many requirements of a supervisor, the group developed this hypothesis: *Skill in human relations is an essential qualification of a good supervisor.*

It should be noted in passing that the group agreed on their conception of what constituted a "good" supervisor. By a good supervisor, the group meant one whom they would still select for the same position if they had a free choice to do it again.

Members of the group verbally presented cases which, in their judgment as executives, involved good, bad, or both kinds of supervision. The essential elements of each case were discussed and tabulated. Each case was examined to determine that elements present were of an operational nature or could be tested by the question: "What happened?"

An analysis form was designed which provided the following: (a) the type of case as judged by the member of the group presenting the case; (b) a brief statement of the case; (c) analysis of "What happened?" (operational events); (d) summary (did the evidences of the presence or absence of human relations skill support the hypothesis?).

Task forces, each composed of three members of the group, were assigned to study one or more of these cases. Each case was analyzed and classified, and a condensed description entered on the form. Next, all essential elements of the case were tabulated. Each of these elements was then examined to determine if the event was operational. The operational events were then classified as to whether human relations skills were present or absent in the element.

When more than one supervisor was involved in the case, evaluation of each individual was made on the one form. Elements not operational but required for complete understanding of the situation, though entered on the form, were not evaluated.

The findings of each task force on each case were reviewed by the group as a whole, and after such reexamination revised as needed to reflect the judgment of the entire group. The detailed analysis of the cases follows.

CASE 1. Electric Company crew engaged in installing lights at a company ball diamond. Crew composed of volunteers for the job, working on own time, without pay.

	EVIDENCE OF HUMAN RELATIONS SKILL *Supervisor*
What happened	
1. Foreman solicited ideas from crew.	+
2. Foreman selected a course of action from among alternatives.	+
3. Crew carried out orders at normal pace.	
4. Crew periodically asked for directions.	+
5. Some group decisions were made.	+
6. Orders were given in the form of a request rather than a command.	+

Summary: This man displayed excellent human relations skill.

CASE 2. An employee, with a good record, and with twenty years' experience in meter reading and collecting, was chosen to be a supervisor of meter reading. This employee was selected by the manager of the department because of his experience and good record. There was also a lack of other candidates.

	EVIDENCE OF HUMAN RELATIONS SKILL	
	Supervisor	*Manager*
What happened (Operation)		
1. Supervisor, prior to appointment, stated he thought job was too big for him.	+	
2. Manager influenced him to accept position.		−
3. Manager introduced supervisor to group. Supervisor remained silent.	−	+
4. Supervisor, after two months, told manager job was too much for him.	+	
5. Manager provides supervisor with temporary assistance.		+
6. Supervisor yelled at men.	−	
7. Supervisor discourteous during telephone conversation with wife of sick employee.	−	
8. Supervisor refused flashlight supplies to employees.	−	

EVIDENCE OF
HUMAN RELATIONS SKILL
Supervisor   *Manager*

What happened (Operation)

9. Supervisor, after nine months, requested demotion to old job.   +

10. Manager asked supervisor to give the job a further trial.   —

11. Supervisor was gruff with employees.   —

Summary: The Supervisor showed evidence of good human relations skill in his relations with Manager, and absence of human relations skills in his supervision of employees.

The Manager's actions in this case indicated an absence of human relations skills.

CASE 3. A line superintendent, operating autonomously in an assigned territory has, in the eyes of his superior, a good working record, a good safety record and an outstanding reputation for good community and employee relations. A new general manager is appointed who directs that some changes be made in operating policies.

EVIDENCE OF
HUMAN RELATIONS SKILL
Superintendent

What happened

1. Superintendent objects to management decision placing the maintenance of all radio dispatching equipment on a system, rather than a local, basis.   —

2. Superintendent will not accept criticism.   —

3. Superintendent's department has no grievances.   +

4. Superintendent does not follow instructions concerning system standards.   —

5. Other departments complain to general manager that superintendent will not coordinate his work with theirs.   —

6. Superintendent refused to follow established routine on connection orders.   —

7. Superintendent (previously a strong advocate of company social affairs) loses interest in company social affairs.

Summary: There is no evidence here of poor human relations skill with subordinates. However, this supervisor shows an absence of human relations skill in dealing with his superiors and with other departments.

CASE 4. A fifty-year-old unmarried female clerk in cashiers department had always been a slow but accurate worker. Of this her supervisors were aware. Eventually, however, her inability to process the work with more speed created a bottleneck.

	EVIDENCE OF HUMAN RELATIONS SKILL	
	Immediate supervisor	*Superintendent of other departments*
What happened		
1. Her supervisor talked to her several times. When reporting to superior was vague as to details.	—	
2. Supervisor prone to praise without good reason.	—	
3. Decision was made to transfer her to other department.		
a. She was not informed of this by her supervisor.	—	
b. She was informed of this by superintendent of the other department.		+
4. Her supervisor was vague answering her statement that she had not been informed of poor performance.	—	

Summary: Supervisor showed an absence of human relations skills.

CASE 5. This case concerns the removal of an old regulator station and the installation of a new one located fifteen miles from the company shops. The people involved are a superintendent, a gang foreman, and his crew. The superintendent was thoroughly competent in the technical aspects of his job, as was the gang foreman, who had a good production record.

	EVIDENCE OF HUMAN RELATIONS SKILL	
	Superintendent	*Gang foreman*
What happened		
1. Night before job was to begin foreman saw to it that all expected necessary materials and tools were loaded on truck.		+
2. Encountered difficulty cutting pipe next morning, cutting tool was slightly damaged.		

	EVIDENCE OF HUMAN RELATIONS SKILL	
	Superintendent	*Gang foreman*
3. Superintendent arrived on job just prior to noon and immediately remarked, "This looks like a bunch of WPA workers."	—	
4. Gang foreman attempted to explain difficulties encountered.		+
5. Superintendent refused to listen to or accept the attempted explanation.	—	
6. Superintendent observed worker struggling with cutting tool.		
7. Superintendent asked for and was handed cutting tool.		
8. Superintendent inspected cutting tool and found it slightly defective.		
9. Superintendent threw cutting tool over a nearby hill.	—	
10. Superintendent said, in presence of foreman and crew, "Any foreman who would bring such a tool on a job should not be a foreman."	—	
11. Without another word, superintendent left the scene of the job.	—	
12. Worker said to foreman, "Why do you take that kind of abuse from him?"		
13. Foreman defended superintendent on grounds that he had recently recovered from typhoid fever, and didn't mean what he said.		+
14. Foreman said he would talk to superintendent that night.		+
15. Foreman had private talk with superintendant that night.		+
16. Superintendent visited job the next day. Talked amiably with the men.	+	
17. After two or three weeks, superintendent reverted to his usual tough personality pattern.		
18. Some years later that superintendent was still a superintendent; the gang foreman was a district manager.		

Summary: Evidence indicates that the superintendent generally failed to use human relations skills; the gang foreman consistently used them.

CASE 6. The manager of an accounting division employing 40 people questions coordination of work schedule in the accounting department. This case also concerns a manager of a real estate department who was the instructor of a course in human relations.

	EVIDENCE OF HUMAN RELATIONS SKILL	
What happened	*Manager*	*Instructor*
1. Manager complained to his superior about other manager not meeting work schedule.	—	
2. Manager's complaints are found to be false.	—	
3. Manager, at his option, elected to take company-sponsored course in human relations.	+	
4. Manager ridiculed course before his employees.	—	
5. Instructor overheard manager ridiculing course and privately questioned if manager liked course.		+
6. Manager did not answer instructor's question.	—	
7. Instructor, at next meeting of course, stated his own need for course, desire to help, and so on.		+
8. Instructor further stated that any participant could withdraw from course if he so desired.		
9. Manager asked instructor if his remarks referred to any particular participant.		
10. Instructor answered that he was referring to manager.		—
11. Manager visited instructor the next day and discussed the events in the class.	+	
12. Manager during discussion broke down.		
13. Manager was changed man following discussion with instructor.	+	
14. Manager, prior to trouble regarding human relations course, had been slow in filling a vacancy in his organization.	—	

Summary: The manager showed an absence of skill in his human relations with the instructor and employees of equal and superior rank.

The instructor, although generally displaying a presence of human relations, showed under pressure a weakness in these skills.

Case 7. Company was recently reorganized with ten department heads reporting to the president and two vice-presidents in staff capacities as assistants to the president. Later, one of the vice-presidents was appointed operating vice-president in charge of production, distribution, and service departments, and the other was appointed administrative vice-president in charge of other departments. The case from here on concerns the operating vice-president.

	EVIDENCE OF HUMAN RELATIONS SKILL	
	Operating vice-president	*President*

What happened

1. Used "cat and mouse" techniques in dealing with subordinates. —

2. Was very critical of *all* his department heads in comments to others. —

3. Even if wrong, would never admit it. —

4. Face-to-face communication with him was difficult. —

5. President discussed method of handling people with operative vice-president with no apparent results. —   +

6. In anticipation of operating vice-president's retirement an assistant was appointed and operating vice-president was instructed to gradually relinquish his duties.   +

7. The operating vice-president never really relinquished his duties. —   —

8. The operating vice-president retired.

9. During the period from the appointment of the operating vice-president to retirement (5 years):

   a. A subordinate, the power production superintendent, had a heart attack.

   b. A new power production superintendent, after nine months on the job, attempted to orgainze resistance to the operating vice-president. This failed and the power production superintendent failed.

   c. Another subordinate, the superintendent of substations, was hospitalized and psychiatric treatment recommended.

EVIDENCE OF
HUMAN RELATIONS SKILL
Operating
vice-president   President

What happened

10. After the operating vice-president re-
    tired, the third power production super-
    intendent remarked to the president,
    "I have just about been going crazy
    for the last two years and a half."   —

Summary: Operating vice-president showed an absence of human relations skill.

CONCLUSIONS

The examination and analysis of the human relations skills demonstrated in the cases presented proved to the satisfaction of the group that these were the distinguishing characteristics of a good or bad supervisor. Throughout the study, the element of technical knowledge was accepted as being important to the job, but it was observed that in those cases in which failure occurred, it was due to the absence of skill in human relations rather than to the lack of technical knowledge. This would tend to the conclusion that, whereas in the past much emphasis has been placed on the technical abilities of the prospective supervisor, a shift of emphasis to the human relations skill requirement of the job will produce better results in supervision. During the study the following principles of effective supervisory conduct became evident.

1. Better results can be obtained when members of the working force are free to make suggestions as to how the work is to be carried out. (Control must be maintained.)

2. Proper planning by a supervisor eliminates confusion and improves morale of working force.

3. Orders given in the form of requests or suggestions are much more effective than commands.

4. A man's willingness to accept responsibilities must be considered before promoting him.

5. Be sure a man's abilities are commensurate with the job before promoting him.

6. Excessive overtime can often be traced to poor supervision.

7. It is necessary to be technically competent.

8. Only such conversation should be carried on with subordinate about his job as will produce positive results.

9. Show confidence in your subordinates by accepting reasonable explanations about deficiencies or problems in a sympathetic manner.

10. Develop responsibility by checking work through subordinate supervisors.

11. Discuss work matters with your subordinates in a quiet, sympathetic manner.

12. Reprimand—if need be—your subordinates in private.

13. Build up your subordinate foremen by deferential treatment in presence of rank-and-file employees.

14. Do those things which will set a good example for the rank-and-file employee to (a) create a good atmosphere for employment, (b) develop loyalty, (c) give the man pride in his job.

15. Give proper training when the occasion demands.

16. Defend your boss and the company to your men because (a) you will gain respect for yourself personally, (b) you will help the *esprit de corps.*

17. If you have a difference with your superior try to resolve it by frank discussion under satisfactory conditions of time and place—do not nurture a misunderstanding.

18. An employee must be correctly informed as to where he or she stands.

19. Sincerity is important both in complimenting and in reprimanding.

20. Take responsibility away from a man and you destroy his incentive.

21. Human relations are as important with your peers and superiors as they are with your subordinates.

22. Do not delegate responsibilities rightly belonging to you.

23. Good supervision reduces accidents; poor supervision permits accidents.

24. Good communications between different levels of authority are necessary in accomplishing the goals of the organization.

25. A supervisor must ensure harmony in his department.

26. A supervisor should not place a subordinate in a position of fear.

27. Good human relations require the heart as well as the mind.

Part Four

COMMUNICATION AND MANAGEMENT

INTRODUCTION

COMMUNICATION is the nervous system of society; without the one, the body is paralyzed and without the other, all human activity would come to a standstill. Industry literally could not exist without communications interlacing its entire fabric. Not only must we have communication channels, but also an intelligible system of signals to transmit through these channels. Every word, gesture, tonal modulation, and facial expression carries a message, as do all our written material, electronic signals, and other means of transmitting intelligence.

To send a message is one thing; to be sure it is received is another; and to be sure it is understood by the designated recipient is still another. In industry the last phase is the important one, as only through proper understanding of directions can we hope to control and direct the actions of subordinates in accomplishing the goals of the enterprise.

One of the serious problems encountered by some of the underdeveloped countries of the world in their programs of industrialization is the difficulty of communication. Often the top echelon—the educated, technically competent manager—is unable to make his directions intelligible to the less well educated worker recently elevated from near-peonage to the unfamiliar world of the factory. Or, even though the producer is experienced in his job, the message may fail to pass unchanged through an "insulating layer" of locally educated but inexperienced "technicians" serving as middle management. With the best of intentions, the people through whose ears, minds, and lips the directions pass change the signals to fit their own concepts of what should be done. Let it be said, also, that this situation is not unique to the underdeveloped countries—it exists to a greater or lesser degree wherever people try to communicate.

Communication in industry is a multidirectional matter. The boss gives orders down the line, but he must receive reports coming upward on the progress of operations, advice and information from staff people and other collateral sources and, unless he is the chief executive officer, he receives instructions and orders from his own supervisor.

In order to be clear and intelligible, communications must be couched in terms and symbols which are typical of the level at which they are used. This frequently involves status levels as well as technical levels. The language of the office differs markedly in many cases from that used in the shop.[1]

Furthermore, communications may follow one of several systems of channels in the average concern. There are the regular formal channels set up by the organization chart, but there are also a number of informal routes—such as the grapevine—which, for some reason, often seem to be more efficient and more expeditious than the formal lines. They are surprisingly accurate too.

THE PAPERS

Livingston analyzes the communication process in terms of its three main factors: the originator, the intermediator, and the receptor. He indicates some of the problems and obstacles encountered in attempting to "get the message through."

[1] An interesting example: The National Labor Relations Board ruled that foul and abusive language used toward a union business agent did not violate the legal ban on derogatory references to labor representatives, if such language is common in the shop. See Fred A. Snow Co. and UAW–CIO, 53 NLRB 184 (1943), p. 977.

Exton carries on the discussion in terms of direct vs. non-direct communication between the originator and the receptor. He considers the problem from the standpoints of the audience involved and purpose of each communication, as each one must be tailormade to fit both audience and purpose, if the desired effect is to be obtained.

In his first paper Hertz concentrates on the variables encountered in communicating within structured groups. He analyzes the steps in communication typical of the management cycle and distinguishes the general classes of information ordinarily transmitted. As a basis for decision-making, information has a value-age relationship which must be weighed against the cost-age relationship in its acquisition.

Rudge suggests three industrial objectives which good communication will accomplish. He cites examples from experience and shows some of the collateral benefits derived. One of the principal conditions prerequisite to reaping these benefits, however, is full information for all echelons of the organization.

Hertz's second paper, "Management is Communication," distinguishes between mechanical communication (which may involve human beings acting only as recorders) and the management communication system which affects people. Our purposes in communicating with each other, the kinds of information transmitted (conceptual, empirical, procedural, stimulatory, directive, and policy) are discussed and a framework established for assuring effective communication by managers.

THE PLACE AND PROBLEM OF COMMUNICATION IN MANAGEMENT AND ADMINISTRATION

by Robert Teviot Livingston

EVERYONE communicates in one way or another, but, before talking specifically about managerial communication, it might be well to generalize a bit. To some writers in this field, everything we do is a communication or an attempt to communicate; as a matter of fact, we are here today because of communication. Our whole culture has been communicated to us by prior generations. Every move in the operation of an organization has been communicated from the manager. So, obviously, the more we know about communication the better.

However much we are concerned with formal, conscious, purposive messages we must not forget that there is a great deal of communication which is neither oral, visual, nor overtly noticeable. There is literally constant communication going on within ourselves; we are highly specialized animals and the various parts must know what to do and what the other parts are doing and will do. For the same reason, within a large and complex industrial or utility organization, much internal communication goes on, coordinating the activities of the com-

Excerpt from the Workbook of the Sixth Utility Management Workshop, July–August, 1957. Mr. Livingston is Professor of Industrial Engineering, Columbia University, and Director of the Utility Management Workshop.

pany; this internal flow of information is administrative communication.

Thus, communication is an essential part of management. Were it not for effective communication there could be no successful management or administration of any enterprise. It is my purpose to locate communication and the act of communication in the total picture of management; later I shall discuss the problem as it affects the individual.

CLASSIFICATIONS OF COMMUNICATION

The act of communication is an interaction and, hence, is from *A* to *B* with an anticipated change of state in *B*. Therefore, a natural method of classification for identification purposes would be by direction.

1. As related to the individual, organism or association:
    (a) outward
    (b) within, or introspective as related to the unit selected
2. In respect to direction in the organization:
    (a) vertical
    (b) horizontal
    (c) diagonal or cross

A study of these would include formal provision for frequency and duration and specific identification of who talks to whom. Another way of looking at direction is in terms of specificity. Thus, a communication may be individually directed, group directed, or undirected.

Another classification might have to do with the originator's purpose or the cause for the communication, the situation, and the occasion. This is not as simple as the directional classification. Thus, there may be communications serving different levels of purpose, such as individual, group, organ, organism, or association. Again, a classification may be made as to the goals and purposes involved. For example, an individual may communicate in respect to his work or because he wishes to carry on a conversation; the question sometimes arises as to whether a conversation is serving the company's purpose. It may not do so directly but, certainly, the better two people know one another (and this is furthered by even casual conversation), the more efficient their formal communication is likely to be. At all events, it is possible to classify communication as being organizationally or personally directed, and it is important to remember that the apparently nonorganizationally directed communication may be as important as the formal; certainly it must be recognized and provided for.

GENERALIZATIONS

It has been proposed by Lasswell that when one knows the following things about a communication he knows the whole story: [1]

1. What is the situation in which *
2. Who
3. Says what
4. For what purpose *
5. In what channel
6. To whom
7. With what effect
   (a) upon the receptor *
   (b) upon the transmitter *

Russell Ackoff, in discussing communication, says "a communication can change the probability of choice of an indi-

[1] The items starred (*) were added by Livingston to Lasswell's original story. It is obvious that only 2, 3, 5, and 6 can be accurately recorded. The first and the last can be observed in part (but not wholly) and the fourth is often a matter of speculation to the observer.

vidual in choosing one set of available courses of action. Such a communication *informs*. Where a communication changes the efficiency of these courses, it *instructs*. One that changes the value of the outcome to the recipient *motivates*." This is an interesting presentation and gives us one more classification to add to our collection. Thus, communications may:

inform   instruct   motivate

A GENERAL MODEL OF A COMMUNICATION SYSTEM

Figure 1 illustrates a model in which the principal phenomena of communication can be located and studied. It presents a three-element system consisting of an originator (A), a receptor (B), and an intermediator (I). It has been reduced to the minimum which can rationally explain the process of communication in a manner which is useful for a better understanding of this important aspect of management.

The process which uses the system is considered in five steps, each of which can be seen in two directions.

1. Stimulation—Receipt
2. Evaluation—Consideration
   (leading to a decision)
3. Media selection
4. Symbolization—Evaluation—Coding
5. Emission and/or acceptance

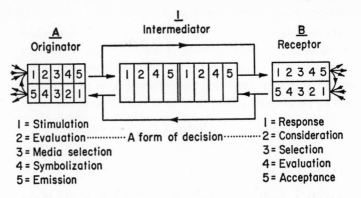

Figure 1. A Model of a Communication System

The third step is not in the intermediator which is shown as a two-directional process with a space in between representing spatial, temporal, or other distance. These general terms may become clearer if we consider a complete unidirectional communicative act in the table below:

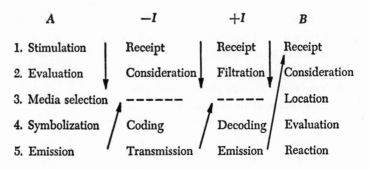

It may be set as the goal that $B5 = A1$; that is to say, that B reacts in the same way to the same stimulation that A received. It is to be noted that the I element—the intermediator—is the area in which the communication people have developed their so-called information theory. It is suggested that this model demonstrates that the problem is far greater than the one they have studied and that the potential sources of error outside I are much greater than within I.

We may assume that any entity is physically able to receive a spectrum of stimuli. At any given instant, whether an entity will or will not receive depends upon (a) the state of the stimulus, (b) the state of the entity, and (c) the combination of the two, or the situation. Entities (human or otherwise) are designed to receive (accept) a certain set of stimuli with given spectra—this is built in.

Having received a stimulation, a very complicated process is doubtless gone through which is similar to the process which is detailed under A above. It may be summarized as consideration leading to a decision of some kind. The first decision is whether to react overtly. If not, then there is a wide field of psychological internal action which we need not pursue here. It will be assumed that consideration leads to the decision to communicate (this decision will include such associated subdecisions as to whom and when, and that the communication is to have a purpose). The purpose might be phrased in a number of ways but, for simplicity, let us say that the purpose of the communication is to get B to do something (X) associated with the stimulus (Y) which A has accepted.

Following the decision to communicate to B about Y (the stimulus A received) in order to get response X, a sequence of interrelated actions takes place. The selection of the medium is largely determined by the physical relationship of B and A. In the model shown, the intermediator is any one of the total possible media. The medium selected determines the class of symbols to use; the message or symbols depend upon both individuals, upon A's understanding of B and X and Y, and upon the circumstances. Following symbolization there is emission, or release, or the message. All of these actions have been shown as sequential, but it is to be understood that there is also a process of recycling, of both feedback and feed-forward.

The intermediator is in two parts; the first, with the exception of the choice of media, is similar to the set of actions of the originator, ending with transmission. The second or positive part is similar to the sequence of actions within the receptor B. The intermediator may be anything from the air in the space that separates two people to the telephone, a letter, or even a book written long ago (in a very real sense, Shakespeare is communicating with everyone who reads one of his plays or sonnets).

The receptor can be considered a mirror symmetry of the originator. However, some explanation is required. There is first the problem of reception; the emission of the intermediator is the stimulus and, hence, is of a lower order of potentials than in the case of A. However, having accepted the stimulus, it is considered and translated from its coded form into impressions, consequences, estimations, and expectations, and finally a primary decision is made—either to respond or not to respond. Next, there is the problem of locating resources, both internal and external, and, in a word, setting up a design for reaction. Two classes of reactions are apparent: (a) to do, and (b) to find out more. If the decision is to find out more, there is the response which is a communication in return. The process of the return communication is the same as the original; thus, a circuit has been completed.

The intermediator is shown as being symmetrical and two-directional. This may or may not be so. It may also be that there can be interference and external noise. All of these are possible and, if it is desired, can be introduced into the model.

However, it is believed that it would be wise to study the simple model before introducing the complications.

COMMUNICATION AND THE INDIVIDUAL

So far we have been talking about the problem of communication in general. We have presented a model to help us study the process. As the model was set up, the individual entered in two capacities: as the communicator and as the receiver. On the surface the problems associated with these two capacities seem different; but, behind the obvious differences, there is a fundamental psychological similarity in the fact that, in each case, there may be a stimulus which can lead to a response. With this similarity in mind, consideration of the individual as the originator of a communication may be helpful in understanding the whole communication process. There are some useful classifications of communications, all centered on the individual. Among them are:

1. External
     human and nonhuman
          and, if human,
     specifically or nonspecifically directed
          and, in any case,
     personal or non-personally directed
2. Internal
     concerned with external stimuli:
          answers
               acceptance
               recognition and identification
               location
               evaluation
               response
     concerned with internal stimuli
          internal want-need satisfactions,

mainly concerned with maintenance of the state of the system, but possibly cued from the outside.

THE NODE/MAN SYSTEM

A second viewpoint which we can take is to consider the position occupied by an individual on a communication system. Three major systems must be taken into account: (a) the formal internal network, (b) the informal internal network, (c) all external networks. It must also be recognized that nodes act in different capacities.

1. Physical locations which are determinants of the topology of the networks; in other words, they are fixed points to which one or more of the networks must be connected.
2. Archives or record stations—the repository of information of various kinds in accordance with which action systems are designed and upon which actions are based.
3. Switching stations—in two capacities; to select connections directly and to switch on or trigger otherwise self-energizing circuits.
4. Two-way filters, screening out non-pertinent information, some kinds of redundancy and noise, and reducing the volume of flow, expanding the message, etc.
5. Monitors—to scan, with different degrees of directedness and thoroughness, and to feed selected information in indicated directions on different networks.
6. Self-energized and externally-energized controls on the results of their monitoring.

It is to be assumed that a node, within certain tolerance limits, is completely predictable. On the other hand, when an individual becomes a part of the node, the objective and mathematical comparison and consequential action system becomes a subjective human system. While the node remains a physical location, in all of the other categories a human element is inserted which may change performance considerably. Two apparently identical node-network unit systems may have different operating characteristics because of differences in the individuals occupying the positions.

These differences arise from several causes. In a physical node switching is completely automatic and unbiased, action following consideration of the stimulus and selection of a response: it is built in. A human being's reaction will not be automatic. A person's feelings and consequent behavior are determined by his perception of the situation. He will be governed not only by his own frames of references but, also, by his feeling toward and understanding of the competencies of the people with whom he communicates. The ability of the individual to draw conclusions from the scanning is a distinctly individual matter; each person has his own set of stimuli to which he responds and there may be quite different responses to the same stimulus at different times and on different occasions. Finally, individuals differ greatly as to the degree to which they will act. This depends not only upon energy level but also upon the individual's attitude toward delegation and toward the whole organizational philosophy.

So far we have considered the node as an entity in a communication system and pointed out that the node/man system has important points of variability which the node alone does not. While these points of variability can cause managerial difficulty, they also make the man-process system superior to any other system as far as creativity and adaptability are concerned.

SUMMARY

The foregoing discussion has involved the relation of the individual to the situation to which he is exposed, largely from the basis of the transmitter. It can be summarized as:

1. There is a situation
   in which an event of some kind occurs
2. A (perhaps the manager) is exposed to it
   he may notice it, in which case
3. He is stimulated
   he develops "feelings"
4. He arranges his feelings
   which leads to some internal action; that is
5. He decides to do something
   The decision may be to forget the whole thing, or to
   do something physical about it himself or to initiate a
   communication

Thinking in terms of the receiver and his processes, five levels of process can be recognized, even though not every message goes through all these stages or in this order:

1. *Alerting,* recognizing that a message is being transmitted, locating its source and generally relating it to the self.
2. *Decoding,* hearing in detail, recognizing the symbols, making some kind of sense out of the sounds or symbols.
3. *Understanding* or comprehending what the message means as a message—objective interpretation.
4. *Evaluating,* telling fact from fancy and building from message to surface meaning.
5. *Imputing* or comprehending. What does the receiver really mean? Empathetic listening as the ultimate at one end, suspicion and hostility at the other.

THE SITUATION AND THE INDIVIDUAL'S REACTION

A schematic model has been developed which may be useful as a reference map when discussing the communication process, whereby two or more people share their knowledge, experience or feelings. The diagram below illustrates the over-all process, the blocks showing physical entities and the arrows indicating processes.

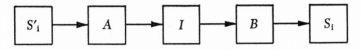

1. There is a situation (S_i)
2. There is an individual (A)
3. There is another individual (B)
4. A and B are separated by an intermediator system (I)
5. S'_i is the understanding of S_i that B obtains due to the communication from A

Now we are interested in the "situation," the word being used generally to mean the particular set of circumstances in which a person finds himself.

Let us say that a situation has a content which exhibits interrelationships and is the potential of the situation. What, then, is in the content and what kind of interrelations are there?

1. A situation contains:
   Things, inerts
   Machines and processes, dynamics
   Records, memory and history
   People, purposives
2. These contents have
   an intrarelationship, a configuration
   interrelations with other situations
   a location in time and/or space
3. The perceived interaction of these form the *potential* of the situation which exists in a *value system*.

A situation, then, may be considered a "space" somehow bounded from the total space. One method of delineation which has been used with human groups is the relative frequency of communication. Membership in a given group includes all who communicate more frequently than an arbitrary frequency/time span.

Three relationships are indicated. The first describes the intrarelationship between and among content items. It is probable that the physical or topographical relationships are first perceived, following which there is usually a searching feedback process by which the situation is gradually figured out; the observer moves to the interrelations; the relations between the current situation and others and between what is in the situation and what is outside. It is probable that the first process tells *what is* and *how*, while the second gives some answer to *why*. In the field of management, the third relation—"location" —is useful in studying a past event or projecting the potential into the future, because values and value systems do not remain constant in time.

INTERCOMMUNICATION

The Basic Process. The process of communication may be considered as proceeding from stimulus to response, but it is also a complex, multipersonal situation rather than a simple case. We can see four focal points:

1. What does A want to communicate?
2. What does A actually communicate?
3. What does B receive?
4. What does B do upon receipt, which is related to A?

The word *what* applies to something different in each case. Before the what, the *why* is important. Why does A want to communicate (w)? What is A's purpose and, further, why does he have that purpose (p)?

A list might be:

1. (p) He wants to share an emotion
   (w) He needs or wants support: a beautiful sunset, a musical phrase that he enjoys, a sense of boredom

from which he wants relief, something he does not understand and wants explained, a fear of the consequences of an unexpected event on which he wants help

2. (p) He wants to get attention
   (w) A variety of reasons—always a necessary prerequisite for good communication
3. (p) He wants to give (or get) information
   (w) A problem to be solved; it is part of his job; the answer is not in the book
4. (p) He wants someone else to do something different from what that person is now doing
   (w) He thinks that what is now being done will not work out, he sees trouble ahead

What Does A Want to Communicate? In managerial communication the actual communication is a means to an end and the *why* is the important thing. It is important to consider how A "sets up" his message, because the stimulus to the receptor (subordinate) is received through communication. The actual communication in many cases is but a cue for a signal; in most cases it is a code or shorthand which depends for success upon what the expected receiver already knows or is expected to know.

In considering the communication situation which exists between A and B, there are four important aspects: (a) the situation itself; (b) the potential, with and without the communication; (c) the degree of control, of and by the participants; (d) the states of knowledge of the participants. Every situation has a potential; regardless of any action taken by A, something will happen and that something is to some degree predictable. When A takes action, it is expected that something different will happen. The outcome of the communication A makes to B is related to the degree of control that A has over B and B has over the situation. The design of the message should take this into account. The result will also be related to the degree of freedom and of control which those included in the situation have. It is a waste of time to tell or ask people to do things which, for physical or psychological reasons, they cannot do.

All of the above is dependent upon the amount of knowledge possessed by the various people involved, not only of physical properties and relationships but, more especially, the knowledge one person has of the knowledge possessed by another. There is an old saw which says: "Never understimate the intelligence of others; Never overestimate their knowledge."

What Does A *Actually Communicate?* This means the signs or symbols he emits, which will depend upon a number of things, such as (a) cause, reason, purpose, and necessity; (b) relation to the individuals and their attitudes—in contradistinction to their skills, know-how, etc.; (c) relative immediacy—in some cases there is plenty of time.

We shall direct attention to the interchange of managerial information between and among people within the organization, although there are many types of nonorganizationally directed communication. It is well to remember that any communicative act, regardless of the number of people to whom it is directed, is considered from the personal point of view by the person who receives it. Communication—good communication—is never an impersonal matter.

What Does B *Receive?* Between the first and second points is the area with which the people in telecommunication are concerned. We could say that A emits a signal consisting of a message of information; between A and B is an intermediator; there is noise, etc. In face-to-face communication a message is carried in a variety of ways simultaneously, and we must remember that the message input may not be the same (the communicator may not mean what he says) and there is confusion on the receiving end, but, also, there is the probability that the various messages will reinforce one another. There is the problem of different codes, and, finally, *B* may not want to receive *A*'s message correctly—this may be conscious, but it is more usually unconscious. It is not to be hoped that the message will be precisely transferred very often unless it is a simple one. (A simple message need not be unimportant.) The complexity of the message, rather than its importance, increases the probability of error. There are other barriers to reception such as (a) not really hearing—other interests, impatience, boredom, apathy; (b) hearing the words only; (c) distortion; (d) bias, prejudice, preconceptions.

When a person is otherwise occupied there is an almost complete block to comprehension. A message received may be written down as a reminder, but when seen again it may convey no impression; in fact the whole matter may be forgotten. Mercifully, a majority of the things that happen to us every day never enter our consciousness or, if they do, are soon forgotten. It is, therefore, apparent that the first step in assuring a successful communication is for the initiator to get and hold the attention of the receiver.

However, even if attention is obtained and held, the communication may not be successful; interest as well as attention is needed; the message must be related to the hearer's action system. This is a reason why one of the cardinal rules of speaking to groups is to close with a call to action. In spite of people's desires to be independent, they are often easily aroused to directed action if the proper appeal is made.

For a variety of reasons, messages become distorted, usually accidentally. For example, words mean different things to different people, and listeners often misunderstand idioms and colloquialisms. In consequence, although the message may be received in exactly the same form as sent, it may yet be distorted in the interpretation of the sounds or words. For example, the French "mon Dieu" is a mild exclamation; when literally translated into English it conveys an impression of urgency. Also, in the English language there are words which sound alike and yet have different meanings and are spelled differently; there are sounds which are only slightly different which mean different things, and difficulty is increased when people speak with a foreign accent or a local twang or drawl.

Due to bias, prejudice, or preconception, a person will hear or read only the things he wishes. He screens out those things which he does not want or need, admitting to his consciousness only those ideas which are acceptable to him. However, at times we are forced to "hear" things we do not wish to accept. It has been said that no one is ever persuaded to change his mind by discourse; what may happen, in such cases, is that the hearer transfers his nonacceptance of the communication to the communicator and, thereafter, is unwilling to accept anything that he is told. In the ultimate, this causes him first not to hear, as in (a) and (b) above, and, finally, to avoid the person physically.

What Does B *Do upon Receipt?* We shall assume that some subsequent action of *B* is related to his receipt of a communication. This action may cover a considerable range: (a) *B* does what *A* wanted him to do; (b) *B* does something like what *A* wanted him to do; (c) *B* does the opposite; (d) *B* does nothing apparently related to what *A* wanted. Why may these different things occur? *B's* reaction to the message *A* sends is very similar to *A's* reaction to the "situation" to which *he* is exposed; as a matter of fact, as far as *B* is concerned the message is one element of a larger situation in which he is a member. One thing *B* may do is to communicate back to *A* for more information; or, *B* may deliberately not do what *A* wants him to; or, it may be that *B* does not understand what *A* said. This is often true, but, as Irving Lorge points out, even the word "understand" may mean a number of different things, such as:

    to get the idea of

to apprehend by way of information

to have information about

to accept as significant

Communications back and forth establish a communication sequence in which there is interaction and in which each person learns more and more about the others; equally important, he imagines more and more about them. People constantly assume roles and shift from role to role, but one person does not grasp quickly the role the other is playing and must build up his understanding gradually as the interaction goes on.

INTERMEDIATION

Between the originator of a message and the receiver(s), there is a space, physical and/or temporal and, in many cases, a mechanical or electronic device. This intermediator plays an important role in the effectiveness of the communication and is subject to a degree of modification and control by the originator.

Different Viewpoints. We can view the problem of managerial communication from the point of view of the manager or from that of the managed. In all the work at the Utility Management Workshop the point of view which has been assumed has been that of the manager; although none of us, who *are* executives, like to think about it, we *are* managed. Perhaps we can obtain a new and useful viewpoint on our own managerial behavior and communication facility if, at some time, we put ourselves in the receiver's place.

There are five important points in any communication sequence to be considered by the originator:

1. Did what he said mean what he wanted to say?

2. Did the person(s) to whom the message was directed receive it?

3. Was it understood?

4. To what degree was it accepted?

5. Was the originator informed of points 2, 3, and 4?

Each of these has importance and location; that is to say, the first is related to the originator and his abilities, the second and fifth to the system, and the third and fourth to the recipient. While still considering face-to-face or, at least, person-to-person communication we should recognize that, in such conditions, an originator (a) has the use of various subsidiary media; (b) has the advantage of the possibility of instantaneous feedback; (c) can adapt and improvise—not only the actual communication but also the situation in which the communication takes place.

As we expand our study to consider other situations, it becomes obvious that the situation controls the media which are available. Specifically directed communications include letters, reports, commands, orders, petitions, requests. Non-specifically directed communications, to groups of different size and interest, include newspapers, magazines and books, radio and television, and signs.

While direct communication has many advantages, the nondirect field is equally important, especially in a large association. As a matter of fact, the invention of writing is considered one of the important turning points in history, and a culture is judged by anthropologists and others to a large extent in terms of its written language. It is believed by many that a common written language is an essential for the building of world peace.

Because the communicants are not face-to-face, nondirect communication has both the advantages and disadvantages of partial impersonality. When communication is written, another group of advantages and disadvantages is encountered. A writer, taking more time, is able to say what he means in the best way, but the reader is deprived of the support he receives from gestures, facial expressions, tonal inflections, and the presence of the other person. If there is a time displacement, the meaning of what is written must stand by itself and cannot be supported by the immediate circumstances, nor can feedback be immediately effective. Another question about non-direct communication is whether it is specifically directed: is it a letter or a notice? All of these factors are important determinants in the design of the communication.

The written record has a far greater degree of permanence than the spoken word; this also applies to public speeches, which are usually recorded, and to semi-public letters which are reprinted.

We may summarize by saying that the problem consists of (a) designing a message for a selected medium, to a specific recipient, in such a way that he can receive and comprehend the particular message the sender intended; and (b) arranging the receipt in such a manner that the "state" of the recipient will most nearly approximate the conditions which were considered in the design of the message.

Thus a message is designed and transmitted. What other problems of intermediation may arise, beyond the very obvious one that B may not receive the message? In industry the latter cannot be disregarded. Every secretary appoints herself a screen between her boss and written communications of all kinds. The mere arrangement of the morning mail, in order of what she considers importance, is a potential source of difficulty.

The receiver's attitude will be affected by the medium and the form used. In descending order of urgency and attention-getting potential, we have:

Registered and special delivery letters, telegrams
Regular letters, telephone messages, and newspapers
Mail other than first class, radio, and magazines
Books, signs

These form a hierarchy; we have been conditioned to feel that any registered letter carries a message of importance to the sender and we feel some sense of responsibility or urgency. A special delivery letter, however, seems urgent from the viewpoint of the receiver—something he needs in a hurry. A knock on the door at night must be an emergency; the telephone has a different meaning to the man of the house than to his teenage daughter. Second-class letters always have second-class contents. News in newspapers always seems more pressing than that in *Time* or *Life*, yet, in many cases, we find the newspaper reproducing photographs the day after *Life* brings them to the newstands. Books are never urgent; their physical permanence seems to convey in a certain sense that their contents have an importance in time, that it is truer, deeper, more thought out.

One may ask, when there is a choice of media, what is most effectively conveyed in writing. The following have been suggested as examples:

Specific and relatively uncomplicated do's and don'ts

Highly general and abstract information designed to convey background, culture, mores, and official feelings

Facts and information about which no action is required

Detailed explanation of more or less complicated procedures and the like, in which it is anticipated the receiver will be self-involved

Audience Communication. There is a great difference between a written communication and the same message when spoken. A literal transcription of even a good speech is often very poor, so poor that it may not make sense when read. If the speaker is wide-awake and reacts to his audience and makes a real appeal to them, the transcript may be even worse. Almost all of the books on public speaking make the point that a speech should not be read. This is generally true only if (a) the speaker is unskilled in reading, (b) the appeal is to be primarily emotional, (c) the action to be called for from the audience is relatively unimportant, simple, or preparatory. One important consideration is what message you wish to convey. Another, and equally important, thing is to understand the audience "situation."

What is the situation of the meeting, its purpose or occasion

What is the constitution of the audience

What do they know in general

What do they know about the subject

What do they know about the speaker

What is the attitude of the audience

Toward the meeting

Toward the subject

Toward the speaker

Public or audience communication is used for a variety of purposes, among them the very important one of merely opening a communication channel. But, usually, the speaker has something he wishes his audience to do—at the very least, he wants the audience to like him and not to walk out on him or be obviously uncomfortable. In most cases, what he wants done is something different from what is now being done, and, in order to get action, he must prove that (a) there is a need to change and (b) the change proposed by the speaker is the right one. There are several kinds of proof:

Logical proof—the facts

Ethical proof—the person who presents the idea

Emotional proof—the feelings about the subject

The wise speaker uses them all and in the proper proportion, depending upon the circumstances.

SUMMARY

Communication takes place in all our contacts with people, but it assumes special importance in managerial relations. Every communication involves an originator and a receptor, separated by an intermediator of greater or lesser extent. The problem facing the originator of the message is to get it to the receptor in a form that can be understood, interpreted, and acted on in the way the originator desires. The medium selected, the attitude of the receptor, and other factors tend to modify the effectiveness of the communication. Much thought, planning, and monitoring are necessary if the manager is to communicate effectively with his subordinates, colleagues, superiors, and the world outside his own concern. This is a necessary—nay, essential—activity of managers, as it is the only link connecting the manager's decision with the subordinate's action.

DIRECT AND NONDIRECT COMMUNICATION

by William Exton, Jr.

FACE-TO-FACE communication and other kinds of communication have certain basic differences which must be understood if each is to be used appropriately and effectively. When we are face to face, communication is like using a *guided* missile. After launching, progress can be observed, and the course can be corrected. There is the opportunity for continuing observation and control. If it is too high or too low, too far left or right, the face-to-face situation offers opportunity to shift rudder or elevators, angles or speed—to get on target and stay there.

But, when originator and intended audience are not face to face, a communication is like an artillery projectile or a ballistic missile. Once these weapons leave cannon or launcher, they are on their own. They fly out of our sight in the direction we have chosen, but nothing can be done to correct their range or course; we may never know where they landed, or if they hit the target or missed—or by how wide a margin, or why.

We know that face-to-face communication can be time-consuming, that it is often difficult to arrange, and that it can lead to misunderstandings when there is no written record available for correction or reminder. We know that, for these and other reasons, its advantages over other forms of com-

Reprinted with the permission of Exton-Aids, Dover Plains, New York, Copyright, 1957. Address presented at the Sixth Utility Management Workshop, August, 1957. Mr. Exton is President of William Exton, Jr., and Associates.

munication, for *most* of the purposes of large organizations, are not greater than the disadvantages. But we know also that, for some purposes, face-to-face communication does offer advantages so important that it should be utilized, and it should be utilized as well—as effectively, as appropriately for the purpose—as possible.

We know that there are many kinds and varieties, methods and techniques of nondirect communication, with innumerable combinations possible; and we realize that each purpose, each situation, each need may best be met by some adapted, specifically applicable communication, planned to do *that* job. And we realize that nondirect communication can supplement face-to-face communication, and vice versa.

Before entering upon any communication, it is useful to clarify several points about the intended recipients, our audience, and also about our purposes. Concerning our audience, we should try to have reasonably complete answers to at least the first two of five important questions:

1. How much do we have in common with them, and how much do they have in common with us? Do *we* know what *we* need to know, to originate effective communication with them? Do *they* know what *they* need to know, to understand, and to react as we wish? Is there a sufficient basis of common interest, and of mutually satisfactory relations?

2. Are they subject to *other* attitudes, influences, interests, conditions, pressures, and the like, or have they had experience that may affect the way they react to our communication? Do we know enough about this? Have we overlooked any important factors?

We may not be able to answer these two questions with completeness and certainty; but, at least, if there is any part of the answers about which we do not know enough, we should realize this. Then we can either seek the necessary knowledge, or allow for the possibilities indicated by the unknown factors.

Obviously, when we are face to face with one person, it is easiest to answer these two questions and to keep answering them, as the situation develops and changes occur. But, as our face-to-face audience grows in size we can, at best, aim at a part of it, or some sort of "average"; and we can still observe some reactions as we are speaking.

But, when we are not face to face—when we are communicating nondirectly—our opportunity to evaluate audience reaction is postponed, at best. Also, it must be accomplished, if at all, through the reports of others—which may introduce distortion—and through the use of methods which are themselves subject to errors and differences of interpretation.

Concerning our own *purposes,* providing answers to three further questions may help to clarify the situation:

3. Is our object to *transmit* or *impart* information or direction? Are we concerned with accuracy of transmission?

4. Is our object to *motivate,* to influence, to persuade, to move, to change attitudes and behavior? Are we concerned with psychological effect—with dynamic acceptance and identification?

5. Is our object to *confer,* to consult, to bring about an interchange of knowledge, evaluation, and guidance? Are we concerned with *contributory participation?*

Actually, any communication will have *some* effect—whether intended or not—in all three ways. They are interrelated; they affect one another. We can give accurate, objective information in ways that influence and change attitudes, though we may not realize this effect at the time. An attempt to motivate may "give away" reasons we thought were hidden, or may have other unintended informational effects. And it has been shown that *participation* is an important key to motivation; people who participate in developing a policy or arriving at a decision are more likely to want to help to "make it work" than if they are merely directed.

In any specific instance we shall be emphasizing one or another of these three areas of communication purposes. But we should never neglect the other areas, or we shall be less effective. And, perhaps even more important, we shall be undermining our future effectiveness with the same audience.

Again, in face-to-face situations, it is simpler and easier to adapt as required; to combine the offering of information with working on motivations. And, of course, with two or a few people, the face-to-face situation is ideal for *participation*.

As the size of our audience grows, these advantages are diminished. When a speaker faces a large audience, the possibilities of participation are greatly diluted. Informing and motivating must be aimed at "the group," rather than at one individual or a few; and there is likely to be a loss of specific effectiveness.

With communication that is not face to face, immediate participation becomes impossible (except through use of circuitry, such as telephone or television). Immediate adaptation of communication for more effective informing or motivating is also out of the question. The communication is sent on its way, and the originator can no longer change it or affect the results.

Direct (face-to-face) communication between individuals usually involves important advantages which provide maximum opportunity for effectiveness. These advantages apply through the availability of techniques, and through corrective adaptation and adjustment.

Among the more important of these advantages are:

1. Supraverbal communication; not only the words spoken, but gestures, expression, and the whole personality which enter into the communication.
2. Simultaneity of utterance and reception; speed.
3. Immediate "feedback"; not only in spoken reactions, but also in other observed audience behavior.
4. Continuity of interchange.
5. Visual presentation and manifestation.

6. Intimacy; presence.

7. Selection and control of environment.

Where the direct communication involves groups, these advantages are diluted. Conferences, committee meetings, and the like offer diminished opportunities to exploit the advantages suggested above. In the case of "unilateral communication," as with a speaker addressing an audience, this dilution is even greater. When the conditions eliminate face-to-face or direct communication, serious problems must be met if reliable effectiveness is to be maintained. Usually there is some major loss among the above listed advantages.

When the communication is *not* direct, *not* face to face, then the means available are drastically affected. The advantages listed above may be diminished to the point of disappearance. Techniques of varying applicability are available, and offer a certain selection among the advantages to be partly maintained. However, some techniques and some media may be incompatible or mutually exclusive; and consideration of applicability, appropriateness, feasibility, and cost usually operate against utilization of techniques and media of maximum effectiveness.

The problems of indirect communication, therefore, usually involve maximization of results by combining a large number of variable factors, each one of which is subject to its own special considerations. Consistently satisfactory results with indirect communication necessitate a high order of judgment controlling the integration of the available dynamic factors, together with adequate weighing of related considerations. The communication situation may be regarded as an organizationally interrelated complex, requiring specifically applicable stimuli to achieve desired organizational responses.

For instance, only closed-circuit television will preserve any substantial part of all the advantages listed above, and this will suffer a loss in points 6 and 7. Motion pictures can offer some of 1 and 5, but only at the sacrifice of the others. Other photographic media are usually less effective than motion pictures. Telephone circuits can provide much of 2, 3 and 4, but are weak in 1, 6 and 7; they fail in 5. A combination of other photographic media and telephone circuits could in some cases approach the effectiveness of closed-circuit television.

However, these media are expensive. Also, they usually require careful preparation; there may not be enough time to utilize these media effectively enough to justify the high cost. For these and other reasons, they are used only in exceptional cases. Of all communication that is not face to face, the greatest part is on paper.

Assuming, then, that our indirect communication is to be *read*, we are faced with a number of possible media and techniques and of forms of parallel, supporting, and reinforcing communication. To help us make a wise selection among the available procedures, we should clarify several vital aspects of the situation affecting the intended recipients, as indicated in the first two questions suggested; we should also clarify the purposes of the communication, as indicated in the last three questions. If we can answer these five questions, we are in a better position to proceed.

In clarifying the audience situation, it is important to realize the full implications of past contacts, and of the organizational and functional relationships involved. Will the communication be considered an exercise of authority, or an act of helpful leadership? Will it be integrated into an "upcurve" or "downcurve" of recipient attitude? Is it "something new," calling for new evaluations and substantial adjustments by recipients, or is it "old stuff"—immediately categorized and reacted to according to its predecessor communications?

Will it be judged on its own merits, in the light of present needs and purposes, or will it be judged according to existing prejudice, attitudes, expectations, "set"? Will the reception of the communication be seriously affected by the recipients' feelings toward the originator, and in what way? What local, special situations may influence reception? Where the audience is cohesive, well indoctrinated, adequately informed, and has a common motivation, there is an important and useful foundation for communication. Then a relatively high effectiveness can be attained with relatively little effort. On the other hand, when the audience is diffuse and varied in degree of indoctrination, information, and motivation, there is a very different situation. Individual communications may be necessary; and it may be difficult to make even these effective.

In any organization we have certain regularities of relationship, with allocations of function and authority and with designated status, specified responsibilities, and stipulated controls. We provide motivation through present earnings, status, and prerogatives, and the expectation or hope of future earnings, status, and prerogatives.

Where the interactions and functions are regulated and support of organizational objectives is enforced within the power of the organization to reward or punish, we have *discipline*. Discipline attempts to enforce uniformity of reaction and behavior. When successful, this simplifies communication. It is usually an error, however, to assume that all or most of the individuals in an organization with similar status and performing similar functions, will react in the same way to the same communication. If when attempting to communicate with a group of individuals we *feel the same way* toward *each one* of them, if we see them as a group, then we are very likely to fall into such an error.

Even the soldiers on a parade ground react differently, *inside*, to the sergeant's commands. The sum of their *visible* reactions presents a splendid picture of well-drilled men moving as one; but we cannot tell how they *feel* about their presence there, their uniforms, the sergeant, the drill, the command just given, the immediate or recent past, or what lies ahead. We can be fairly certain they will not all feel the same way about *any* such matters. Here, the movements are relatively subject to enforced conformity; the thoughts are not.

The reactions of individuals are, of course, more reliably predictable in some areas than in others. The reactions of members of a group to a communication, likewise, may be more predictable for certain subject areas than for others. For instance, assuming that there has been overt consideration of the question of increased remuneration for a group of employees, let us consider predictability of reaction to several possible communications, all *denying* a general increase. Let us assume that the announcement appears on plant bulletin boards, over the signature of the plant superintendent.

1. "There will be no raise!" (Nobody likes to have a total negative aimed at them.)

2. "There will be no raise at this time!" (New employees will be least disappointed and most encouraged by the implication of future possibilities.)

3. "Management conducts a continuous survey comparing our pay structure with competitors, and with those of other employers in the community. It is management's intention to maintain a pay scale as high as or higher than any competitor or neighbor." (If observable facts confirm this policy, only individuals can complain plausibly.)

4. "Supervisors have been instructed to give special consideration to merit increases, and to recommendations for promotions to fill existing vacancies." (People who think they are in line for special consideration will perhaps feel that this announcement is "promising.")

5. "The over-all business situation, and this company's competitive position and recent earnings, do not warrant a general wage increase." (This may alleviate resentment, to the extent that the reasons given are believed valid, and to the extent that

the individual employee feels "identity" with the company. Effect on long-service, older, and security-minded employees will be different from that on younger and newer employees. Such a statement may subject supervisors to economic arguments, and provoke unions to question the facts and demand detailed financial information.)

In all of the instances suggested above, reactions will be greatly affected by the past experience of the employees with company pay policy and with the reliability of company statements, as well as by their understanding of the alternatives open to them, their other experience with the company and elsewhere, and their past and present contacts, inside and outside the company. Nevertheless, there will be at least one fundamental regularity: the denial of a raise is frustrating. There will be infinite variations and degrees of negative reaction, but all reactions will be negative. On this there will be virtual unanimity.

But now, let us suppose a different issue arises, one in which there will be no basic regularity of reaction. Suppose the plant is to be "moved." Let us assume that the new location is a desirable one, perhaps, for many employees; or preferable in many ways to the present location. What can we predict? Long-term, higher paid, and "identifying" employees will tend to want to go along. Age and home ownership will influence toward "staying put."

1. "All employment at this plant will terminate March 31. This announcement constitutes legal notice to all employees." (This is a general layoff.)

2. "This plant will close March 31. Employees desiring re-employment should apply during July at the new location." (This doesn't encourage any one. Those most interested will demand more information, with probable resentment at lack of consideration.)

3. "In connection with the plant removal, all employees who

would like to move with us are requested to inform their supervisors, who will provide them with full information about the
new location, interim pay, housing facilities, transportation assistance, etc. Management hopes you will 'come along,' and
has arranged help for you." (This offers great encouragement
and, by the same token, will arouse maximum resentment
among those who stay; especially home owners, who will anticipate a decline in real estate values. The community generally
will also resent loss of population even more than loss of
industry.)

However, in this case, while some employees will have a very
adverse reaction to the situation, however communicated,
some will be *pleased*. A certain proportion will welcome the
opportunity of moving to the new location. Employee reactions
will be manifested along a continuum, from the strongly
negative, on through the more or less neutral, to the strongly
positive.

Here there is a basic difference from the previous case, where
employee reactions would run a wide gamut, but *all* on one
side—the negative. Furthermore, the reaction of any *one*
employee to either of these situations would be affected by
largely different considerations, working out into complex
tangles of conflicting influences. No two employees would have
just the same reaction to these two situations, nor would any
two arrive at their reactions in the same way. And a man at
the negative extreme of one continuum might be at the positive
extreme of the other; that is, a man who resented the refusal to
increase pay most strongly might most heartily welcome the
opportunity to move to the new location.

The considerations raised in this discussion of two differing
communication situations suggest the diversity of possible reactions and the possible "regularities" upon which some degree
of predictability may be based, also the degree to which such

predictability may be affected through changes in wording of simple announcements.

The first and second of my original questions should elicit, or indicate the need for, information indicative of possible reactions. All available predictable, "regular" reactions should be examined. Questions 3, 4, and 5 should clarify or lead toward the clarification of *purpose*. Determination of purpose provides the basis for evaluating the predictable reactions that are available. The problem, then, is to communicate in such a way as to maximize the desired reactions and minimize the undesired reactions, also to contribute incidentally to the future of the relationship.

In other words, to communicate with consistent effectiveness and success, we must:

1. Know enough about our audience, the relevant knowledge and attitudes of that audience, and the actual or potential dynamics of reaction of that audience, based on past experience and existing or contingent influences, to predict the results of various possible communications on the present subject.

2. Realize adequately the effects we desire to achieve, through our communication, in terms of transmission of information, changes in behavior (determining the related reactions and attitudes to be stimulated) and mutual participation and interchange.

3. Plan and execute our communication procedures with appropriate choice and combinations of media, techniques, timing, etc., to bring about the desired effects to the highest degree obtainable, through maximizing desired results and minimizing undesired results in accordance with our predictions.

Obviously, this is easier said than done. But if any of these steps is inadequately carried out, the communication procedures will fall short of their potential effectiveness to a related degree. The most clearly envisioned and tenaciously held purpose will fail, without understanding of audience and competent carrying out of the communication process. The most impressive communication performance, *technically,* will be relatively ineffective if not geared to purpose and audience; even the most intimate and empathetic understanding of the audience is not enough for successful communication without clarity of purpose and adequacy of execution.

PROBLEMS OF COMMUNICATION
by David B. Hertz

FROM THE STANDPOINT of a business organization, the communication problem refers largely to communications among individuals in the organization. There are additional problems associated with communication of information within other groups. A statement as to communications systems in business usually assumes (a) a structure and (b) a decision framework within which one may examine questions relating to "management information."

GROUP COMMUNICATION VARIABLES

As outlined by Festinger,[1] the variables involved in communicating information in structured groups are as follows:

1. The relevance to the group of uniformity in respect to a specific state of information.
2. The pressure upon members of the group to communicate with one another concerning specific states of information at specific times.
3. The discrepancy between the information of specific members and the "average information" of the organization as perceived by the organization at a specific time.
4. The cohesiveness of the group with respect to specific

Address presented at the Sixth Utility Management Workshop, August, 1957. Dr. Hertz is a partner in the firm of Arthur Andersen and Company.

[1] L. Festinger, "Informal Social Communication," *Psychological Review 1950*, pp. 271–82.

members—that is, the average intensity of the desire to retain such members of the group at a specific time.

5. The perceived receptivity of specific members to influence by other members of the group at specific times.

6. The average pressure towards uniformity of the group with specific members as felt by the group at a specific time.

7. The cohesiveness of the group *qua* group.

Festinger has set up certain hypotheses with reference to the relationship of these variables, and we shall discuss these relationships in detail as they pertain to certain other communication problems.

ORGANIZATION COMMUNICATION VARIABLES

From a communications standpoint the management cycle for a reasonably stable system includes the following:

data-gathering

data-processing

preliminary report

data analysis, preliminary decision, and, if required, request for more data

additional data-processing and, if required, additional data-gathering

final reporting

final decision-making

implementation of decisions

systems response to the decisions, generating new data.

From a strictly mechanical viewpoint one can confine his attention to the first three elements of this cycle. Within these elements we find the following variables:

events being reported on

age of the information

cost of the information

value of the information

These are not necessarily independent. The age of information is a result of the interaction between two time sets having to do with the interval over which the information is generated and the delay in gathering and processing. The costs for communicating in a mechanical sense depend on both the information interval and the delay, as well as on the specific events being reported on. Value depends on the event being reported on, as well as some functions of the age of the information such as maximum age, average age, or minimum time.

Furthermore, from a mechanical standpoint in an operating system we can distinguish between two classes of information states:

1. condition information, which is the actual state of the system at a given time, such as the cash balance at the close of business on a certain day
2. operating information, which pertains to a set of states of the system during a time period

We can define age as the amount of time which elapses between the event or events under consideration and the availability of process information about such events. Average minimum and maximum ages of information can be determined.

Cost/age relationships are of considerable interest in dealing with the problem of information. In general a system which produces information with a small average age costs more to operate than one that produces information with a larger average age. The value/age relationships must be related to the change in significant decisions arising from either earlier or later utilization of information, because it is obtained for shorter or longer intervals. Organizational action must be attuned to the availability of information. A question arises as to the optimal time of management action and its relationship to age, time, and availability of information. Obviously, the volume of information depends, among other things, on the dynamics of the events involved, the level of management, the historical circumstances, and the states of information technology.

Long intervals have the disadvantage of averaging out unusual events; short intervals magnify unusual events. History plays its part in such things as calendars, rules, laws, regulations, plans of management as to the ability to obtain and use information with a given frequency and nonmanagerial demands on the system.

Simon[2] indicates that Dr. Tukey has pointed out that processes may be classified into rapid (high frequency), slow (low frequency), and intermediate (intermediate frequency) in every analysis of empirical time series. He pointed out that the over-all period of observation T places a lower limit on the frequencies that can be examined and the interval of observation at an upper limit.

In this mechanical view of communications problems from a management standpoint we are interested in examining the relationship between cost, value, delay, and interval.

COMMUNICATION AND BEHAVIOR

In general, individuals communicate when one of the individuals responds to a set of information signs selected by the other in a specific way. One definition of the measure of responsibility as given by Ackoff[3] is that a communication can change the probability of choice of an individual selecting one of a set of available courses of action. Such a communication informs. A communication which changes efficiency of these courses of action towards given ends instructs. One which changes the value of the outcome to the recipient of the communication motivates. Any single communication may, of course, do any combination of these simultaneously.

[2] H. Simon, *Models of Man* (New York, 1957), p. 144.
[3] R. Ackoff, *Towards a Behavioral Theory of Communication* (Case Institute, 1957).

MANAGERIAL TECHNOLOGIES

by Fred Rudge

IF ALL that has been written about industrial communications in the last decade were to be put in one pile, I would not be surprised if it would reach all the way to complete confusion. As a matter of fact, the output, both spoken and written, has been so profuse that many people have come to think of communication as an end in itself. Clearly, it is a means and not an end.

As a means, let us examine together, first, some of the ways it can facilitate corporate growth and development and, second, how it can assist the individual executive in the performance of his job.

Naturally, with an audience such as this, it is unnecessary to dwell on such well-recognized ABC's of communications as clarity, exactness, and simplicity. Rather, it is my objective to point to certain areas where corporate and individual practice, in some cases at least, may be subject to improvement.

In promoting corporate growth and development, I would like to suggest, for example, that intelligent use of communications will

1. *Motivate* people at every level in the organization to do a better job.
2. *Expedite changes* in policy and practice with minimal friction.

Address presented August 2, 1956 at the Fifth Utility Management Workshop, Arden House, Harriman Campus, Columbia University. Mr. Rudge is president of Fred Rudge Associates, Inc.

3. *Provide management a desirable and proper balance of power in its relations with other groups.*

Motivating people to want to do a good job is a familiar objective and a familiar subject to all executives. From piece-rate systems, incentive plans, group bonuses, and rate ranges through merit rating, Christmas extras, and stock option plans (to name but a few), we have sought to make it desirable for the individual to produce. Through seniority, pension plans, and promotional opportunity, we have sought to win a measure of loyalty and cooperation. No company can afford for long to disregard those areas that assure reward for a job well done.

Quite a few companies, however, do disregard a companion effort—that of building an interest beyond "me," the individual, and "my" pocketbook, to a comprehension of "we" and the good of the group as a whole. Is it possible, you may ask, in a day and age of mass production and wide-spread unionism, to create among employees an interest in, and desire for, group as opposed to individual, take-home pay and security, objectives and, if it is possible, is it worth-while? Let us consider each in turn briefly.

The reasons why the individual can—and even wants to—be a part of a team to which he is willing to give an added measure of support, include among others, these:

1. The vast majority of people are shrewd enough to realize that their own security and their own chances for advancement are linked to the success or lack of it in their company.

2. Most people, whether at the president's desk or at a lathe, want, through their work, to feel they are contributing to worth-while ends, beyond the receipt of a pay-check.

3. Almost everyone wants to be able to speak with knowledgeable pride to his family and neighbors of "the swell company I work for."

The individual's sense of security, his feeling of worth-while contribution, and his pride in his company can be considerably enhanced by a management which takes the time and trouble to explain, and keep on explaining, its goals to its people. To some executives, admittedly, the task of talking or writing about their thinking and the reasons for their plans for the future does not come easily. They find it difficult to believe that other people will be interested.

The president of a multiplant operation, for example, protested that he would be embarrassed to give a speech on his philosophy about the company's future growth and the added contribution it might hope to make in the years ahead. "Why, most of the people I'll be talking to," he said, "have known me from ten to thirty years and certainly don't want to hear my theories about running a business." After giving the speech, which he finally graciously agreed to do, he said, "Well, I *was* embarrassed." When asked why, he replied, "Four of my oldest friends warmly congratulated me at the conclusion and told me it was the best speech I'd ever made. Naturally," he continued with a grin, "being an honest man, I had to tell them that I hadn't written it." The same speech, incidentally, was used as the first of a continuing series of mailings to all employees. The objective was employee understanding and support that would relieve the company of responsibility as a principal pattern-setter of its industry. That objective was met.

Another situation involving management communication and its goals had salutary results in two directions. The first result was with the union and the employees, the second with top management itself. What happened was this. After 52 days of a bitter strike, it was decided that the company president personally should lead an effort to break the deadlock. In a series of communications he addressed himself, not to the contract clauses on seniority and management prerogatives which were at issue, but to the broad questions of: What kind of a company is this? What are the competitive problems we face? And what kind of a working relationship do we have to

have so that the company can provide opportunity and security?

Against this backdrop of fundamentals, he then discussed
the *why* of management's position, from the standpoint of the
employees and the union, as well as that of the company. The
union president, who, to say the least, could never be accused
of being pro management, responded after the third message,
that at long last the company was making some sense, and said
"Let's get down to business and get this mess settled." It was,
and with the very contract terms which management had
sought from the outset.

The second effect was, as I have said, on top management
itself. In attempting during the strike to write a factual story
of company plans for the future, it was revealed that long-
term goals had never been established. There followed, over
a six-month period, an intensive study of corporate objectives,
coupled with considerable restructuring of the executive organization itself. Within a year, that company began, in another state, an operation which may well dwarf the parent
plant in the next decade.

It must be granted, in discussing the worth-whileness of
explaining and reexplaining to people at all levels where the
company has been and where it is seeking to go, no exact
measure of results has been developed. This much, however,
can be said categorically. In many cases where labor and
employee relations have been unsatisfactory, communications
on the broadest aspects of corporate growth and development
have been a keystone of the effort to build mature and stable
relationships. Where such programs have been energetically
pursued, they have never in our experience failed to produce
a revolutionary change for the better.

In speaking of the role of communications in expediting
changes in policy and practice with minimal friction, I shall
not dwell on the need for explaining management's new plans

to the people concerned. Most executives have learned by now that, when the work practices of anyone, at any level, are to be changed, well-chosen words, spoken early in the proceedings, are apt to prevent a spate of trouble later. A comment is perhaps in order, however, about upward communication as part of the process of easing change because it is this process of upward communication, or listening to the other fellow, that is most frequently neglected.

When a new inventory control system, a new production control system, a new organizational structure, or whatever, is under consideration, usual procedure is to appoint a task force to analyze, to recommend, and to instrument. As jobs must be delegated, and as we live in an age of increasing specialization, this is understandable and logical. But the result is apt to be that the worth-while change, which is perfectly understandable to those who have thought it through, is incomprehensible to everyone else. As a result, those who have to operate under the new system oppose it instead of supporting it. What is the answer?

The answer would appear to be to bring along the thinking of those concerned from the very beginning. Instead of waiting to do the selling job when the program is fully rounded out, experience testifies that it is worth-while to take the time and have the patience to explore the need, examine the objectives and discuss the development of a new approach from the start. The ideas emerging from discussion and review with the larger group will not necessarily be any better than those which would have come from the study of the task force group. But the effort will help materially in winning the complete support of those who must implement the change.

Let me cite an example. Some years ago a rubber company planned a complete shift in manufacturing method from a bench-type operation to a production line. Union and employee resistance was anticipated. After study, it was decided to build

the new production line in available warehouse space. Before
the changeover all employees, in small groups, at preliminary
meetings, saw and talked about the new operation, both generally and as it would affect their individual jobs. Later,
supervisory and employee ideas as to improvements were
solicited and some excellent changes in procedure developed.
When the entire employee group finally moved from the old
to the new method, it was without a protest from the union, or
the filing of a single grievance.

The trick of expediting change, in oversimplified terms, is to
put change in *with* people, rather than to impose it *on* people.
Speaking of my own company's experience, it certainly has
been clear that the consultant's report will be valuable *only*
if mutual understanding and joint agreement of line and staff
executives have been developed at each stage of the project,
as to the facts, as to the needs, and as to the thinking underlying the specific recommendations on policy and method
changes. Conversely, unless there is considerable participation
between client executives and the consultant, the final report
gathers dust instead of leading to action.

Communication as a factor in growth and development, it
has been suggested, can help provide management with a desirable and proper balance of power in its relations with other
groups. As time is limited, I shall address myself only to the
area of union-management relations. In this area, it is no news
to you that corporate practice varies tremendously—all the
way from complete disclosure of what management thinks
(and why) on a continuing basis, to the opposite extreme of
no communication, or communication only on subjects as non-
controversial as mother love.

As of three years ago, Fred Rudge Associates, Inc. checked
the practices of some fifty large and medium-sized companies
representing a cross-section geographically and by industry.

In terms of the efforts of management to have some control over their destiny vis-à-vis union relationships, the pattern, broadly speaking, was this. A majority communicated during representation elections and, of that group, most found it had been effective. Most communicated *after* a strike had begun but, not surprisingly, many felt a late start frequently produced minor rather than major changes in union and employee attitudes and action. Relatively few of those checked in the survey communicated before and during negotiations about the economics of the company and the contract objectives and the reasons for them. Those few who did, even where industry wage patterns were set by one or a few major companies, were unanimously convinced that it was of real assistance in reaching contract agreement with minimum difficulty and maximum speed.

In major industry, where the monopoly power of unions is used to set a pattern and then enforce it on others, there is, to my knowledge, only one pivotal pattern-setting company (and one not unknown in Bridgeport) which is doing a thoughtful, extensive and effective job. That company has pioneered, for a dozen years now, in stating explicitly what it stands for and why this stand makes sense. Further, it does so in respect to union policy or action with which it disagrees, with utmost frankness and without the fear of reprisal which has muzzled many in American industry. During the earlier years of this company's effort, many of the so-called experts in labor and industrial relations predicted the most dire outcome. Their theory was that an admittedly antagonistic top union leadership would have enough power through the support of its membership, to teach the company a lesson about minding its manners. To date, the results speak for themselves; the company in question persuaded the employees to accept a long-term contract of its own devising, while a principal competitor, which had minded its manners in respect to any statement of its management opinions, suffered a long and bitter strike.

Whatever the experience of the major corporations, it is certain that smaller companies can, to some degree, control their own destiny at the bargaining table. A part of the "how-to-do-it" that is often neglected may be of interest to you. That aspect of winning support for management, which I have touched on previously, is *upward* communication, i.e., *listening* before *telling;* or *seeking to understand* before seeking to sell a point of view. Many examples of the importance of listening first might be given. Here is just one which is typical.

A large brewing company was faced last year with a strike of its engineers and firemen. The expiration date of the contract agreement with a small union immediately followed the signing of contract agreements with the other two, larger unions in the company. All issues, consistent with these other two contracts, had been agreed upon, with the single exception of a new demand for time-and-a-half and double-time for Saturdays and Sundays, as such. Time-and-a-half and double-time for the sixth and seventh days of the work week in an around-the-clock operation were already being paid.

Operating management properly felt that, in light of industry practice, the demand was unjustified, and that the company had an excellent case and should stand by its position even if there was a strike. In communicating with itself, that is, talking over the problem and its possible solution, management interestingly enough discussed only the unresolved issue. At long last, however, it was finally suggested that perhaps the failure to settle was on factors about which management was uninformed, and which might have little or nothing to do with the Saturday-Sunday issue. There followed individual, off-the-record interviews with the handful of supervisors involved.

These interviews revealed four cases of employee discontent—none very difficult to handle once given attention—but all *very important* from the point of view of the men on the job.

Having *listened,* the company *spoke intelligently.* Each supervisor talked individually to each of his men about the four issues which the supervisors had thought—and rightly—were causing discontent. Each supervisor said that the problems had come to the attention of the company president, who was up from the ranks and both liked and respected. The president, they reported, was upset and embarrassed that such things as unclear lines of authority led to conflicting instructions to the men—and wanted to get each of the four problems sensibly resolved as quickly as possible.

The day after these individual talks with the men the employee group met with their business agent to take a strike vote. Having had their chance to blow off steam, and being no longer anxious to prove their annoyance by whatever means at hand, the unanimous sentiment was "To hell with making a fuss, let's sign up."

I think it is fair to draw the conclusion that, if management had not listened and there had been a strike, communications about the correctness of management's position on the Saturday and Sunday issue would have been wide of the mark. Clearly, that was not what the men had on their minds.

Considerably more difficult circumstances were faced by two companies last year. Each involved major modernization of old plants. In neither case, however, would modernization pay off under existing union contracts with antiquated piece-work wage systems, with, for example, buffers' and polishers' annual incomes running as high as $12,000. The alternative to rehabilitation, coupled with a satisfactory contract, was building at a new location, at a probably increased cost in one instance of about $5 million and, in the other, about $7 million.

With such amounts of money involved, each management

said, "Let's take a shot at the seemingly impossible, and try to win employee and union leadership acceptance of revolutionized contracts that will make plant rehabilitation desirable." Step number one was *listening*, in hour-long, anonymous interviews, to hundreds of people, including management, supervisors, rank and file, and union leadership. Policies and practices in both cases indicated rehabilitation was needed in the human area as well as in the physical area. A host of problems, running all the way from organization restructuring to supervisory development to window washing were attacked, with as many people as possible participating in the discussion. Community luncheons, speeches, in-plant informative meetings, problem-solving get-togethers, letters to homes, visits from the top officials at company headquarters all played their roles.

Ahead of any expectable results, from management's point of view, one of these two plants voted in a new slate of union officers just three months after the program of research, new policy and method formulation, and communication began. The incumbent union president, who had held that job for 14 years, was replaced by a man whose political platform had one, and only one plank. It was, "Let's try getting along with management for a change." Within six months, and without a strike, a new contract permitting a modernized wage system and incentive plan was signed.

In the other corporation, there was not *one* union but *eight* unions which were pivotal to success. All eight had been in the plant for more than ten years. To install and maintain a satisfactory plant-wide wage and incentive system required that the eight unions agree to joint bargaining in the future. Seven of the eight accepted the proposal and then materially assisted management in selling the one hold-out during a strike which terminated on the tenth day, with full agreement to management's objectives.

No doubt most managements of operations involving 3,000

to 6,000 people would hesitate to invest several hundred thousand dollars to build understanding of corporate problems and goals, and to establish a very close-knit working relationship. It is, however, noteworthy that when, as in the two cases discussed, the economic pressure dictates such efforts, they *do* get the desired results, however impossible it may seem.

Arguing from the specific to the general—admittedly a dangerous practice—I maintain, in the light of experience in many individual situations, that the American industrial worker will accept a fair, honest, *well presented* management position. Ninety-five percent of those at every level are interested in facts about their company, shrewd in analyzing the facts, and, if you do not push your conclusions at them, will arrive for themselves at about the same point of view as management. Finally, they will be effectively articulate with their union leadership, if convinced that union policies and actions are unwise.

So much for communications as an aid to corporate growth and development. Let us turn briefly, in conclusion, to communication as an aid to the individual executive and supervisor. I shall not belabor its usefulness in helping the individual with his daily job, or in accelerating promotion. It is evident enough that the boss who uses the right words, in the right way, and at the right time, gets the best results from those whom he directs. Similarly, the man who handles his relationships, upward, with thoroughness and skill, is the most apt to be in line for advancement.

Herewith, then, are a few ground-rules which may be helpful. I suspect that they are known to all of you, but may be worth repetition, as they are frequently honored by breach rather than observance.

First: Concentrate in putting your ideas and messages across in terms of *why* the recommended action will be productive. And, for most of us, this does take concentration, because once we have a picture in our own minds, we too frequently conclude unwittingly that others see the same needs we do. We tend, therefore, to leap into what should be done and how it should be done before establishing mutual understanding that anything at all should be done.

Selling the *why* was second nature to the rugged looking, 285-pound superintendent of a beet sugar plant. His foremen, when interviewed, unanimously gave him the highest rating for leadership and effectiveness we have ever encountered in any type of plant. Unanimously, too, they said that, after explaining in detail *why* some change was desirable, he gave them a free hand to decide what to do and how to do it, unless they specifically asked for his help. Incidentally, his subsequent promotions have indicated that his bosses as well as his subordinates liked his brand of leadership.

Most of you have read many engineering reports. Perhaps you have found that the excellent substantive ideas in some of them have failed of adoption. The reason, not infrequently, in our experience, is that the decision-makers who received the report were insufficiently briefed on *why* the improvement was worth consideration.

Second: The act of communication lies in talking or writing. The *art* of communication lies in listening, so that the ultimate *effect* of communication lies in being understood. One can go even further and say that, without listening, let alone being understood, one may not even be heard.

Just prior to negotiations, the operations vice-president of a furniture plant wanted to present the facts about the competitive position of the company. The process of listening to several hundred people prior to talking to them revealed that a thoroughly chaotic shipping department was the number one matter on their minds. Not only was it cited generally by virtually everyone as a prime example of management inefficiency but, specifically, it had interrupted chair- and table-line production, and thoroughly disgusted those who had lost incentive earnings. In that climate talking about competitive pressure and why a wage increase should be 6 cents an hour and not 8 cents would have been like water running off the proverbial duck's back.

The first step was the development and full disclosure, in meetings with everyone in the plant on all shifts, of a 13-point program for cleaning up the shipping department. Management was then in a position to talk the economics of bargaining, having put its own house in order. Listening, of course, is not always as easy, or the results as focused as in the case just presented.

Both in individual and group situations, those whom you address listen in terms of their educational background, their experiences generally, their racial and religious connections, and their current state of mind (affected not only by in-plant goings-on, but by how their children behaved last night, or the way the coffee tasted this morning). These complexities do not lead to the suggestion that you all become amateur anthropologists, sociologists, or psychologists. They do suggest patience in the process of feeding people ideas and, usually, rather frequent check-ups through questioning as you go along to determine whether they are absorbing the mental food set before them.

Third: Finally, effective communications call for two kinds of faith: faith in the people you seek to lead or direct; and faith in the ideas you are presenting.

How much faith you have generally in those in American industry, and specifically those with whom you work, you have already decided for yourself. It is not the purpose of this address to try to lead you to believe, as I do, based on some hundreds of thousands of interviews in all types of industry throughout the country, that we are greatly blessed in having a majority who will more than gladly do the right thing if they know what it is, and are permitted by circumstances to do it. It is my purpose to suggest that, in communicating, you have at least enough faith that, before you question your addressee's intelligence, you question your own effectiveness in putting the story across.

Similarly, faith is required in the merit, the decency and the worthwhileness of the ideas you are presenting. That this is not always easy in a fast-changing industrial society, you are well aware. We have gone from concepts of authoritarianism to all kinds of new experiments in permissiveness, participation, committee management and what have you in the last several decades. We are struggling with new philosophies and new methods of stimulating, rewarding, and judging—and none of them by any means proved out to the last decimal point. Occasionally, too, we are apt to become frenetic—if we care about the science of management—as the professional critics look with detached humor and cynicism at our management efforts.

It can be said fairly, however, that we can be proud of the ferment in management thinking and practice without which we will never make progress, let alone reach exact conclusions as to the best method of handling people's problems. In short, you can properly have faith that, even if your ideas are not the ultimate in perfection, they are a good and useful part of the evolutionary and never-ending development of management abilities. In that light, you can have the faith and you can feel and communicate the sincerity without which full acceptance of your message is impossible.

MANAGEMENT IS COMMUNICATION
by David B. Hertz

The word *communication* will be used here in a very
broad sense to include all of the procedures by which
one mind may affect another. This, of course, involves
not only written and oral speech, but also music, the
pictorial arts, the theatre, and in fact all human behavior.—WARREN W. WEAVER [1]

COMMUNICATION is simply the transfer of information from
one place to another. It may or may not pass through the human mind in the process—thus, a meter reader writing a set
of numbers in a book or on a mark-sense card is acting as a
mechanical intermediary in the transfer of a simple set of information. On the other hand, the same information can be
transferred automatically from the meter to the same card, and
the human mind may be unnecessary. In fact, it is possible to
develop systems which would automatically deal with this
same simple set of information all the way from the meter to
the return of this same number, properly manipulated, in the
form of a bill to the customer. Obviously, the decisions to *use*
such an automatic system involve economic considerations,
among others. It is not the purpose of this paper to deal with
the economics of such system design, important as they may
be. The handling of this class of information is what we may

Address presented at the Eighth Utility Management Workshop, August,
1959. Dr. Hertz is a partner in the firm of Arthur Andersen and Company.

[1] C. E. Shannon and W. W. Weaver, *The Mathematical Theory of
Communication* (University of Illinois Press, Urbana, 1949), p. 94.

designate as mechanical communication, whether performed by machines or by human beings—the sense of our definition being that the effect on people during the process is essentially negligible. This is not to be construed as minimizing the importance to management of such communication systems. Rather, it is intended to make the subject more manageable.

For this purpose, then, we shall start with the premise contained in Dr. Weaver's definition, which is that the important communication systems for management are those which affect people, and take for granted both the existence and importance of systems which merely move information in time and space. The net results of such movement of information must ultimately be reflected in the behavior of people, of course. If this were not so, we could ignore the matter completely. For example, the bill received through such a system by a customer could:

1. Lead to the simple action of writing a check and mailing same, with either pleasure or pain—there certainly *could* be customers who pleasurably pay for the services rendered by the utility.

2. Lead to evasive action—no payment.

3. Cause anger because the customer feels: (a) the bill is wrong, i.e., the information is in error; (b) the bill is late, i.e., the "time location" of the information is incorrect; (c) the bill is not his, i.e., the "space location" of the information is incorrect and so forth.

In any event, the results of such transfer systems are to be analyzed in terms of behaviors—whether the information is dealt with automatically through computers such as load analyzers or billing devices, or through human minds, as, for example, the meter reader or bookkeeper. Management's job is to use such mechanical systems, and much more complicated ones, to achieve the objectives of individuals and companies. Nothing can be accomplished in the first instance without initial communication at least, and nothing can be changed subsequently without additional communication. In this sense then, "Management is Communication."

WHY DO WE COMMUNICATE?

Aside from the broad purpose of communication (which, as we noted, is a necessary mechanism of management), what are specific communication acts, or information transfers used for? The remainder of this paper will deal with various ways of describing and thinking about this question. Thus, we may classify information transfers as to their direction, i.e., "In" (to me, to my department, to my firm, etc.) or "Out" (to others, to my boss, to my subordinates, to other firms, etc.).

Clearly, both these classes must be considered seriously if a system of communication is to meet the test of being "management." "In" communications serve different purposes than "Out" communications; one or the other is often neglected or handled poorly in almost every management center. Let us look at the reasons for "In-Out" communications and how they may be described.

Usually, the reasons we arrange to receive information (or, perhaps more precisely, *it is arranged for us*) have to do with decisions or actions we may wish to take. Clearly, the timing of the action or decision is crucial, as is the magnitude of the effect our action or decision may have. As examples of extremes of timing, consider first the investment house trading desk man, who is buying and selling stocks on an hourly basis for the firm's account. His objective is to have a profit on his transactions at the end of the day with a minimum risk or exposed position. He needs information on every sale of the stocks he is interested in, virtually at the time it is made. He tries to keep the "magnitude of the risk" attaching to each individual decision within certain controlled limits. However, he could not operate with daily or weekly averages—which are aggregations of the very same information he must use.

On the other hand, the institutional investor is hardly interested in each sale; the information contained in each sale of the stocks in his portfolio might well confuse rather than assist him in the decisions he must make. He is much more likely to be interested in the averages or aggregations which would be useless to his counterpart. At one step again removed, the Federal Reserve Board, in considering over-all margin policy, might be interested in averages of averages.

Thus, information "in" must be useful to the purposes at hand, considering the timing and risk involvement of the decisions or actions resulting from its use. Obviously, you have to know what you want to know, why you want to know it, and most likely where what you need to know is. This is, undoubtedly, half the mark of a good manager. Of course, the same bundle of information can yield different sets of intelligence (or material on which decisions or action can be taken), as we have demonstrated. No doubt you could be informed as to the size of Mrs. Jones's bill for July, by say the 15th, if you really wanted it—or, for that matter, the size of each of the bills—but there is little use to which information in this form could be put. On the other hand, this very same information, properly aggregated, weighted, remembered, and so forth, is the basis of many, many important decisions.

WHAT SHOULD BE COMMUNICATED TO WHOM?

If communication "In" should be designed to facilitate our own decisions and actions, if it should be timed and aggregated so as to eliminate or reduce "confusion" (noise, clutter, error) and "unnecessary decisions," what of communication "Out"? It seems clear to me that communication to others falls into a different category. Presumably, the objective is to influence other peoples' actions and decisions. Here we are at some disadvantage compared to our own selves. Presumably, we have "some" insight into what we, individually, need in the way of information to make decisions concerning the tasks we undertake. (We can, of course, be quite wrong about its efficacy; for example, a stock trader may insist on having the hourly temperature in London fed to him on his ticker and may, in fact, use this data to make decisions, thereby reducing his net profits). With respect to others, this may be a difficult task.

As managers, therefore, we must design systems of communication, either consciously or unconsciously, to provide other action-takers or decision-makers with a wide variety of information *plus* information sources to enhance the chances of or odds on their making decisions which will further some set of objectives. An excellent example of the need for thinking through these requirements lies in the field of responsibility accounting. Many utilities still operate with the uniform systems of accounts as prescribed by a commission. These almost invariably leave decision makers with a totally confused picture of the operations under their control. Only the expert accountant understands the codes and allocations involved; at the levels where costs must be put into one slot or another, the individual cannot relate the language of the accounting system to his tasks or functions. At levels of management control the massive accounting data provide no way to signal or pinpoint areas requiring action, much less point the way to what decisions might or might not be helpful.

Revision of these accounts into functional terms—into responsibility areas—removing arbitrary allocations and aggregations from the operating information, reduces the "noise and clutter" and provides control-chart-type signals for action. Further, the information presents a logical picture which can be used for decision-making analysis—"if this, then that."

Thus, a change in the structure of the information system improves (1) the ability of the functional operator to *classify* the empirical data, (2) the ability of the supervisors to understand the data, and (3) the signals to management that something is out of line.

WHAT KINDS OF INFORMATION DOES MANAGEMENT COMMUNICATE?

When designed to achieve management objectives, such systems almost always, implicitly or explicitly, include information which is intended to induce action and decisions which management feels it would like taken under circumstances, known or unknown. In general, the system is used to provide various individuals with the following types of information:

1. *Conceptual information:* concepts, theories, ideas about the business world, the firm, economics, labor, etc.
2. *Empirical information:* data on various parts of the business world. Such information is often obtained by the individual himself as a result of (a) curiosity, perhaps induced by conceptual information, and (b) instructions issuing in the form of procedural information (see below).
3. *Procedural information:* instructions for sets of actions to be undertaken by the individual and others, in general or under specific circumstances.
4. *Stimulatory information:* "get-in-there-and-fight" communications, to provide motives, incentives and drives, both individual and social.
5. *Directive information:* instructions as to the problems to be "thought about" in given contexts.
6. *Policy information:* "information" as to how those above him in the hierarchy "think" about the activities and communications of the individuals and others, in the firm and

out. An attempt to spell out, without setting forth procedures and directives, the general areas of allowed, approved, and desired behavior, and vice versa. In one sense, policy information provides the necessary medium or background which allows the other types of information to be integrated into a single coherent network.

It must not be assumed that all of the information described is written—far from it. Much is verbal, but a great deal is nonverbal, as well. Further, a single communication event often carries all of these types of information bundled up together. Thus, a statement from a foreman to a supervisor such as "My shop repaired ten meters today" can, depending on tone, expression, urgency, raising of eyebrows, and the like, range from a simple communication of empirical information to one containing empirical, procedural, stimulatory, and perhaps even directive information; and, of course, "discussions" on more complex matters are usually loaded with all six types. It will be useful, therefore, to examine in somewhat greater detail some of the requirements and problems surrounding each of these information categories.

Conceptual Information. The concepts held by an individual are fundamentally ideas, theories, and hypotheses he holds about relationships among various entities or variables in "his" empirical universe. (Note: To a certain extent, each of us lives in his own universe of "fact" or "fiction.") The background of conceptual information in the individual is, of course, developed gradually from birth to maturity. As a rule the individuals management must deal with have a rather complete set of concepts and, for this reason, communication—in a general sense—may be quite difficult. This is primarily due to the fact that these concepts will differ from individual to individual and communicative acts designed to reach one type of person very likely will not touch another. In communicating concepts the rate of transfer of information is low—very low. For this reason, propaganda efforts are usually very massive compared to the amount of information being moved. In business, this kind of information transfer has distinct educational overtones.

Empirical Information. Empirical information is the "life's blood," so to speak, of a business communication system. It is necessary to keep track, if only in a routine way, of the state of the various units of the business. Empirical information is easy to transfer—for this reason perhaps too much of it is transferred. The rate of transference is high, but it is subject at the same time to high "noise" levels, to the introduction of error, to the inclusion of "clutter," to repetition, to lack of utility to those who receive it. Since empirical information is so easy to get and move about in space and time, the problems with which management must concern itself are whether what is moved is helpful in the light of specific objectives, whether it is timely, whether it will be needed later rather than now, etc. A note of caution as to the changing (almost fleeting) needs for specific empirical information should be sounded— in developing methods for solving decision problems which depend upon empirical information for their continuing solution, the empirical data are rarely if ever received in the form the decision-making method requires; if they are, one might say that the problem is virtually solved.

Procedural Information. It goes without saying that management must communicate information about procedures which it desires to be used. Many of these are explicit and are formalized in manuals, tables of organization, and the like. The major problems are: (1) the recognition of what should be procedurally formalized, and (2) stating the procedures in a straight-forward, unambiguous way. The latter is probably one of the most difficult communication problems, since the language used to make procedural statements is subject to semantic ambiguity. In addition, illogic and incorrect syntax or grammar are apt to creep in, leaving procedures wide open for misinterpretation as well as misunderstanding.

Stimulatory Information. Management generally wants information translated into energetic action. Lethargy and chillness are the opposites of energy and stimulation. What makes for stimulating communication? This is a long subject in itself, but the best short lesson is that to be unaware of the need to keep individuals "anxious to get a job done" is the best way to insure that there will be little or no stimulatory information communicated.

Directive Information. The coordination of actions in *any type* of organization (small group, workshop, department, company, etc.) implies "direction." Information whereby the coordination is achieved is in some sense directive. In essence, directive information—proceeding both upwards in the hierarchy as "recommendations" and downwards as "suggestions" or "directives" for things to be thought about or problems to be solved—states the management objectives. For example, we might say that, by sending executives to a management conference, management is conveying to them information about certain kinds of problems about which it wants the executives to think.

Policy Information. The individual is in a better position to put all other kinds of information (both retained in his memory and currently received) to work if he knows (1) where the firm is going and why and (2) where he is going and why. Proper communication of the reasons management has for doing things or wanting others to do things provides a context within which the other communicative events can tend to become mutually consistent. (They can never become wholly so!)

These kinds of information—conceptual, empirical, procedural, stimulatory, directive, policy—are not the only types of information which are transferred, but they seem to be the most important. While they may be discussed as though they were independent, in practice they are overlapping, concurrent and highly interdependent. Some of the categories are not used simply through neglect or lack of encouragement. Others are misused through lack of effective means or media. Management can only be as effective as the effectiveness of the information transferred by means of its various communication systems.

CONCLUSIONS

This paper has been an attempt to provide a framework for thinking about communications and information in the context of management problems. The proper transfer of information—the structuring of communication systems so that the behaviors and actions of individuals mesh with the objectives to be achieved by the organization—is a problem which requires the exercise of considerable thought and practice. Much of this exercise is apt to be routine and uninteresting. In fact, for a long time, it may seem to be a formal exercise and sometimes a useless pursuit for those who are not able to handle the difficult substantial problems involved.

There is no more virtue in the development of the communication systems themselves than in studying what others have done. A pragmatic framework embodying the possible in communication systems certainly must discipline theoretical thinking about the content of information transferred; but theoretical thinking is the wherewithal to provide any substantial advance in improving communication.

I suggest that the best way to go about stating communication problems in management is to state a specific information transfer problem in such a way that as much as possible can be solved by reason alone. By reasoning we try (a) to isolate each question of fact that is unresolved and (b) to ask these questions in such ways that the determination of the answers would help advance the communication problems of management through further reasoning.

To get at communication problems in this way, one can follow these steps: (1) ascertain the elements and requirements which, from awareness of the topic, issue or area of concern, will have to be taken into account; (2) determine the logical relations between these elements and requirements, in terms of who is to know what for what purpose (this is a stage of preliminary model building); (3) make sure this is a true picture by checking for omissions of needed elements, for improper or unclear definitions of terms, or undue emphasis on some part of the information content; and, finally (4) statement and restatement of the way in which the information is to be transferred, what its content is intended to be, and the purposes it is intended to achieve. At this point, one can say that the communication system under consideration should in fact not only be at the service of management and reflect management's objectives, but also that it should be an efficient part of management in action.

Part Five

DEVELOPMENT OF MANAGERS

INTRODUCTION

WE HEAR a good deal about "management development programs" and "management training programs" but very little about "manager-oriented programs." One suspects that they are probably about the same in actual practice, but, to put the emphasis where it properly belongs, it should unquestionably be directed to the managers, as people, and not to the profession. No profession can grow and develop independently of its practitioners—even if it were possible, the result would be a sterile set of principles and practices with no one to put them to use. If, as most authorities agree, managers get things done through people, we are still a long way from push-button management. We need—desperately—executives who have the ability to view the factors of productive enterprise in balanced perspective, not, as too many of today's managers do, from the narrow basis of the single department or activity in which they grew up.

Leadership and management are so closely akin as to be almost synonymous; native ability in leadership must be supported and developed if it is to be converted to the skills of management. This is often a long and tedious process but, as yet, we have not found any better way of providing the men to guide our ever-growing enterprises to successful operation. Executive development, as a field of serious interest for corporate training directors, is relatively new. There are probably a number of reasons why so little attention was paid to the problem in the past. Among them, one suspects that resistance by executives themselves was by no means the weakest. Mere election as president of an enterprise was held to be proof positive that the individual was competent to handle the responsibilities of the job and needed no training. This philosophy happily ignored the fact that the responsibilities, both within the company and with the outside community, were heavier and more complex than those of any other job in the organization. Another reason, which still has its effect, is that the higher a man climbs in his company, the fewer are the people who can tell him he needs training for his present or prospective job. Perhaps one of the other important reasons was that the industrial operations of bygone days were generally on a smaller scale and less complicated than they are today. All of which brings us to the point that manager and executive development is now a "must."

Manager development must begin early, in the lower supervisory levels. By the time a man is elected president of his company, it is too late for training. In selecting candidates for development it must be recognized that "many are called but few are chosen" for the highest echelons. Industry owes to its employees an opportunity to progress to the highest level of which each person is capable. Lest there be any misunderstanding on this matter, we must recognize that competitive conditions may be such that highly qualified persons may find a job ceiling short of the top. This does not mean, however, that their capabilities cannot be used and should not be developed; it does mean that industry should make maximum use of its supervisory manpower resources, developing them by every available means. There is little enough genuine ability as it is.

THE PAPERS

Livingston and Waite define and describe the terms "education," "training," and "development," concentrating their attention on the third, because of its pertinence to management. They point out that performance is the criterion of accomplishment and give certain means by which the development program can be geared to enhancement of performance.

Lippert's paper follows a typical industrial training program through its various steps and suggests ways in which the instructor, too, can learn and grow in the process. The reader should bear in mind that, although the terminology is that applied to lower-level training, the principles expounded are equally applicable to all levels of supervisory and manager development.

The reports of the White and Blue Groups were prepared at Arden House by conferees at the Utility Management Workshop. The members of the working parties were practicing public utility managers, and their collective experience was brought to bear on the problems analyzed. The Blue Group presents ideas on the identification and appraisal of potential managers, while the White Group takes over at that point and suggests methods for improving the quality of management through proper indoctrination, various types of training, current appraisal, and counseling.

Acker spells out the criteria for determining the effectiveness of a program of executive development. It is only through evidence of such effectiveness that a company can justify the expense of operating the program.

Smiddy's paper describes the Manager Development Program of General Electric Company. He points out that the operation required considerable time to prepare and launch, because it had to be "sold" all along the line first; this has paid off in greater acceptance by all levels of managers. He develops at some length several of the guiding principles in the plan and closes on the thought that any development program must introduce new ideas on management methods, as well as teach the application of traditional methods.

NEW HORIZONS FOR MANAGERS

by Robert Teviot Livingston
and William W. Waite

"TRAINING," "EDUCATION," AND "DEVELOPMENT" are all terms used to describe what goes on in that branch of an organization devoted to imparting knowledge to employees, improving their job skills, and modifying their attitudes. Regardless of the title assigned to the manager of this activity, there are few concerns indeed which can afford to neglect it altogether. It may be well to define some of the terms which will be used later, in order to avoid misunderstanding, after which the discussion can proceed in more detail.

DEFINITIONS

"Education" means the exposure to and acquisition of certain degrees of familiarity with and understanding of specified areas of human knowledge, experience, and beliefs. It is not related directly to a given task. "Training" involves the learning of certain skills and abilities and the acquisition of at least minimum proficiency in their application. It is specific and directed toward the requirements of certain jobs. "Development" is growth—growth in any dimension. Basically, we are

Adapted from an address presented before the Connecticut Chapter of the American Society of Training Directors, Hartford, Connecticut, May 21, 1959. Mr. Livingston is Professor of Industrial Engineering, Columbia University, and Director of the Utility Management Workshop. Mr. Waite is Professor of Industrial Engineering, Columbia University.

here concerned with the development of effective human beings, and it should be emphasized that a person must *do* the developing himself—it is not something we can do *to* him.

Education. The importance of education lies in the broadening of horizons and the deepening of the appreciation of life in general or, more obviously, of definite areas. Education is a determinant of the kind and amount of training required and, most especially, of the effective means available for use in training. Education is related to the ability to comprehend instructions, among other things, and this is its principal tie to specific tasks. It is a part of the natural process of growth. We learn things other than conditioned responses and skills. Education permits one to understand more things and form more different viewpoints and, perhaps most important, it expands one's sense of values.

Education is not generally recognized as a responsibility of management. It can be argued, if it is assumed that education is learning facts, that some forms of education are a company responsibility. A course in "Know Your Company," for example, is good on the assumption that, if a person knows "why," he will understand as well as know "How." We believe that this matter of knowing "why" is the key to being effective at every level from the worker's bench to the president's desk. Of course, the "why" at these different levels is different. This is an important fact that a person learns—sometimes with surprise—when he moves from level to level in an organization. Fundamentally, however, it is the same problem—an understanding of the special world in which each of us lives and the values he lives by. This is often used to justify industry's entry into the field of education, as distinguished from training, in order (1) to improve understanding (the "why") and (2) to make training more effective.

Education leads to a new set of values and, hence, in many cases, to a certain degree of discontent. It may become constructive discontent and can be channeled in two directions. The first will help make training more effective, if the training department adapts the program individually to the educational level of the person being trained. And it can also be used by the individual himself, for education not only can make him discontented, but also can make him sufficiently aware of the limitations which he has set on his own progress that he may not only be willing to be trained but even anxious to develop.

Training. As has already been suggested, this usually involves the development of a mechanical ability. Even the ability to program a computor, paint a picture, write a book, or, for that matter, manage, requires certain mechanical capabilities, and in these a person can be trained to perform as adequately as his physical, mental, and psychological characteristics will permit. In distinguishing between education and training, it is important to realize that a person *can* be trained with little or no education but the level of education provides an ecology, a climate for understanding. However, in the basic sense, training does not demand education.

Everyone in industry needs training, and this goes all the way up to the top man in your company—he should get training in interpersonal relations, if nothing else. You may find it hard to persuade him to take it. Whether it is publicly admitted or not, you know that your own boss and doubtless others right up to the top in your organization would be much more effective if they had a little more understanding and appreciation of you and your job—if they had a little more finesse and skill in human interrelations.

Development. It was stated earlier that "development" of effective human beings is an important concern of present-day industry. The word "effective" is the key, as it applies to the situation as well as to the person. Where, then, does self-improvement enter into a company program? It comes in two ways: Development involves a change of behavior, not just a change of situation, a change of audience, or a change of opportunity. It is true that all of these occur, but the fact of their occurrence does not mean that there has been development. It would seem that there are four dimensions to this problem:

1. A change of horizons and of perspective; thus, more things are seen in their relations to one another.
2. A change of understanding, an appreciation that there are different sets of knowledge, appreciation, and understanding besides one's own.
3. A change of value appreciation, a realization that the values other people have are to them as rational as the ones we have are to us.
4. A greater acceptance of responsibility, with a corresponding decrease of dependence; greater freedom from fears, greater readiness to stick one's neck out and accept the consequences.

These are all things which a person must accept unto himself, and these acceptances do change his behavior and his overt personality.

It is a *social* responsibility of our modern corporation to provide the opportunity for a person to develop into an effective human being, but it is not the company's responsibility to provide *unlimited* opportunity. This has wide and deep significance, as it means that the job itself must be so designed that the person may be effective in that job. In that connection, a well-designed training program may very well alter existing jobs.

The modern corporation has a responsibility *to itself* to develop managers as required at every level, and this is a different matter from the first. The company must provide incentives and, if necessary, instill sufficient discontent so that people will strive to develop their abilities and competences to the point where they can perform effectively in jobs other than their present ones. Thus, there seem to be two apparently conflicting objectives: (1) to provide the means whereby each individual has the opportunity to develop into an effective individual where he *is,* and (2) to provide the means whereby some (not all) individuals may develop for larger or different responsibilities.

These are different, and there are some important problems in the determination of incentives and stimuli which should be applied—as well as the obvious "to whom" and "by whom." There is also the problem of those to whom these stimuli are *not* applied.

In order to consider development intelligently, it is important to ask the question "development for what?"—just as in rating programs, when answering the question "promotable?" it is wise to consider "promotable to where?" "Development," as the term is used in industry, has to do with movement upward within the company's organizational hierarchy as well as development of the effective human being.

It is useful to consider company management as a sort of stepped pyramid, in which there are at least three distinct levels of behavioral change required: (1) from direct supervision to the top level of operative management; (2) somewhere within middle management, where the individual moves from being a technician or specialist to becoming a real manager—a generalist (many never succeed in making this transition); (3) from middle to top management, when the individual assumes complete responsibility, with all that implies. There is a fourth step, the movement to principal executive, but this is so completely an individual matter, and the situation by which the position is attained is so unique, that this will not be discussed here.

The three initial steps require recognizably different behavioral changes. The first step requires learning to delegate physical accomplishment, to accept different ways of doing things, to have confidence in subordinates' technical ability. The second step requires (a) learning to plan in time, to evaluate men's potentials, and to assign unspecified responsibilities for unforeseen contingencies: (b) the ability to adjust to other equal and, at times, competing personalities; and, finally, (c) the recognition that the company's personality is dominant. The third step requires the development (a) of confidence in the honesty and the intellectual, as well as technical, competence of associates in fields in which the manager may be uninformed: (b) the ability to see the consequences beyond the results: (c) the patience to permit subordinates to make what appear to be errors and to assume the responsibility for such errors; and (d) the self-confidence to make ultimate judgments and see them through with the recognition that there are times when retreat may be the best road to victory—in a word, to learn the true meaning of compromise.

Delegation. Finally, there is the courage that flows from confidence, the courage to play the game through to the end with assurance that those to whom responsibility and authority have been delegated will form a strong, winning team. A moment's thought will show that delegation of the manager's job is one of the important elements. There is an old truism that "no matter what you delegate, you still remain responsible." Of course this is true, but it is not so categorical as it sounds. Delegation cannot be understood without also understanding the meaning of control. In these three steps, while there is delegation, the control changes.

Step One: There is complete control, little anticipated second-degree delegation, and substantially zero time displacement. Detailed reporting is also anticipated; the reporting may be the communication which comes from job completion.

Step Two: Control is incomplete. Second-degree delegation is anticipated; consideration, corrective action, and time displacement are implicit. However, goals, resource use, and time duration are specified, as is required reporting.

Step Three: There is delegation largely without corrective control. Goals are general, resource use and time duration are judged, not specified, and reporting is usually only on request in the case of emergency or innovation in general terms.

Obviously, the paths to making these behavioral changes are not identical. It follows that the three areas of manager development mentioned earlier, and the techniques used in each area, cannot be identical. The first and third levels are generally recognized, and there are means available for handling them; the second is seldom considered or, if considered, is not considered apart from the other two.

We can express this basic concept as follows:

1. The more the subordinate can do, the better.

2. The more the subordinate knows about the objectives (goals, restrictions, etc.), the better.

3. The more the subordinate *understands*, the better.

4. The more the subordinate does not disagree, the better. (This does not mean that he should keep quiet, nor does it mean slavish acceptance.)

5. The more the subordinate is personally involved with the success of the group, the better.

6. The more the success of the group is dependent upon the success of the organization and vice versa, the better.

7. The more the person who is responsible for training knows about training, the better.

THE BASIC PROBLEM

Performance of a task depends upon the abilities of the person to whom the task is assigned, and better performance is possible if these abilities are developed and the task organized to make the most effective use of the individual's ability. It is apparent that there are two aspects: (a) the development of the individual's ability, and (b) the organization of the task.

Generally, a task is organized on the assumption that any operator will possess certain generalized skills; with a minimum amount of individual training he can perform a certain set of operations. The directions and orders given to the operator select the particular skills to be applied to the particular job. It is characteristic of today, as distinguished from, say, fifty years ago, that the tool or process is *given;* the individual is selected and trained to service the tool.

This is probably a satisfactory method when applied to the performance of essentially routine and repetitive tasks, but it does not allow for any psychological or creative satisfaction on the part of the worker. Looking a bit beyond this, there is the performance of tasks which, while perhaps routine, are not identical and where the operator puts something of himself into the operation. In such performances the operation is specified as to outcome, but the factors are not completely under management's control. Questions arise and can only be answered by the operator; among such choices is the sequence of application of the skills he has available; this will depend upon the particular characteristics of the job at hand. In productive industry this is a characteristic of the "job shop," the maintenance worker, or the repairman, and it is also characteristic of any job where people, different people, are involved, but especially where they are being serviced.

To some extent, such jobs can be foreseen; the operator can be trained to recognize situation X, and from the n procedures in which he has been trained he can select the particular sequence of skill applications which have been laid out to handle situation X. Preparing a man to operate in this way involves two training elements: skill development, and cue (or situation) recognition.

No matter how well the former is done, the second is equally important, but it is often overlooked because it is not considered a "training problem." However, let us assume that both of these are handled adequately. What is the end product? A group of individual operators who will perform adequately as long as they are scheduled or programmed, the materials are available, and the equipment is satisfactory.

Such a situation requires very close and precise supervision, and all the responsibility for production is on the shoulders of supervision. This does not make even adequate use of one of our great resources—the minds and the imagination of men. Also, the people involved will be so uninterested that they will have to find something with which to occupy themselves, and what they find to do will probably not be company-directed.

It is important that the operator know not only about his job, but what it means and where it fits in. At a minimum, and as a starting point, every job should be related to whatever other job comes before and what happens next. We may, therefore, add a third aspect to the basic elements of training: physical job relation comprehension.

At this point it is important to realize that ability and understanding of the job are not enough to assure good—let alone outstanding—performance. Performance is what a person does, not what he ought to do, or what he can do, or what management wants him to do. Performance is what the operator contributes from himself in doing what *he* wants to do. It is the function of the company to provide such a climate that the operators (and this applies at any level) will want to perform, and it is suggested that this is a basic element of a good training or development program.

Performance depends upon competence, attitude, and willingness, and upon motivation or drive. It is almost impossible to teach anyone much more than a few simple responses; he has to learn, and this involves attitude and motivation, which are as important as competence. Provision of motivation and attitude is the heart and soul of a good program, be it in education, training, or manager development.

The development of managers differs principally in terminology and detail from the training program provided for workers or lower-level supervision. We are still faced with the problems of task organization and individual development. Motivation must be provided, albeit in somewhat different form, and a certain ability to recognize cues is requisite. However, job relation comprehension takes on increasing importance as a manager advances up the ladder; at the apex of the pyramid, the chief executive officer must have a working comprehension of the entire organization. As was stated at the beginning of this paper, "development" envisages growth in many directions. What better application can we make of the techniques of development than in promoting the growth of the knowledge, ability, and comprehension of the managers of industry?

INSTRUCTION—A TWO-WAY PROCESS

by Fred G. Lippert

MUCH of the unsolicited advice that is offered to the supervisor has to do with his responsibility as a teacher or instructor. But one very solid precept is often overlooked: "The learner must do the learning; the instructor can't do it for him." The instructor may know his subject, have prepared his material with care, and have polished his technique to the ultimate in smoothness—all to no avail if the learner just doesn't get it.

And this may be because the learner simply is not interested. He may not be lazy, or hostile, or stupid. But, for some reason or other, he is not motivated to learn. Here follows a brief survey of the essentials of effective instruction—from the viewpoint of both the instructor *and* the learner.

PREPARATION BY THE INSTRUCTOR

Good instructors are *made*, not born. Good instruction is not delivered extemporaneously or "off the cuff." It often happens that more time and effort are required for adequate preparation than for the actual instructing.

For example, when preparing to instruct:

1. Determine the objective. What is the purpose of the knowledge or skill which is to be transmitted? Is it intended

Reprinted from *Supervision,* XX (January, 1958), pp. 10–12. Copyright 1958, Supervision Publishing Co., Inc. Address presented at the Seventh Utility Management Workshop, August, 1958. Mr. Lippert is Director, Personnel Administration, American Electric Power Service Corporation.

to provide background information which will increase the learner's understanding of his over-all job? Or, is it intended to equip him to perform a certain group of operations, that is, a specific task or job? Instruction in background information is more general and may be broader in scope, since permanent retention of details is not necessary. Conversely, instruction in specific operations or skills requires great attention to detail, much repetition, and actual practice by the learner.

Thus, deciding first on the objective of the instruction enables the instructor to eliminate lost motion in his preparation and to develop an approach which will best serve the immediate need.

2. Be sure your material is pertinent to the objective. Once the objective is established, it becomes easier to select material which bears on the subject and which serves the purpose of the instruction. If you are lecturing on welding to a group of machinists who are not going to do any actual welding your material will differ from that which you would use with a group of apprentice welders.

3. Put your points in logical order. Arrange the components of instruction so that each leads logically to the next. Ask yourself "which will he do first?"—or "What must he know first, and second, before he can grasp the *main* point?"

4. Be sure the dosage is tolerable. The learner can absorb just so much at one sitting. Five distinct ideas is about par for the course. Beyond that confusion sets in, attention wanders, and interest dies.

PREPARATION AND THE LEARNER

Isn't all this effort wasted on the learner? Isn't this kind of attention to small points just so much wasted effort? Maybe yes, maybe no—but listen to what one learner said: "He gets me in there and beats around the bush about how we have to

speed up during the fall rush season. He starts telling me how
to tie a package—but he drops that for a lecture on stacking
the pieces straight—and leaves *that* to tell me how to allow
for moisture when I figure the net weight of the bundle. Then
his phone rings and he tells me to come back tomorrow! Some
instruction!"

Was this a case of poor learner attitude or lack of preparation on the part of the instructor?

THE INSTRUCTION PROCESS

What is involved in the instruction process? The nonprofes-
sional instructor—the supervisor who must instruct his people
as part of his day-by-day job—will do well to rely on the four-
step method that became so well known during the Second
World War as J.I.T. (Job Instruction Training). But the four-
step method predates Pearl Harbor by many years. It had its
beginning early in the century and has had its value proved
over and over again by vocational instructors.

Understanding of the purpose behind each step will improve
the application of this technique.

Step 1: Preparation of the learner. This step is concerned
with conditioning the learner to receive the instruction. It is
not to be confused with the advance preparation done by the
instructor. By telling the learner the purpose and scope of the
instruction—and by getting *him* to tell what he already knows
of related subjects—the instructor establishes a "jumping-off
point." He has aroused the learner's interest, attracted his attention, and possibly overcome the learner's fear of not being
able to learn.

As the farmer plows and harrows before he sows, so the instructor similarly prepares the learner for the seeds of knowledge he is to receive. This is a crucial stage in the process. If

the learner has not been brought to a state of receptivity there will be no learning.

Step 2: Presentation. In this step the instructor presents the new ideas or demonstrates the manipulations necessary to do the job. Here, the instructor's advance preparation comes into full use. He has already decided on the scope of the presentation, the order in which the steps will be presented, and the details of the explanation which he gives. He is setting a new work pattern in the learner's mind and a concise presentation will set a clear and easily followed pattern.

Step 3: Application. Now the learner is ready to try it on his own. Under the instructor's close scrutiny he attempts each step in the same order, and in exactly the same way as presented to him by the instructor. Insistence by the instructor that the learner follow the exact pattern of the presentation will help in the development of a clear-cut habit or way of doing the job. It eliminates the growth of sloppy methods and dangerous shortcuts.

In this step the instructor is quick to correct mistakes and to require the repetition of any step wrongly done. This is the learning process at work, and it pays its reward of satisfaction to the instructor who has laid a good foundation with thoroughgoing preparation and presentation.

Step 4: Test. This is the payoff step. The instructor stands back and lets the learner perform on his own. If a proper pattern has been set, and correct habits have been formed during the application step, the learner will pass a satisfactory test. If he bobbles, the instructor must be quick to reinstruct in the part of the operation in which the mistake was made, in order to prevent damage to the habit pattern which he established during the presentation step.

VALUE AND USE OF SKILL AS AN INSTRUCTOR

The ways and means to good instruction which were surveyed briefly in the preceding paragraphs are applicable in any situation involving interchange of ideas between two people. They are not limited to the classroom, the training shop, or the lecture hall. In less complex situations the user merely compresses the steps. In an effective transmission of a thought or a bit of know-how they are all there.

Consider the giving of directions to the "nearest drug store." Advance preparation—form a quick mental picture yourself; is it three blocks down and two over, or is it the reverse? Now for the four steps.

Step 1: Preparation. "Do you know the neighborhood?" If the answer is "Yes," you can tell him it's in the 1700 block of X Street. If "No," you will have to give detailed directions.

Step 2: Presentation. "Go to the corner." (Point to the corner.) "Turn right, walk two blocks to the first traffic light; turn left, and you'll find one in the middle of the third block."

Steps 3 and 4: Application and Test. "Now, *you* tell *me* how you're going to get there."

Or, perhaps you are explaining the new sick-leave plan. Advance preparation—study the purpose of the plan; its provisions; what it does for employees. And, again, the four steps:

Step 1: Preparation. Why a plan at all; its purpose; the benefits.

Step 2: Presentation. Give details of the plan: eligibility, time allowed, how to apply, physical exam, returning to work.

Step 3: Application. Call on various members of group to explain the points you have covered.

Step 4: Test. Give three typical cases and require group to apply the procedure to figure the sick leave entitlement in each case.

THE LEARNER'S VIEWPOINT

What does the learner think about his instructor's technique? Well, that depends on what the learner gets out of the transaction. Here's what one fellow had to say, after exposure to a session of rapid fire "force-feeding":

"I don't care whether they put me through *four* steps or *ten* steps! What I *do* want is to know *what* I'm learning and *why!* If there is some meaning to what the man is showing me, I'll pay attention. By meaning I'm talking about 'What's in it for me?' That may sound crude, but after all, who is interested in something that doesn't hold out the promise of a benefit.

"Then he shouldn't snow me. I'm no Einstein, and when he shoots so much so fast it just makes my head spin. And, if he wants me to get in the act, how's about letting me do something—get my hands on the tools, or let me explain it back, the way *I* see it?

"But none of this business of a once over lightly and then, 'Take it away, bub, it's all yours!' Let me try it a couple of times on my own before he hands out the diploma.

"Pictures and sketches help too, I see things better than I hear 'em.

"Most of all—if I flub it, I don't mind him telling me so. But if I make the grade, is it going to kill him to tell me I'm doing all right?"

So, what happened in this instance? You don't have to be a mental giant to figure it out. The man wanted to learn and was willing to put all he had into the deal, but the instructor shortchanged him.

A TWO-WAY PROCESS

Instruction is a two-way process. The instructor *comes to the learner* with his knowledge and skills neatly organized for best possible presentation. But there is failure unless the learner *comes to the instructor* fully relaxed and with his attention, interest, and perceptive powers in high gear. In many respects the learner's attitude reflects that of the instructor. Patience, tolerance, and strict attention to the fine points will motivate the learner to draw near and be taught. And, from the effort expended in preparing and instructing, the instructor himself finds that his own knowledge and skills are better organized and more usable than they were before.

Report: A METHOD FOR SELECTION, APPRAISAL, AND DEVELOPMENT OF FUTURE MANAGEMENT PERSONNEL

Fifth Utility Management Workshop, August, 1956

RESOURCES of the Blue Group were ten men representing ten different utilities—telephone, electric, gas, and water—located in ten cities scattered over six states. The combined experience of these men totals 211 years in the utility business—113 years having been spent in management assignments. During the initial study sessions it was soon realized that, even though the men did not have company affiliation or geographic location in common, they did have common interests and problems. A detailed discussion of individual problems resulted in the evolution of a theme for study: the method of selection, appraisal, and development of future management personnel.

As study of the theme progressed, some felt that selection, appraisal, and development were all a continuous process, the components of which existed simultaneously. Those who hold this concept see continuous selection, appraisal, and development leading like a stairway to eventual promotion.

The support of the stairway is composed of eight keys to selection:

1. community acceptability
2. compatibility within the organization
3. somatic characteristics

4. intellect
5. emotional capacity
6. predictable behavior
7. background
8. managerial skill

It is felt that these factors run through all levels of management.

Another concept is that selection is a "spot" occurrence with continuous appraisal and development leading to simultaneous selection and promotion.

We have developed a plan for management selection, appraisal, and development which includes standards for three levels of management. The framework around which we built it is based on the concept of the "total man," which is that he is at least tri-dimensional in nature—somatic, emotional, intellectual. To these three should probably be added a fourth dimension, the spiritual.

We decided that there were eight basic criteria by which this "total man" might be measured. An attempt was made to determine all the pertinent factors under each of the criteria, despite our inability to devise objective standards on many of the factors.

Not only are selection, development, and appraisal closely related in time, but it is generally agreed that criteria for selection and appraisal and, hence, the guides to development, are the same. Appraisals are simply indications of how well the man performs in comparison with the criteria of the job for which he was selected. Thus, criteria and clues of performance were put under the general heading of appraisal in our chart.

A study was made of the difference in performance criteria at various management levels. It was found that these criteria differed more in degree than in kind. As a result, three general levels of management—initial, middle, and top management—

were used to illustrate the relative standards of performance on the criteria established.

The general tools of management development were surveyed, and the basic types of development available are listed in the fourth column. In the fifth column there is space to provide for the individual needs of the man being appraised. These individual needs should be geared to the general tools available and to the recommendations for improving the weaknesses in the man's performance as shown in the appraisal column.

Following the appraisal and development plan are the standards established on each of the eight criteria for the three general levels of management. No attempt is made to measure or identify the specific productivity of a man or any peculiar technical aspects of his job. In addition, the combination of any rating on the eight criteria into one over-all appraisal rating is not treated in this report. This would depend upon such factors as the importance of the individual criteria to a specific job, company policy, and the like. We would recommend the development of such an "appraisal weighting guide" to future groups at Arden House who have, as we did, a feeling that the proper selection, development, and appraisal of management personnel will be the most important problem facing public utilities for decades to come. Management development is a threefold responsibility to the enterprise, to society, and to the individual. Survival depends on tomorrow's management.

Plan for Management Selection, Appraisal, and Development

APPRAISAL			DEVELOPMENT	
CRITERIA		Clues to		Personnel
Man and Job Factors	Standards	Performance	Tools	Needs
Satisfactory to community	[Set up for initial performance and for middle and top management]	[Indications of man's strengths and weaknesses]	Examples: Supervision Techniques	[Recommendations to overcome weaknesses in man's performance]
Compatible with organization			Safety Job planning Job simplification	
Somatic			Customer relations Executive training	
Intellectual			Executive development Business administration	
Emotional capacity			Letter writing Report writing	
Predictable behavior			Rapid reading Trade magazines	
Background			Company library Films	
Managerial skills				

CRITERIA

1 = acceptable   2 = good   3 = outstanding

* = should be developed   ** = should be encouraged

		STANDARDS	
Man and Job Factors	*Initial*	*Middle Management*	*Top Management*
1. SATISFACTORY TO COMMUNITY			
Environment	1	2	3
Social sensitivity			
Appearance	2 *	3	3
Sincerity	3	3	3
Poise	1	2	3
Civic interest and participation	1 **	3	3
2. COMPATIBLE WITH ORGANIZATION			
Social relationship	3	3	3
Sense of humor	3	3	3
Tact	3	3	3
Acceptance	3	2	3
Dedication	1		

Plan for Management Selection, Appraisal, and Development (Continued)

CRITERIA

	STANDARDS		
Man and Job Factors	*Initial*	*Middle Management*	*Top Management*
3. SOMATIC			
Physical fitness	Must pass thorough entrance examination and receive annual check-up at all levels.		
Drive-energy-endurance	Ability to supervise several projects simultaneously over a relatively short period of time.	Ability to supervise numerous projects simultaneously over greater period of time.	Ability to coordinate great number of projects over indefinite period of time.
4. INTELLECTUAL			
Educational background	High school or equivalent	College or equivalent; specialized knowledge in his particular field.	Broad, general knowledge of his company, the industry and the political, social and economic factors which affect them.
	CUMULATIVE ⟶		
Intelligence	I.Q. above average	I.Q. above average of those he supervises.	I.Q. above average of those he supervises.

Intellectual curiosity	Interest in acquiring information and skills to advance him in his job.	Interest in areas other than his own.	Broad interest and foresight in all phases of general business, industry, and science.
Problem solving	Ability to solve personal and job problems, learn from mistakes.	Ability to consider and correctly interpret all facts in solving problems; to recognize the irrelevant; to recognize importance of prompt decisions.	Same as Middle, but greater scope and greater skill necessary.
Communications	Ability to listen; to recognize and report significant information; to give clear instructions.	Ability to speak with conviction; to prepare concise, understandable, and conclusive reports; to interpret company policy.	Ability to organize and maintain effective channels of communication.

— COMMUNICATION ⟶

Plan for Management Selection, Appraisal, and Development (Continued)

CRITERIA			
Man and Job Factors	*Initial*	*Middle Management*	*Top Management*
Job experience	Nominal in breadth and depth; ability to assume responsibilities.	Considerable in breadth and depth; ability to learn and profit from experience; over-all knowledge of job; resourceful.	Substantial in breadth and depth; ability to learn and profit from great variety of experience; over-all knowledge of the company.
5. EMOTIONAL CAPACITY			
Adaptability	Ability to get along with people under varying situations.	Willingness to make changes, accept criticisms and suggestions.	Flexible to changing conditions.
Stability	Ability to take success or failure in stride; actions based on reason.	Ability to retain equilibrium under pressure.	Same as Middle, but under greater stress.
Courage of convictions	Willingness to present new or different ideas to superiors; to carry his decisions through.	Same as Initial but at higher level.	Ability to make decisions best for company, regardless of personal consequences.

	Happy home life	Desirable situation at all levels.	
6. PREDICTABLE BEHAVIOR			
Personal conduct	1	2	3
Respect for personal dignity	3	3	3
Impartial handling of disputes	1	2	3
Freedom from prejudice	3	3	3
Discretion in use of power	1	2	3
7. BACKGROUND			
Variety of interests: Leadership Recreational	Varied interests, such as civic, recreational, professional, and social.	Same pattern with emphasis on leadership.	Leadership qualities should predominate on a local, district, and national level.
8. MANAGERIAL SKILLS			
Planning & work organization	Ability to plan work of several people or small groups.	Ability to organize work of several elements and relate to company goals.	Ability to formulate policy, long-range plans, and goals for company.

Plan for Management Selection, Appraisal, and Development (Continued)

CRITERIA

| | | STANDARDS | |
Man and Job Factors	*Initial*	*Middle Management*	*Top Management*
Delegating	Ability to delegate minor aspects of job; concern for coordination.	Ability to delegate responsibility with limited control over routine operations.	Ability to delegate all but most important factors; to counsel and advise.
Control of operations	Ability to maintain orderly output of small groups.	Ability to coordinate efforts of several company operations; appraise performance; communicate effectively.	Ability to evaluate all or major parts of company performance and relate it to industry and economic conditions.
Training	Ability to train people in specific skills; to counsel for advanced training.	Ability to coach supervisory techniques; to bring high-caliber people up through organization.	Qualified as sophisticated judge of people's abilities; to insure future management of company.

Report: SOME TECHNIQUES FOR DEVELOPING MANAGERS

Fifth Utility Management Workshop, August, 1956

MUCH has been written regarding the need within every organization for a program to insure the proper selection and training of managers. The premise is accepted by the White Group with the observation that little has been written concerning techniques which will implement the establishment of such a program in an organization where no program is in existence, or will assist in the evaluation of programs already in operation. It is the purpose of this paper to develop some of these techniques.

The magnitude of this task is such that the paper will be limited to those aspects which have to do with the development of managers (i.e. the indoctrination, training, and appraisal of the trainee). Further, it is based on the assumptions that (a) the manager has already been selected and placed in the job, or that the individual has actually been selected for promotion to a managerial position; and (b) managerial positions include those in which the individual has supervisory duties, has the authority to hire and discharge employees under his supervision (or effectively to recommend such action), and spends less than 20 percent of his time performing the work he supervises.

It is not the intention of this group to set up a definite program for a particular company. Rather, its objective is to set forth various techniques for developing managers, regardless of the nature of the company. The group recognizes that not all the suggestions contained herein are essential to the establishment of a manager-development program in any given company, but feels that all of the points covered should be considered and carefully related to the peculiarities of the company before implementing a program for that company. It is also felt that, once a program has been established, it should constantly be reviewed in light of these recommendations and the changing conditions within the company, to insure the best possible results.

INDOCTRINATION

One of the most important and difficult aspects of the training of first-line managerial talent is to reorient their thinking from an identification with the workers and their problems to management and its problems; therefore, to be effective, such reorientation must begin immediately when the man becomes a member of the management team. Having reached management status, it is at this time that he is most receptive to this new concept. Unless he is integrated into the management group promptly and successfully, full application of his managerial ability may be seriously delayed. Many of us have not recognized this problem at once, with the result that efficiency has been slow to develop and morale has been impaired in many cases.

Employees are individuals with differing personalities, with a whole makeup of traits, emotions, and characteristics. At almost no other time are the development of these characteristics and their relationships so subject to influence as when a man goes on a new job. It is important, therefore, that the indoctrination be carried out in a thoughtful and well-planned manner.

The indoctrination of a new manager in his new job is that

part of his training which consists of introducing him to his new surroundings and acquainting him with the things he needs to know about working conditions, relations with other employees and other departments, as well as new or different company rules and regulations. Such introductions should be made in an atmosphere of hospitality. He should also be advised on company policy and objectives of the organization of which he has become a part and the management opportunities that lie ahead.

Some suggested techniques for indoctrinating managers are:
1. Interview with a top executive officer
   a. company history
   b. company organizational structure
   c. company policies and objectives
   d. company's tie-in with affiliated or associated companies
2. Full explanation of duties, with emphasis on responsibilities and authority
3. Visits to other departments
   a. meet department head
   b. explanation of various functions of the department
   c. detailed explanation of his relationship with the various functions of the department being visited
4. Explanation of management-union relationships
5. Explanation of community social, civic, and moral aspects, especially if a new location is involved.

These steps should, in all cases, be a continuing process as the manager advances through the various phases of the organization. Such indoctrination should be directed by the manager's immediate superior; however, as occasions dictate, higher echelons should participate.

TRAINING

Management training is a managerial function; it is a responsibility that should not be delegated to a specialist or staff officer who does not have managerial authority, unless the person to whom such responsibility is delegated is recognized as the personal representative of a company official. Training of operators and clerks can be done by a competent person under delegated authority, even though he is not in close touch with higher executives; management training cannot. Probably the single most important contribution to the training of a manager is his immediate boss; this is particularly true in his first managerial job.

Some companies carry on well-coordinated training and development programs for managers. Others scatter attention in so far as this problem is concerned, and some appear to trust to luck to produce candidates for higher management positions when and as they are needed. Trying to solve the managerial training problem by intermittent attention accomplishes little more than the luck-trusting policy. The most effective policy is that of having a planned program whereby an adequate supply of candidates who have the necessary personal qualifications, training, and experience is being developed for key management positions of greater responsibility.

Even though a positive policy of management development is in operation, the procedures and practices differ from company to company. Not all the suggested techniques listed below can be utilized by all companies; consequently, application must be dictated by attendant circumstances and requirements for the particular manager. Full recognition must be given to the fact that the only responsibility the company can assume in a training program is to provide adequate tools and a conducive environment. The real responsibility as to how well he develops lies with the individual.

Some suggested training techniques are:

1. Movies and Sound Slide Films. The use of movies and sound slide films as training media may be helpful. There is, of course, the problem of selecting the proper type of material,

something that has a direct bearing on the type of training the particular company is trying to give. Many companies are now making their own films. With the type of equipment available today, this is not a difficult procedure.

Some excellent films are available, both movie and sound slide, from organizations such as EEI, AGA, AMA, and other industry-associated organizations. The American Economic Foundation has prepared some excellent films dealing with the subject of free enterprise, which should surely be an important part of any management development program.

When using movies or sound slides for training, it is important that someone be present who can answer any question or explain in detail any part of the film. Only those films should be used which can make a real contribution to the total program. No time should be wasted on questionable or borderline material which may simply have propaganda value or merely be entertaining.

2. Schools. In addition to on-the-job training, valuable aid in the training and development of managers is available in many schools, colleges, and universities.

Extensive programs are carried on in practically all cities or towns of any size and in state-supported colleges and universities. In many communities, the business interests are cooperating closely with the schools in working out special and part-time courses. Many schools offer the cooperative plan of education, and still others offer extension programs. In addition to company-sponsored programs in such schools, there is also the opportunity for self-improvement by the individual, which should be strongly recommended.

3. Handling Personnel Problems. One of the most important phases of the young manager's development is that portion dealing with personnel problems. While it is true that he may have a personnel officer to handle most of these problems, the manager himself must make many decisions regarding this

phase of the total management job. The following are a few of the items with which he should be familiar.

a. *Recruitment of good personnel.* The recruitment of personnel is a never-ending job in industry today, due to retirement, death, resignation, expansion, and the like. It follows naturally, then, that the manager should be familiar with such things as the sources of labor supply and methods of obtaining desirable personnel, which includes the problem of good selection.

b. *Turnover.* One of the foremost aims of management is the maintenance of a relatively stable working force. Those who are responsible for the management of labor relations are cognizant of the fact that effective methods of recruiting, selecting, and placing the labor force avail but little in the absence of adequate ways and means of retaining those who have been selected and placed in an organization after intensive training periods and at considerable cost.

c. *Absenteeism and tardiness.* Modern industry, with its high degree of specialization and interdependence of operation, requires the regular and prompt attendance of all employees in order to insure steady production at a cost which enables it to meet competition.

d. *Promotion.* The manager must recognize early that promotion cannot be effected in a haphazard manner if a strong organization is to be maintained. Training in the skills required for proper evaluation and appraisal of personnel must, therefore, be made a part of the development program.

e. *Discipline, discharge, and demotion.* A well-defined policy with regard to these matters is essential in the maintenance of good labor relations and is, therefore, an essential part of manager training.

f. *Wage and salary administration.* This phase of the manager's job is important because of its relation to good will and efficiency. Since wages and salaries affect both personnel and profits, emphasis should be put on training in this area.

g. *Human relations.* We speak of a manager today as one who must deal with several publics: employees, stockholders, customers, and others. Since all of these publics are people, the manager's job is essentially one of human relations. That being the case, it is obvious that he must develop his ability to deal successfully with his publics. This requires a knowledge of behavioral causes and effects, the ability to understand what makes people tick: their interactions, conflicts, differences, motivation, and the like. In addition to the above, a manager must thoroughly understand the union contract, personnel policies and practices, and other company policies affecting the personnel in any way.

4. Conferences and Group Discussions. The conference method is widely regarded as an essential in most training programs today. Because of this, those in charge of training programs have placed much emphasis on the requirements of successful training conferences. Special courses in conference leadership have been developed in order to insure success along this line.

In the training conference, mutual problems form the subject of discussion. Participants pool their ideas and experiences in attempting to arrive at improved methods of dealing with them. The whole attitude in this type of procedure is one of joint exploration. Members of the group come together not to be taught, but to teach themselves.

It is usually found advantageous to hold these conferences on company time when conditions permit and the subjects considered are those with which the participants are familiar. Experience has shown that best results are obtained when groups are fairly small (ten to twenty-five) and when surroundings are informal. Such conferences may be held every week or month, but experience indicates that weekly meetings are more systematic and tend to get and hold interest more readily. In some instances, companies take a group of managers away from their work for a three- to five-day training conference at some resort in order to devote all their time and effort to the consideration of the problems involved.

The conference is essentially a method of comparing, considering, and discussing, and to these ends managers should be trained to plan and conduct such meetings and to use them as a training technique.

5. Rotation of Assignment. Rotation of assignment is used primarily to broaden an individual or to strengthen individual weaknesses. Carefully used, this technique can be a valuable tool for developing a manager. A rotational assignment should be tailored for the individual involved. Two types of rotation are:

a. Assignment as alternate for another manager during vacation or other absences, given full responsibility and authority for carrying out the activities assigned.

b. Assignment as a manager or to an administrative position in another part of the company, either in another activity or in another geographical location. In this assignment the manager should be completely divorced from the position occupied formerly and given complete responsibility for the new position.

6. Delegation of Responsibility and Authority. The technique of delegating responsibility and authority is useful in determining a manager's potential. If he satisfactorily accepts and fulfills the responsibilities delegated, he can be expected to be able to advance. In this area it is very important that a manager be permitted to act within the scope of his job. Managers who appear to ask their superior's advice too freely may be coached by being asked: "What would you do?"—then, "Why don't you go ahead and do it?" This technique will be helpful in training managers to determine when they should seek specialized advice or help.

7. Community Activities. Every company should and must be a good citizen of the community. This is particularly true of utility companies, where substantially all members of the

community are its customers. To be a good citizen a company should participate in and contribute to community activities. It follows, therefore, that training in this field is essential. About the only training that can be given is by participation in these activities. The trainee, however, should first have explained to him the company policy regarding the degree of participation. After such an explanation, he should be encouraged to join in such activities as service clubs, commerce associations, fund drives, and similar community endeavors.

8. Outside Consultants. Some companies are using outside consultants in their management training programs. There are firms that have set themselves up in business to do this kind of work, and some college professors also do this on a part-time basis. Such a program may be especially desirable in a small company which does not have a high-calibre training program. Consultants or specialists may also be used by the larger companies in an advisory capacity to tie in with their training programs.

9. Professional Societies and Trade Associations. Professional societies and trade associations should have company support. They provide an excellent medium for the training and broadening of managers. Here the manager comes in contact with others in a like field of endeavor. The attendant committee work in such organizations helps in teaching him to assume additional responsibilities and to work with and get along with others.

10. Staff Assignments. At times it is beneficial to ask a manager to undertake a special temporary task for the experience it will afford. A well-selected work assignment can help an individual to develop in many ways; however, the assignment should be made with his educational needs in view. Special assignments may be used effectively to change attitudes and prejudices brought about by a lack of information and understanding. Such assignments should be real and sincere. Suggested special or staff assignments may include:

a. Critical study of an established method or of a proposed method
b. Preparation of comprehensive reports of departmental activities
c. Preparation of annual budgets
d. Inspection tours
e. Preparation of routines or procedures
f. Temporary observational assignments

APPRAISAL OF THE MAN AND HIS PERFORMANCE

Training does not serve its full purpose unless results of the training are observed and analyzed. Appraisal of the man during his progress on the job is essential to his development. Appraisal provides the basis for post-appraisal interviews and counseling. It pinpoints the areas in which the man is weak and needs additional training, or a different approach. It identifies those men with exceptional ability who may become available for other managerial positions. Properly done, appraisal is a motivating force toward improving job performance. Appraisals may be formal or informal, but usually a combination of both is desirable. The informal, or on-the-job, appraisal is the continued critical observation of day-to-day performances. The formal appraisal is made according to practices established by the company, and is usually done at stated intervals through the use of appraisal forms.

Many types of forms are proposed in books and other published material, and as many more are in use in industry today. It seems important that an organization should use considerable care in selecting the form. The simplest is the essay type, on which the appraiser is free to write as little or as much as he cares to about the trainee. A modification of this is the essay-type appraisal which shows paragraph headings. The opposite of the "pure" essay type is the checklist type of printed form on which is shown a list of character or personality traits and job performance factors, together with gradations of performance.

Perhaps the most popular form is a combination of the two —a form which requires the appraiser to check certain specific points and also requires him to use his own words in describing the trainee. The combination checklist-essay form is a thought-provoking appraisal, designed to make certain that the appraiser concentrates on the job at hand; it also assures consideration of the specific factors listed.

A thought that apparently has some merit involves changing the standard form every few years. This tends to prevent an appraiser from becoming so familiar with the form that he merely goes through the mechanics of making out the appraisal without really thinking.

It is important that all supervisors understand fully the use of the appraisal form. Therefore, a set of instructions for the correct use of the form is necessary. This guide should be kept as simple as possible, yet it should cover in detail the mechanics of appraising a trainee. Sometimes the necessary instructions can be printed on the form itself, making a separate sheet or pamphlet unnecessary.

Appraisals are usually made periodically. The period may vary between trainees. Sometimes an older employee is appraised less often than a new one. Certain jobs seem to point toward appraisal at a specific time of year, or at the end of a job cycle. In general, too-frequent appraisals tend to become stereotyped, but, if they are not frequent enough, any fault indicated may be difficult to correct after it has become a habit.

In addition to the periodic appraisals, provision should be made for special appraisals as occasions warrant. These additional appraisals take the form of a commendation or a reprimand for behavior at a specific time or in regard to a specific job. Without exception, the immediate supervisor of the trainee should make the appraisal. In some cases the second- and even third-level superiors may also make separate appraisals if they are close enough to the trainee to make fair judgments. In other cases, separate appraisals may be made by a group of the superior's peers who are closely associated with the trainee. In any case, the individually made appraisals should be sent to another party for comparison and review. If there is any great degree of variance among the appraisals, the appraisers should be called together to work out a new appraisal acceptable to all of them.

The panel system of appraisal requires a group of appraisers which should include the trainee's immediate superior and others selected from the level of the immediate superior or higher levels. The group meets with a leader (usually a man with special training) who sits on the panel for all trainees. His job is to ask leading questions to stimulate discussion and draw out answers which compare the trainee fairly with the other trainees. The results of the conference are included in a summary which all the appraisers sign.

A good appraisal should point up the trainee's strong points, weak points, degree of promotability, and recommended action. Careful follow-up of the recommended action is essential. In all cases, after final appraisal has been made, it should be routed back to the immediate superior, who within a specified time limit should counsel with the trainee.

COUNSELING

Although this phase of the development program is treated as a separate subject, it is in reality an integral part of each of the other phases. It is considered separately merely to add emphasis to its importance.

The most obvious time for counseling with the trainee is at the completion of the appraisal cycle, at which time the results of the appraisal should be discussed with him. This counseling should include, in addition to criticism, praise of the trainee's performance in those areas in which he has shown aptitude. Notes should be made by the counselor of his reactions to the discussion, the employee's attitude toward the discussion, and the need, if any, of further counseling with the trainee as a result of the appraisal and discussion. If such is considered desirable the trainee should be advised of this fact and of the approximate time at which further discussions with the counselor will take place.

Regularly scheduled counseling periods are essential to the entire program. Naturally, those resulting from the appraisal will be fixed by the appraisal interval, but there should be other regularly scheduled counseling periods in order to permit a closer observation of the trainee's progress and attitude and to insure that the training program is proceeding as planned. The times of these regularly scheduled counseling periods should be made known to the trainee, and he should be made to feel free to request additional ones if he sees fit.

The counseling of the trainee should preferably be done by his immediate superior, but, as circumstances dictate, other persons may also participate. All counseling discussions should be held in private with the trainee and under circumstances which will encourage him to feel at ease and talk freely. The trainee should be encouraged to discuss matters other than those pertaining to his job or to the training program, for it is through such discussions that the counselor may gain insight into the motivation of the individual and his progress which cannot be disclosed in any other manner.

All counseling discussions should be aimed at improving the progress of training the individual and with the ultimate goal of assisting in producing good managers. They will also assist in forming evaluation of the individual and the adequacy of the training program.

EVALUATING THE DEVELOPMENT PROGRAM

One facet in the management development field which is often overlooked is the possibility that it is not always the trainee who is at fault when the appraisal points up an apparent shortcoming. Therefore, evaluation of the program becomes necessary if it is to be successful. Close scrutiny of the program itself should be a continuing process. As the program progresses, certain check-points for evaluation of the program will appear.

One of the first logical check-points would seem to be the post-appraisal interview. During this interview either the trainee or his immediate superior might suddenly realize that not only is the trainee perhaps partially at fault, but also that the program is very definitely at fault. In the next few days, as both parties reflect on the interview, the idea might strike either that the program is inadequate.

Another spot closely connected to the interview, which might point up a shortcoming in the program, is the recommended action. If, for example, the recommended action frequently turns out to be "further training" or "different types of training," this might indicate a weakness in the program and the necessity for revision.

The person responsible for the coordination of the management development program should have periodic meetings with superiors of trainees in order to review the progress made. At these meetings, provided there is free discussion, new ideas for improvement of the program will arise. Suggestions of trainees should be given consideration.

Some of the things that may show up, either in the continuing observation of the program in action or at the check points already mentioned, are:

1. A complete omission of a certain important phase which should be included

2. An unusually large percentage of failures in one particular area, such as human relations
3. A high percentage of failure under one or more supervisors or instructors
4. A section of the program which is obsolete or obsolescent
5. A general breakdown or failure of the program all across the board. This would indicate a serious morale problem and/or a serious lack of motivation. For example, this might be the result of a poor salary schedule or promotion with utter disregard of the management development program. It is very likely to be a result of top management's failure to provide a proper atmosphere and support for management development.

Once it has been decided what the shortcomings in the program really are, the remedy may suggest itself. It might take the form of a complete overhaul of the program or merely a modification in one of its phases. Perhaps it can be brought up to date by changing the content. Perhaps the immediate superiors are not adequate and themselves need training or retraining in certain areas. Along this line, it might be discovered that some supervisors do not fully understand the development program. Even though they do understand the program, some may be uncooperative and not wish to train others since they lack prospects of promotion themselves.

JUSTIFICATION FOR AN EXECUTIVE DEVELOPMENT PROGRAM

by Ernest R. Acker

MY ASSIGNMENT is a discussion of the approach of an executive to the problem of executive development and, in particular, the kind of evidence he requires that the expenditures of time and money involved in the conduct of a formal training program will be justified by the results achieved. This is a challenging assignment because it deals largely with intangibles and with matters of individual judgment which cannot be measured by simple and generally accepted yardsticks. For this reason I would like to have you consider what I have to say with two reservations in mind: first, that I do not consider myself an expert in the field, and second, that my whole management experience has been with a relatively small gas and electric utility whose executive development problems do not necessarily compare with those of any other management living or dead. I am particularly aware of the fact that, while the principles of an executive development program may be the same irrespective of size, the important element of personal contact is so much more readily achieved in the smaller company that my approach may not appear practicable to those of you who represent the larger companies. In any event I welcome the opportunity to review with you the experience of my

Address presented at the Fourth Utility Management Workshop, May, 1955. Mr. Acker is President of Central Hudson Gas and Electric Company.

own company and the conclusions I have reached as to the justification for a management development program.

As a background for my discussion, let me outline briefly my concept of the job for which we are attempting to develop managers and executives and then my specifications of the man we hope to bring out of the hopper. An executive or manager has the responsibility to advise and assist in the determination of sound objectives, policies and programs which will merit and obtain the support of the investor, the customer, and the employee, and to design and carry out basic operational procedures to effectuate the purposes of his company as determined by its board of directors.

He is responsible for the application of those principles of coordination, cooperation, and control which will assure the execution of all company functions in accordance with those principles, policies, programs, and budgets approved by the board of directors; for prescribing and receiving periodic and special reports from officers and department heads to measure conformity with established procedures; for effecting remedial administrative action wherever and whenever necessary; and for submitting reports of operations and financial position to his superiors and to regulatory, investor, employee, or other groups, as required.

He is responsible for the development, maintenance, and motivation of a well-qualified employee group; for the promotion, through his leadership, inspiration, and direction, of sound principles, standards, and practices affecting the selection, development, utilization, compensation, working conditions, and welfare of all employees, to the end that their productivity, teamwork, loyalty, and morale may make a maximum contribution to the total effectiveness of the organization.

Now, what kind of a man is this modern executive or manager on whom we hope to depend for the management leadership of the future. In my own thinking he is essentially a coordinator who respects persons, recognizes ability, and relies upon teamwork to achieve results. He has a broad knowledge of general business principles, but need have only a basic knowledge of the elements of his own particular business. He has an open and inquiring mind trained to analyze and quick to get at essential facts. He loves to play with ideas and readily discards the old in favor of the new. He asks questions, seeks the judgment and advice of others, and listens more than he talks. He leads his associates to the joint solution of organization problems, but accepts the responsibility for final decisions when it is clearly his duty to do so. He inspires others to develop their talents, to excel individually but to work for the best interest of the organization as a whole. He fixes responsibility, delegates authority, and gives full opportunity for the development and demonstration of individual initiative. He presents his case clearly and logically and keeps his associates constantly informed of the objectives and the intent of his management. He inspires confidence by what he *does* rather than by what he *says*, and sets the character of his organization by the strength of his own convictions and the manner in which he comports himself. But above all these things he has a consummate knowledge of human relations. He is sympathetic and understanding, quick to praise and slow to criticize, and sincerely interested in the welfare of the members of his organization. He defends his people jealously, values their friendship highly, but is firm in the execution of his duty when the interests of the company are involved. He is quick to recognize merit and prompt in his consideration of its reward. He is patient, just and true. He inspires loyalty by the character of his management and builds the spirit and morale of his organization on the pleasure and satisfaction of joint accomplishment. Aside from the essential qualities of personal integrity and honesty, these are the qualifications which I believe will secure high productivity and performance in any industrial organization. The question is—how shall we assure ourselves that these qualifications are being built into the executives on whom we must depend for the future. Can we leave it to chance, to the hope that they will learn by example, or to the old concept of sink or swim? Obviously not. The pace of industrial progress today dictates that we will need more competent managers, more quickly than at any time in the past, and I submit that this can only be accomplished by well-conceived and intelligently administered executive development programs.

While the major job in this field is the provision of competent future replacements, we cannot disregard the great need for upgrading the abilities of those members of management who will remain at their present organizational levels. This group constitutes the great majority in management and is responsible for the bulk of the routine management of the business. Their jobs will increase in importance with the growth of the organization and, if they are to meet the demands of the job of tomorrow, it seems clear that they must be made a part of any development program looking to the securing of optimum present and future management performance. I feel, too, that the problem of replacement is not met by merely providing backup men for each important position, but that the whole future of the organization will depend rather on the *character of the training* given these men and their associates in lesser management positions. This, in my opinion, is our hope for the future: that we can lead all members of management to greater joint accomplishments through the adoption of sound and effective management development programs.

If this is the objective, let me outline the procedure in the adoption of such a program. It seems obvious that management must first recognize the need. This may arise from widely differing factors in various organizations. One may be faced with early retirement of an important member of its top executives, another with the need of rapid expansion of its organization to meet the growth of its business, or others with the need for new or upgraded management personnel to deal with questions of modernization, automation, changing economics, and the like. Whatever the reason, the first requisite is a competent and impartial analysis of the particular needs of the organization involved. In this analysis the entire organization should have a part, and the leadership should be such that the organization is convinced the management is sincere in its intent to improve the quality of its performance. It is particularly important that all levels of management participate in the analysis and in the drafting of any new program which may develop, so that the entire group will be stimulated to do critical and constructive thinking rather than to build up defenses for existing methods and practices.

This was the approach adopted by the Central Hudson Company in 1949 when it became apparent that the management techniques of the organization were inadequate to meet the problems of expansion, rising costs, and decreased productivity experienced in the post-war period. The company needed, in particular, to recruit and train new supervisory personnel more rapidly than at any time in the past, and to train existing personnel in improved management techniques to deal with changing economic and employee-relations problems.

In these circumstances we engaged the services of management consultants, and with their help conducted a survey of employee attitudes. The survey covered a broad sample of classified and unclassified personnel and was conducted by our consultants with complete assurance of anonymity to all employees interviewed. The fact that the management was willing to subject itself to this kind of critical review was an important element in the success of the ultimate program. The following high-spot review of the consultants' report may be of interest:

1. There is too much complacency among supervisors. Too many individuals are satisfied with doing what they can under

the circumstances; too few make any effort to change or improve the circumstances even when they are not satisfied with them. Security is too often the prime consideration and security means keeping out of trouble, "do what you're told," "keep your nose clean," "it's best to play safe; after all, you're not expected to make many suggestions." There seems to be very little premium on initiative, particularly in regard to personnel problems or human relations. These attitudes, characteristic of too many supervisors down the line, seem to be due to:

    a. superiors giving help primarily on the mechanics of the work, but not much on how to deal with people;

    b. superiors not enlisting supervisors' participation in solving work or personnel problems. Consequently, supervisors too seldom enlist the advice of their subordinates.

2. Supervisors lack skills and techniques of effective human relations. Supervisors are well meaning; very few are really "tough" or hard to get along with. But many feel seriously handicapped by lack of knowledge and skill in human relations, especially when they deal with the younger employee.

Supervisors are puzzled; some are afraid of the union and the conditions created by it. They retreat in the face of any challenge or threat of challenge by the union.

Some feel that the best way to be liked is to see that men get considerable overtime, rather than do what is reasonably expected during regular hours.

Lacking confidence in themselves and their techniques of motivating high standards of performance, they play safe and put up with the situation instead of making a determined effort to change workers' attitudes and improve the situation. Consequently, they often fail to claim and secure what are really management's rights. They tend to dodge responsibilities; they avoid initiative; they permit slighting of the job, both in quantity and quality. On the other hand, they wish they knew how to deal with these problems. Many are asking for help.

3. Too many supervisors fail to develop group feeling and group responsibility.

4. Too few know how to "sell" ideas. Some don't even realize the value of sharing ideas about company plans and policies with employees. They fail to tell all they should, so communication is spotty.

5. Most supervisors need to improve their planning and assigning of work, their delegation of responsibility and authority, their ways of appraising results. These represent the managerial phases of their supervisory responsibilities. What they know has been learned largely by trial and error; "experience" has been as effective in teaching poor methods as it has good ones. Human relations, motivation and morale would be improved by better planning, delegation and ways of checking results.

These five needs contribute to low productivity, spotty quality, human relations problems, and high costs.

The situation can be changed, first, through better communications; second, through training in supervision; and third, through better direction from superiors and more consultative management.

Let us look briefly at the implications of this situation for the department heads.

NEEDS OF THE MANAGEMENT GROUP

1. Supervisors need more help on communication. Policies, plans, and executive decisions are not always passed down the line; often the transmission is delayed; what is learned by supervisors too often comes first from the union representative, the "grapevine," or even from outside the company.

Communication is too strictly limited to divisional matters; persons do not know what is going on in the other divisions or why. Company loyalties are handicapped. Supervisors are not told enough about how to interpret and apply company policies and decisions even when told what they are.

2. Supervisors need more help from superiors on how to deal with personnel and human relations problems. Supervisors feel that they get plenty of help on the "mechanics" of their jobs, but they too seldom look to their superiors for help on such matters as how to motivate productivity or to build morale and teamwork, how to "handle" the younger element, and how to develop responsibility, initiative, interest in the job.

3. Both supervisors and some members of the management group need a clearer understanding of the organization structure, duties and responsibilities and relationships. This applies especially to "line and staff" relationships, and where two or more organization units are involved in an operation.

4. The organization needs more practice of consultative management by members of the management group. Most superiors would profit from enlisting more participation of their supervisory subordinates in solving day-by-day problems. They need to call for more communication "up the line." Supervisors need to be asked to contribute their ideas and to be given "examples" of how they should enlist participation of their subordinates.

5. More systematic development of personnel for replacements and for new positions.

It may be asked, How do the above needs compare with those common to other, similar businesses or industries? In brief, the situation which Central Hudson faces is not worse or more difficult than the typical company. In many respects the situation is much better than the average.

The situation is really typical of the more progressive companies which have been intelligently and honestly concerned about people and good management. Experience indicates, however, that these are the very companies which are least satisfied with their supervisory and management effectiveness and are doing the most to bring them to increasingly higher levels.

With this kind of report, what better evidence could be presented to an executive of the need for immediate action. The question became not whether we could afford to make the necessary effort and expenditure, but whether we could afford not to—and it was clearly evident that the corrective action lay first, not in employee education, but in management development.

In summary, it was found that the company needed, first, training in supervision techniques; second, clarification of relationships, duties, responsibilities, and authority within the organization; and third, modernization of communication practice, using the term in its very broadest sense.

SUPERVISORY CONFERENCE PROGRAM

Based on these findings and the recommendations of its educational advisory committee, the company initiated, first, a supervisory conference program conducted by its management consultants in weekly sessions following dinner meetings of the management and supervisory groups. The sessions were held for groups of from fifteen to twenty persons, the management and supervisory personnel meeting in entirely separate groups. In the first series of sessions, instruction was given in subjects dealing with the principles and tools of modern management. These subjects included Principles of Sound Organization, Coordination and Control, The Supervisor's Responsibilities, How to Plan and Assign Work, How to Delegate and Audit Performance, How to Communicate and Sell Ideas, and How to Build and Maintain Good Human Relations.

In the second phase of the program, several sessions were devoted to instruction and training in Principles of Consultative Management, Techniques of Conference Leadership, and How to Plan and Lead Problem-Solving Conferences. These meetings were conducted by consultants using the coach and drill procedure, under which all participants received training and practice in all phases of conference leadership.

In the third phase, each group elected a chairman and secretary, chose group leaders on a rotating basis, and conducted a series of problem-solving conferences on subjects of their own choosing taken from their daily work experience. In this phase of the program the consultants acted as observers, critics, and advisors of the group and summarized the results at the end of each conference. Through this procedure the participants gained confidence and assurance and learned how to apply their newly acquired skills in dealing with attitudes and emotions and in reaching joint conclusions.

Some of the specific benefits may be summarized as follows:

1. Supervisors have had the opportunity to meet together and to become better acquainted and better informed as to each other's problems on an interdepartmental basis. As a result they have a broadened viewpoint and have an increased knowledge of all phases of the company's operations.

2. They have concrete evidence of the management's support and appreciation of their efforts, and have the opportunity, through group thinking and discussion, to contribute to the adoption of improved methods and procedures.

3. They have gained greater knowledge of the importance and value of improved communications, human relations, cooperation, and coordination.

4. They have gained greater appreciation of the responsibilities of the supervisor and have adopted the principles of consultative management in their dealings with each other and in their working relationships with those they supervise.

5. Trained conference leaders are available to assist in placing before employees and the public informative or educational material relating to company or industry operations.

6. Above all, conference principles and procedures have been adopted on a departmental basis and the younger men are having the opportunity at an early age to sit with supervisors and managers of all levels and from all departments, and to participate on an equal basis with them in the consideration of common problems.

Last year a report entitled "History and Development of the Supervisory Conference Program and Recommendations for Future Application" was given to each participant and each group met to study and analyze this progress report.

We were pleased to find that the participants felt that the conference procedure with its problem-solving theme had served an important function in providing training and practice in the use of the principles of consultative management and the techniques of conference leadership, but more importantly that they recognized that it was only a part of a broad and effective management development program.

With this new concept, the groups scheduled meetings on group-approved or management-sponsored subjects.

The subjects covered in the meetings can be grouped in two general classifications. Under the first classification, the groups took advantage of the opportunity to gain information about specific subjects in which the majority were interested. The subjects included financing, rate making, budgetary control, plant additions and improvements, and organization planning. Presentations were made to the various groups by officers and department and division heads who were not included as group participants. In the second classification, subjects related to position descriptions were discussed, and various members of the groups outlined their duties and responsibilities with emphasis on the coordination and cooperation with other departments involved in effective performance.

Regardless of the character of the subject matter, all members obtained great satisfaction from the meetings and felt that they were free to choose informative subjects of greater general interest and more directly related to the individual group functions than in the case of specific problem-solving conferences. In addition to this favorable attitude, the participants felt that they had an excellent opportunity for self-improvement. In those groups where individuals described their own functions, the interest was so great that it was difficult to limit the discussion to the allotted time. This may seem insignificant, but it must be remembered that prior to this conference program it would have been impossible to maintain this kind of interest on the part of the listeners and also impossible to persuade some of the participants to take part in such presentations.

It is interesting to note, however, that the problem-solving feature has not been forgotten or abandoned. As various members have outlined their duties and pointed out difficulties encountered because of carelessness, inaccuracy, or lack of understanding on the part of others, the meetings have developed into problem-solving sessions. When the importance and nature of the difficulties became known and understood by others, and as individuals appreciated the importance of coordination and cooperation, they have been working together productively in the conferences and in daily operations in solving each other's problems.

Although no precise formula has yet been devised to measure the results of this form of development program, we are satisfied that the program is highly effective. The participants have accepted and believe in the management principles and techniques presented; they have increased their knowledge of human relations; they have been motivated to apply their knowledge in their day-to-day operations; their efforts have brought about greater cooperation and coordination within the organization—which has resulted in greater efficiency and productivity; they have been provided with a forum for the airing of difficulties and the elimination of misunderstandings; they have available a medium for the widespread dissemination of information; they are learning to think in management terms, to see how the elements of the management problem are tied together, and they have before them the opportunity to broaden and develop themselves so they may occupy an important position in a well-informed and better-equipped organization for the future.

We find that the program is regenerative in that collateral benefits develop as the program progresses. The results are cumulative and progressive. Some of the collateral developments are:

1. Study and emphasis on communications
2. Improved employee bulletin
3. News digest for supervisors
4. Improved introductory program for new employees
5. Employee information and education program
   a. Economics
   b. Rates
   c. Niagara redevelopment
   d. St. Lawrence
   e. Security benefits program
   f. Annual report
6. Speakers Bureau
7. Position analyses. Each supervisory employee assisted in the preparation of his own position analysis.
8. Position descriptions. From the position analyses, position descriptions were prepared and such descriptions were reviewed with and approved by the respective supervisory employee.
9. All of this will logically lead to performance appraisal. The basic material contained in the position descriptions will serve as a starting point for the completion of performance appraisals.

10. Salary administration. With these items completed, the ground work will be completed for the establishment of a sound salary administration program.

We are deeply impressed with the experience which we have had to date. We have noted improved abilities and attitudes of many individual supervisors and are confident that we are making definite progress in the development of our future executive and supervisory personnel.

In conclusion, may I quote Lawrence A. Appley's clear and concise statement that "management achieves its objective (1) by increasing the knowledge, (2) by adding to the skills, (3) by changing the habits, and (4) by influencing the attitudes of people."

The test of the value of an executive development program then lies in the degree to which it achieves these ends with those members of the organization responsible for the present and future management of the business.

In our own case I am convinced that we have improved the attitudes and relationships of our supervisory personnel, that we have achieved increased productivity in our organization and are building a sound management team for the future.

A MANAGER DEVELOPMENT PROGRAM

by Harold F. Smiddy

WE HAVE BEEN carrying on a research program in manager development for the past couple of years. I shall report to you a few of our findings, and also discuss the launching, operating, and sustaining of such a program in an actual working organization.

Only a few salient points have been selected from our research findings for presentation today, and I suspect that some of them will not be new to you. I further suspect that some of them will seem deceptively simple. However, it is my hope that they may stimulate the development of ideas and techniques applicable to your own special problems.

Here are the points. They are not placed in any particular order, as they are general points which, because of the great supporting evidence we found, have the standing of "Guiding Principles" in our planning.

Point 1: Manager development cannot be accomplished by a "program"; it is a way of life, a philosophy of management. Our studies indicated that neat, packaged, printed plans are generally inadequate, not universally adaptable, and generally fail to get sustained, constructive action on the part of the operating people. Time after time, in our own company, as well as others, we found organizations with elaborate, pat

Address presented at the Second Utility Management Workshop, May, 1953. Mr. Smiddy is Vice-President, General Electric Company.

"executive development programs," some of which had been quite widely publicized, but with very little familiarity and very little action down at the operating levels.

Point 2: The method of developing the plan and of installing it in the organization is at least equal in importance to the content of the plan. We are persuaded that few plans for the development of managers will be really successful if they are installed by edict; that is, if the president or chief executive officer issues an instruction that "Hereafter, the Company's standardized Executive Development Program shall be executed in all Departments." As Peter Drucker has so aptly put it, one of the inherent freedoms of an individual is to refrain from doing things with which he does not agree.

The key to this situation appears to be active *participation* by the managers in the company in the *formulation* of the plan. This is the primary reason why we in General Electric have devoted two years to the formulation of our plan. During these two years, using both our own people and high-level outside interviewers, we have interviewed in depth more than five hundred General Electric managers, asking them two primary questions:

1. To what do you attribute your progress and present position in the company? What was it that the company did, or that your individual managers did, to help you develop? What did they fail to do that might have helped you develop faster?

2. Please assist us in developing the General Electric plan by telling us what principles and methods you believe should be incorporated in such a plan.

In addition to this depth interviewing, we have made a particular effort to keep our management people (particularly at the top level) informed as to our progress and our findings at all times. Further, we have presented our findings to groups of General Electric managers all along the line and have asked for their constructive suggestions and criticisms so that they may

derive a sense of participation and so that the plan, when issued, is, in part at least, *their* plan.

*Point 3: The most effective way to get action from managers
is through motivation rather than exhortation.* We are persuaded that motivation of managers to do active manager-
development work has two aspects:

1. The formal and official requirement by the executive officers that the development of personnel is a major part of every
manager's job—that it is written into his position description,
and that it is a part of his formal accountability.

2. The providing of good, simple, flexible services by a full-
fledged service department to help managers discharge this
responsibility.

We believe (and we have strong indications that we are
right) that once managers at all levels fully realize that personnel development is an integral and important part of their
individual jobs, they will respond quickly and will want to
take positive action. If good staff services are easily available
to them, they will reach for them and use them voluntarily and
with enthusiasm. Such an arrangement also has the beneficial
effect of putting responsibility on the service department to
provide continuously good and improving materials and services for use by management people.

*Point 4: The job must be done by all working managers at
all levels in all areas of the business; it should not be done for
them by a service staff.* In our studies we have found some
cases where an individual or a department has been set up
actually to do the manager development work in the organization with staff people making the appraisals and conducting
the schools and conferences for the operating units. This we
conceive to be a dangerous practice in that it relieves the working managers of their responsibility for doing this job, permits
them to say "Manager development is not my responsibility—
the president has set up an outfit to do that job, thereby taking

it away from me." Obviously, this is unsound since, as I shall point out later, and as you undoubtedly know, a large proportion of a man's development is dependent upon his actual working experience, the management environment in which he works and his relationship to his managers.

For these reasons, we believe that the primary burden for the development must be placed on all managers individually and that a small hard-core services unit should be maintained to help *them* to do the job.

The above four points are primarily concerned with some principles for *launching* and *actuating* a plan for the orderly, accelerated development of manager talent. I would now like to set forth a *few principles applying to the nature and content of the plan itself.* It may well be that I have got these in reverse order and that the discussion of the plan should have preceded the principles of activation. However, they are so interdependent and the activation is so important, that I think the order in which they are presented is not too important for our discussion here today. Turning now to some thoughts on planning for manager development, I am not going to rehearse the techniques of appraisal, identification, selection, etc. You have on your program some gentlemen who are better qualified than I to speak on these subjects. What I would like to do is to *sketch for your consideration some* of the *broad principles* which apply to a sound plan for the development of managers.

Principle 1: Any plan for the development of managers should be focused on the self-development of the individual. It is axiomatic that no one can "develop" another individual— that all development comes from within and that the *responsibility* for such development *rests with the man himself* and not with the company. Emphasis on this point seems somewhat irrelevant, but our concentrated thinking about it has resulted in some important changes in our approach to the total problem.

Under this concept the part to be played by the company in a man's development is twofold:

1. To motivate and encourage the individual to undertake self-development
2. To provide (for the individual) opportunities, challenges and help which will facilitate and accelerate his self-development

Under the head of *motivation* the strongest forces probably are, first, fair and adequate recognition and reward for progress, in both pay and status. The second strong motivating factor is the frank discussion with him by a man's manager of his position, his progress, his strengths *and his weaknesses* in a constructive manner so that the man will be moved to try to improve—or else will understand the reason for his lack of progress, or for his removal, if he does not improve.

Principle 2: The sound manager development activity is focused not on promotion alone but primarily on development in present job. There are a good many reasons for this, many of them I am sure, well known to you. Prominent among these are:

1. Inherent to a sound activity is the fact that a man must do the *best possible job where he is* before he is considered to have *earned the right* to progress. This, of course, is very important to the success of *current* operations of the enterprise
2. Any activity which is *primarily* focused on promotion makes men restless and impatient and distracts their attention from the job at hand
3. Since there is a relatively limited number of positions at the top to which men can be promoted, it is essential that progress in present job be fully recognized as good progress and be suitably rewarded in pay and status.
4. Tapping the available but unused capacity of *every* manager is the royal route to greater productivity, inspiration, and satisfaction for all.

I have left till last two very basic factors in the development of managers. I put them last not because they are less important, but because they are probably the *most* important things in development of ability to manage.

These points are, first, *organization,* and second, an *understanding* of the *work of professional management.*

Let me cover them briefly for you.

First, what about organization as a development factor? This leads our discussion to:

Principle 3: The most powerful tool for developing managerial ability is an organization based on the principle of true decentralization. By decentralization I mean of course, not merely geographical decentralization but decentralization of *decision-making,* the very *personal* process of exercising judgment and common sense, based on the best available facts and measurements in working with the day to day problems of the business. And this means decentralization of responsibility and authority, *with commensurate accountability.* The point here is one which is widely known but frequently ignored in practice; that the best and fastest way for a man to develop managerial ability is to *manage*—to carry the responsibility for making his own decisions from learning through mistakes, from facing up to his accountability and being given a free hand in meeting that accountability.

As you probably have heard, we have for some years been engaged in the General Electric Company in the evolutionary process of converting the organization pattern from that of a centralized functional organization to that of a decentralized product responsibility organization. The basic unit in this organization structure is the product department, with its own general manager carrying full responsibility and having all authority necessary to discharge that responsibility—that is, all authority except the minimum which is *withheld in writing* by the higher echelons. Further, this department general manager is expected to decentralize below him, seeing to it that the same philosophy is carried to his section and unit managers. This process of portioning out the responsibility to the periphery where the real work of the day is done is, in our judgment, the *primary* development method.

Principle 4: The manager development activity must be based on a fundamental, universally applicable, understanding of the unique and distinct characteristics of the work of the "professional manager."

One of the first and most frequently repeated questions which occurred during our research was this: What is a good manager? How can you start out to develop managers unless you know what you are trying to develop? There are very wide differences in the characteristics and methods of successful managers. Are you going to try to place them all into one mold —to make them conform to a prototype? If so, what prototype?

Obviously, the wide differences in individuals must be recognized, and, obviously, there must be no attempt to raise a generation of uniform automatons. There are, however, some basic things that *all* good "professional managers" must *do* to be successful.

We believe that this concept of professional management must be emphatically introduced into the development process. Otherwise, if we simply relied on information drawn from the experience of our present managers, we would create successive generations of managers in the image of those we now have. Many of these managers (particularly many of the older men in the higher echelons) are in general often managing in a way they started learning twenty years ago. This way of managing, while quite adequate to the requirements of the past, is only too frequently inadequate to the present and dangerously short of the requirements of the future.

While we fully recognize that manager development must be done on the job and through free-thinking seminars and conferences of managers and potential managers, we are convinced that this alone is not enough and that new and advanced thinking on the *work of management,* as such, must be introduced into the process by every means at our command. Only in this way can we advance the art of management in the General Electric Company, and bring along new, successive generations of managers, educated in the management philosophy and method which we need now and will most urgently need in 1960 and thereafter.

Part Six

DECISION-MAKING

INTRODUCTION

DECISION-MAKING is the lonely prerogative of the manager; logically he cannot share the responsibility with others and remain a manager. This prerogative attaches to every managerial assignment, at every level. Unquestionably the scope of the decisions and the number of alternative choices available will become more circumscribed as we descend the organizational ladder, but, within the limitations imposed by organizational policy and one's superiors, the final selection of a course of action is up to the manager. He must consider as many choices as are available to him, he must evaluate the consequences of each course of action as fully and accurately as possible, and he must decide finally to order one course to be followed.

Because most segments of our society are organized on numerous levels, the vast majority of managers play two roles —they are both supervisers and subordinates. Only the "chief executive officer" falls outside this classification, and even he has a board of directors looking over his shoulder. In his role as subordinate, a manager's decisions are subject to the limitations and restrictions placed upon him by the decisions of his boss. The restrictions may be minimal, leaving him a wide range of discretion in decision-making at his own level; they may be so close that he is forestalled altogether in the use of discretion—he has been told what to do and how to do it; or, he may have any degree of latitude between these two extremes.

The restrictions on managerial decisioning may be imposed from above, from below, or from outside the organization altogether. The first possibility has already been mentioned; the second involves consideration by the manager of the probability of acceptance by his subordinates of various alternative decisions. This is a vital consideration, as any order is no better than its acceptance by those who must execute it. Unless they are able and willing to implement a decision, it might as well not be made. Aside from sheer impossibility, nonacceptance may stem from a variety of causes, from lack of understanding to deliberate sabotage. The clinically oriented manager has a fairly good idea of what he can expect in response to almost any type of decision, and he limits his choices accordingly.

The third type of limitation, that imposed by outside factors, is an important one. Government regulations—at federal, state, county, or municipal levels—set a rigid framework hedging many decisions. Unions exercise vast influence on decisions in fields other than wages, as witness the protracted 1959 steel strike, where the principal bone of contention was management's right to make decisions modifying allegedly lax working rules. Another outside influence of importance is the actions of customers and suppliers. Many concerns find their operations severely hampered and face agonizing decisions when suppliers' facilities become strikebound or are closed by disasters.[1] Similarly, managerial decisions of manufacturers are frequently severely affected when extremely large customers (such as mail-order houses) offer lucrative orders on an "all or none" basis.

All in all, the decision-making process is a complex matter. The manager can, and should, seek whatever assistance, ideas, or suggestions he can obtain from subordinates, colleagues,

[1] One example of this was the great fire which destroyed the General Motors transmission plant at Livonia, Michigan, in 1954, necessitating reappraisal of decisions by several auto makers to use Hydramatic transmissions.

and staff personnel. But, no matter how it is influenced by external or internal factors, decision-making is the sole responsibility of the man in charge at whatever level of the organization he functions.

THE PAPERS

Livingston and Hertz, in their joint paper on decision theory, stress the close interrelationship between the theories of decision and management. They discuss the decision process in detail and present mathematical models illustrating different types of choice. An important aspect of the problem is that of estimating costs and satisfactions deriving from alternative choices in economic terms and also in terms of the degree of acceptance likely to be accorded different choices.

Branch directs his attention to the practical handling of the problems an executive encounters in the course of his work. The author's three steps in the process are (1) to define the problem, outline possible solutions and forecast probable results from the application of each; (2) to select the alternative which is, in the manager's opinion, the *one best* course of action; and (3) to implement the decision.

Wolfe describes three general principles for obtaining effective action on executive decisions. He also suggests how to overcome such obstacles to action as the "time squeeze," failure to delegate, too great reliance on past experience, executive preconceptions, failure to think in terms of the effects of action on people, broad applications of contested decisions, overdependence on statistics, and "group-tight" thinking.

Rudge discusses the matter of corporate responsibility toward the public—a new and unfamiliar role for business executives. This is primarily an educational matter, and most executives have had relatively little experience in making decisions in this field. The climate in which such decisions are made vitally affects all aspects of the decision-making process.

DECISION THEORY

by Robert Teviot Livingston
and David B. Hertz

MANAGEMENT is the process of getting things done, and this is equivalent to the process of making and implementing decisions. The theory of decisioning is an integral part of a theory of management. In a previous presentation decisioning has been described as part of a cycle of continuous action.[1] The action of decisioning was spelled out in considerable detail within the operating hierarchy of an association. It has also been indicated that there are channels of information transfer within an association which constitute a system of feed-back circuits. Static and dynamic information energy levels have been demonstrated to represent "only a small fraction of the energy exchange in the system."[2] The decision is the "triggering" element controlling the alternative releases of associational energies. A decision having been made, the result of the decision, as indicated by action, is fed back and combined with new, or different, information to create a continuous check or governor upon future action.

A paper presented at the Annual Meeting of the Management Division, American Society of Mechanical Engineers, New York, November 30–December 5, 1952. Mr. Livingston is Professor of Industrial Engineering, Columbia University, and Director of the Utility Management Workshop. Dr. Hertz is a partner in the firm of Arthur Andersen and Company.

[1] R. T. Livingston and D. B. Hertz, "The Integration of Organization and Management, *Transactions of the American Society of Mechanical Engineers,* LXXIII (No. 7, 1951), 997–1004.

[2] D. B. Hertz and R. T. Livingston, "Contemporary Organization Theory," *Human Relations,* Vol. III (No. 4, 1950).

When decisioning is removed from the conceptual area of flash of genius or automatic reactive process, a new basis of analysis is available. It leads to the methodological dimensions in a multidimensional concept of action in which other dimensions are (a) content, i.e., kinds of things, organisms, concepts, perceptions, and the like; and (b) sequence, or position variable in a time stream. The process dimension, as we shall show, comprises a number of variables; the actual "instant" of decision, which is usually considered to represent the process, can be no more than an interval separating specific elements.

DEFINITIONS

Definitions may open the door to useful argument, and, as far as better communication is concerned, they may save a great deal of time. The following definitions are presented generally to orient the area we intend to examine.

1. A "decision" occurs at a point in time when observation and analysis end and where action of a specific nature is taken.

2. "Decisioning" is a process of alternative choice, of selecting one path in preference to another. It is, always, goal-seeking. The personal goal of the decision-maker may bear little or no observable relation to the apparent goal for which the decision is ostensibly made.

3. Decisioning is represented by conscious action (or inaction) in respect to a (specific) situation. Unconscious decisions, in the form of elemental reactions, exist and may make up a large part of what we have defined as decisioning, but they will not be explicitly discussed here.

4. Decisions may be classified in a number of ways. For example:

> relative to temporal events (immediate vs. future)
> relative to finality (tentative vs. final)
> relative to the maker (individual vs. group)

relative to the affect (personal vs. impersonal)

In this discussion only *immediate final decisions* will be considered in detail. It is assumed that a distant and/or a tentative decision is a *plan* rather than a decision. Decisions which affect only the decisioner are not of primary interest here. What follows applies equally to impersonal and personal decisions. It is the latter in which we find the greater interest. By personal decision is meant an action by one individual which is intended to alter the behavior of at least one other person.

We shall discuss *how* a process of decision-making might work. In other words, what follows is a model for further analysis and study. We shall consider only single acts of decision, while recognizing that decisioning is a continuous process.

Upon the assumption that a single action may be used to represent the continuous process, the argument may be simplified. We assume that a problem (p) arises which requires a decision (D_i). We shall further assume that the decision to be made by M_d will affect—that is change—something and/or require action or inaction by or in relation to individuals (M_i) other than M_d. Further, this decision is not part of a routine operating procedure, and it is a matter of some importance to both M_d and M_i.

THE DECISION PROCESS

In this decision model there are two distinct steps prior to the instant of decision:

1. *Consideration* of the problem, perception of its nature, the alternative means available to solve it, and who will be affected and how. This connotes recognition and analysis of the problem on the one hand and of discrimination among available means, resources, and anticipated results on the other.

2. *Evaluation.* This is usually thought of as a part of consideration, but it actually is a transformation of the problem variables to a different field. It is the formal evaluation of

alternatives in terms of costs of all kinds, of potential satisfactions, and of acceptances. Whether consideration and evaluation are, in practice, carried on simultaneously is not important. *At some point in time a "decision" is made.* However, making the decision is one kind of process, making it work is another. Two different kinds of action *after* the decision also may be distinguished.

3. *Implementation* of the decision, attempting to tamper with the probabilities of future events. By this is meant attempting to gain acceptance of the decision.[3] It is concerned with making desirable probabilities move backward in time, attempting to make undesirable probabilities move forward. There is an implicit notion here that probabilities, or, rather, the effect of the anticipated events they represent, have a time element. Further, it may be considered that there is an attempt to change the shapes of their distributions. It may be that one would like to flatten an unfavorable probability, or reduce the anticipated relative frequency of that set of occurrences in some larger class of events (the knowledge of which is based on past experience). Actually, one wishes to change the basic cause system. Thus, the dishonest gambler resorts to "loaded" dice. By so changing the cause system, previously undesirable probabilities may become sufficiently small. Similarly, with a favorable event, if we could compress its relative frequency of occurrence (that is, make the distribution more peaked), providing our timing was correct, its influence might become more favorable to the outcomes we desire. Thus Rabelais's Judge Bridegoose threw *loaded* dice to make his decisions so that they would "come out properly in the long run."

4. *Adjustment to Reality.* There is no use, in most cases, in following lost causes. It is often necessary to adjust to non-acceptance of decisions. A 60 percent goal 100 percent realized is, perhaps, better than a 100 percent goal 50 percent accepted.

---

[3] John D. Millett, "Working Concepts of Organization," in *Elements of Public Administration,* ed. by F. Morstein Marx (New York, 1946).

The probability of the acceptance by M_i of the decision by M_d is a variable which must be taken into consideration.

Within the framework of these four categories it is proposed to study the process of decision-making. It is not maintained that this is *how* decisions *are* made, it is intended to indicate that this is a model in which decisions could be made and implemented. It is believed this will help interpret the situations which occur in industrial and other associations. Within this scheme some useful measurements may be made towards a further development of decisioning theory.

Simon presents an interesting and provocative matrix of the evaluative aspect of decision-making.[4] His process represents a model of only the most final decisions. However, it does not lend itself to the type of analysis being attempted here.

Presented below is a logical expansion of Simon's analysis to take into account the "approximately equal" situations.

$$C_1 < C_2 \ S_1 < S_2 \quad C_1 > C_2 \ S_1 < S_2 \quad C_1 \cong C_2 \ S_1 < S_2$$
$$S_1 > S_2 \qquad\qquad S_1 > S_2 \qquad\qquad S_1 > S_2$$
$$S_1 \cong S_2 \qquad\qquad S_1 \cong S_2 \qquad\qquad S_1 \cong S_2$$

When $C_1 =$ cost of a particular decision, and

$S_1 =$ satisfaction resulting from a particular decision.

If we wish to assume a model of categorical vs. noncategorial choice (or decision), relying for the moment upon the accuracy of our estimates of probable costs and satisfactions, the following classes may be distinguished:

Categorical alternative 1	*Categorical alternative 2*	*No decision*
$S_1 \cong S_2, \ C_1 < C_2$	$S_1 \cong S_2, \ C_1 > C_2$	$S_1 \cong S_2, \ C_1 \cong C_2$
$S_1 > S_2, \ C_1 < C_2$	$S_1 < S_2, \ C_1 > C_2$	$S_1 > S_2, \ C_1 > C_2$
$S_1 > S_2, \ C_1 \cong C_2$	$S_1 < S_2, \ C_1 \cong C_2$	$S_1 < S_2, \ C_1 < C_2$

[4] H. A. Simon, *Administrative Behavior* (New York, 1947). It should be noted that Simon has expanded this concept in probabilistic terms in another context to which reference is made below.

However, the model presented in this paper deals with probabilities or the anticipated relative frequency of occurrence of specific events (or expectancies of both costs and satisfactions). The categorical representation is inadequate to express the probability distributions from which actual decisions are to be made. Therefore, we shall describe cost and satisfaction distributions leading to an alternative concept of evaluation.

COSTS

Costs can be divided into categories: metrical and non-metrical, or, as they are more often listed, financial and imponderable. An alternative choice study usually ends up with a "for and against" tabulation in which various imponderables are listed. However, it must be realized that even the so-called

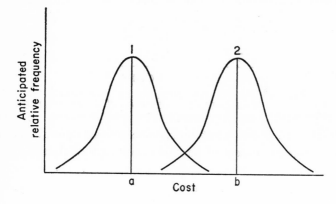

Figure 1. Comparative Expected Cost Curves

metrical costs are but *estimates of probable future expenditures.* Therefore, they should be modified by factors indicating the probable accuracy of estimate and of changes in the cost situation with time. Without loss of generality, these factors may be considered together. Rather than any single number for a set of probable costs there exists a frequency distribution of anticipated cost occurrences. These distributions may differ in both shape and position. For example, position, as in Figure 1.

Here the probable cost of 1 is rather definitely less than 2. However, there is a possible situation in which *2 could cost less than 1.*

Different forms of distributions may affect the decisions made, as in Figure 2.

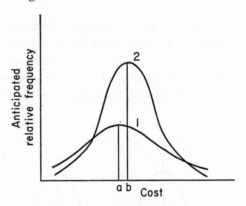

Figure 2. Comparative Expected Cost Curves

In Figure 2 the "most probable costs" are approximately equal, but the different shape may well determine the decisions.

It is to be recognized that what is being considered as "cost" is the present worth of a series of anticipated future "payments." Specific alternative cost estimates may be described as:

$$C_1 = {}_1C_1 + {}_2C_1 + \ldots {}_hC_1$$
$$C_2 = {}_1C_2 + {}_2C_2 + \ldots {}_hC_2$$

(where ${}_iC_j$ = estimated future cost of alternative j at time i) or two series in time, each payment consisting of $\Sigma \, (qu)$, or the sum of a series of quantities multiplied by a unit "cost."

The relationships of the alternative cost estimates will be one to one only if (a) there is a single payment at a given time in both cases, or (b) if each payment in each series is made at the same point in time.

In a real sense, cost estimates must include a distribution (O) expressing the expectancy of the occurrence of events on which the cost estimates were based and parameters to "describe" the shape of the distribution.

Figure 3. Comparative Expected Satisfaction Curves

Evaluation of relative costs among alternatives must be in terms of significant differences among the various time distributions, along with estimates of the confidence which may be placed in these estimates, related to the specific objectives of the decision.

SATISFACTIONS

The problem of relative satisfaction is of similar nature to that of costs, whereby the "utility" of a set of anticipated occurrences is usually transformed into economic terms. Figure 3 illustrates the different ways in which satisfaction may be obtained. The distribution functions represent the probabilities of attaining a given degree of satisfaction by alternative decisions *A* and *B*. In the case of *A*, we may say that we have a very "precise" design which will only satisfy a rather narrow range, but within that range there is a very great probability that the desired amount of satisfaction will be obtained with relatively little variation. Alternative *B* has a very wide range of satisfaction with lower probability of meeting any specified small range.

It may be assumed (although this is not a requirement) that the curves are symmetrical, which means that there is the same probability of failing to meet or exceeding the desired satisfaction *X*, but there is a difference between the probabilities of meeting a given range of $(X_U–X_L)$ between the two distributions.

$$P(_BX_U - {_B}X_L) < P(_AX_U - {_A}X_L)$$

(where $U =$ upper value and $L =$ lower value). There is an interesting corollary, which is:

$$P(_BX_X - {_B}X_U) > P(_AX_X - {_A}X_U)$$

(or that the probability of exceeding an upper value of satisfaction is greater with *B* than with *A*) and, of course, the equally valid corollary that:

$$P(_AX_L - {_A}X_X) < P(_BX_L - {_B}X_X)$$

The natural assumption which one would make is that, if the probability of falling between $X_U–X_L$ is to be maximized, then *A* is the preferred alternative. But this conclusion is based upon an inherent premise that the particular set of events forecasted from previous experience is going to occur. What is the particular set of events? It is the set of events which it has been assumed will occur, and which would make a particular set of utilities the ideal satisfaction. But what will happen if this particular set of events does not occur? It is, of course, conceivable that some other set of circumstances might occur so that the utilities were still the desired satisfaction, but it is also possible that, with this different set of circumstances, the best set of utilities might differ from the first.

This, then, means that the categorical statement, if $S_A > S_B$ then A should be accepted over B, does not hold but must be modified in some manner by an evaluation of the probability of the occurrence of the set of events based on previously experienced relative frequencies. Actually, it is not only this expectancy of the occurrence of the events which is important, for both alternatives might differ in the same manner and the same choice of "suitable" satisfaction might hold for both. It is conceivable that the two alternatives might depend upon the same events in a different manner. What is required is an expression which will indicate the probability that a given ordered chain of events might shift the required satisfaction more than a given amount. The rational answer is what Carnap [5] calls a "fair" bet, based upon complete knowledge of the relative frequencies of past "relevant" events. However, in the long run, it is unlikely that one has a chance to make "fair" bets. The bets must also be based on an estimate of the probable cost of not "knowing."

Satisfaction, in the sense of this paper, means the occurrence of a particular, desired set of events transformed to some utility (or negative cost) scale within a given time interval. To satisfy implies a want or need and some scale including a threshold value of minimum acceptance and a maximum of satiation. The scale may be termed a set of values, and a value function is a function which transforms the value scale from one set of units to another (thus, dollars, or hours, or other measures). The value transformation functions apply both to costs and to satisfactions, although for a given alternative the two functions may not necessarily be the same. A satisfaction-value distribution might be highly right skewed and a cost-value distribution left skewed, since the distance from thresh-

---

[5] R. Carnap, *Logical Foundations of Probability* (Chicago, 1950).

old to satiation may be quite small and the cut-off utility cost quite sharp.

One says "this" is better than "that." But, we ask ourselves, under what circumstances. This is better than "all other things being equal."

Considering the problem from a different viewpoint, "satisfaction" may be viewed as meeting a set of requirements with limits, such as:

$$_1R_L \ldots _1R_U$$
$$_2R_L \ldots _2R_U$$
$$.\qquad .$$
$$.\qquad .$$
$$.\qquad .$$
$$_nR_L \ldots _nR_U$$

where $_iR^*$ is the requirement and R_L and R_U lower and upper limits, respectively.

Let us call $_iR^*$ the actual desired point for any requirement. This we may identify as unity. Then, we may weight these various requirements by a factor W_i and we set the condition that

$$\sum_{i=1}^{n} W_1 = 1.00$$

Then $\sum_{i=1}^{n} (W_iR^*) = 1.00$, and this is the condition of satisfaction.

Within these specifications we can measure satisfaction obtained in terms of the $\sum_{i=1}^{n} (W_iR_i)$, where R_i is the actual requirement achieved.

Having specified the acceptable range of satisfaction, we must describe, as was done with costs, the probability of achieving satisfaction (Φ).

$$\Phi = \sum_{i=1}^{n} (W_i R_i \lambda_i)$$

where λ_i is the probability of the requirements falling within the required limits.

ACCEPTANCE

The problem of "acceptance" has been largely neglected, although in an unpublished manuscript Simon has outlined the employer-employee relationship in formal terms. Acceptance is a part of evaluation of alternatives, and subsequently, a part of adjustment to reality.

It is conceivable that there might be a potentially satisfactory solution of a problem which would fail due to the intransigence of those affected by the particular decision. A certain thing may be "best" for an individual, but he does not accept it necessarily; hence, it may not work out as well as something else which was, in theory, not as good.

As a basic premise we may now note that three elements are involved in achieving a desired objective by means of the decision: (a) estimated costs, (b) potential satisfaction, (c) acceptance.

Just as there are distributions of estimated costs, events and achievements of satisfaction, there are also distributions of probable group acceptances (a). If acceptance is unity then it will not affect the possibility of achieving the potential costs and satisfactions. The acme of opposition would lead to complete nonacceptance and, thus, to a zero probability of successful results.[6]

[6] Very often a decision may be viewed in terms of sub-decisions, the acceptance of all of these being equivalent to acceptance of the primary

What is the cause of acceptance or, more usefully, the cause of nonacceptance? We shall assume that a person M_d is making a decision which will somehow affect another person M_i. The first problem which arises is communication: M_d must convey a message to M_i. There arises an important question: the degree to which M_d understands M_i, which is the source of a potential error which may be expected to affect the acceptance.

M_i is interested in the decision because it will affect him, and his interest is indirectly related to the degree that it will affect him. It may be assumed that the decider has attempted to estimate the probability of acceptance when he made the decision. There are, then, two fairly obvious causes of error. The decider can estimate inaccurately the acceptance, or the recipient can misinterpret the values which are intended to be conveyed by M_d's communications. It may be that potential acceptances are measurable in terms of differences of value functions (as noted by Simon in the employee-employer contract).

---

decision. If D comprises a number of successive partial decisions ($D = d_i \ldots d_n$) the probability of acceptance of any d_i may be greater (or less) than that for D.

If P_i = the probability of acceptance of any $d_i (0 \leqq P_i \leqq 1)$ and

P = the probability of acceptance of $D (0 \leqq P \leqq 1)$, where $\sum\limits_{i=1}^{n} d_i = D$

(in the sense discussed above, then the $\sum\limits_{i=1}^{n} P_i$ may be greater than P).

If the d_i are considered sequentially, and if $P_i > X$, $P_2 > X + \sigma_i$, $p_3 > p_2 + \sigma_2$ (where σ_i is a function of the ordered set of d_i), and, in general, $p_i > p_i - 1 + \sigma_i = 1$, then for any D as $n \to N$, $p = 1$.

$$\lim_{N \to \infty}$$

Thus we introduce the concept of partial goals successively won, building a bridge of acceptance so that each successive decision may have greater probability of acceptance.

CONCLUSION

The selection of alternatives in this model depends upon three probability distributions, Φ, A, O, where

$\Phi =$ the probability of achieving satisfaction

$A =$ the probability of acceptance

$O =$ the probability of the occurrence of the estimated cost events

When these distributions are combined with their associated costs, we obtain a multivariate frequency function as follows:

$$X = \int_{a\dots}^{b\dots} \int \int (\Phi, A, O)\, d\Phi\, dA\, dO$$

where

$X =$ anticipated relative frequency of achieving objective

An intuitive representation of this distribution is shown in Figure 4.

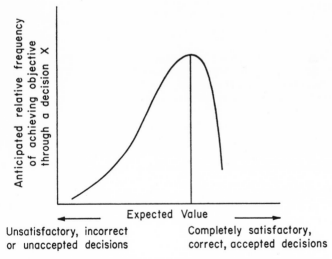

Figure 4. Intuitive Representation of Expectancy of Achieving an Objective through a Decision X

SUMMARY

We have shown that the process of decision-making may be described in terms of:

1. *Consideration* of a problem
2. *Evaluation* of future probabilities (of costs and satisfaction)
3. *Implementation* (including an evaluation of probabilities of acceptance)
4. *Adjustment* to reality, in terms of probabilities of acceptance of partial decisions

The model is shown to be noncategorical and to include various types of probability distributions for costs, satisfactions, and acceptances. The final function is proposed as a model of the decisioning process. Within this model it is now suggested that various kinds of decisioning situations may be described, and that quantitative treatment of the variables and their probability distributions is desirable.

3–D DECISION-MAKING

by Harllee Branch, Jr.

EVERY normal person makes decisions. It is an indispensable concomitant of daily living, at least in a democracy.

But to say that decision-making is almost as common as breathing is not to say that it is commonplace. It is a dynamic, challenging venture that reveals the measure of a man. It is the skill that, more than any other, differentiates the top-ranking individuals in an organization from the lower-rated ones. It has been called "the core of the management process," since the ability to make sound decisions is required of all managers who hope to gain the respect and cooperation of their co-workers, investors, customers and the public.

Decision-making is really the modern executive's only excuse for being around at all. For, if decisions were not required, business firms could be turned over to machines and to machine-tenders.

The opinions regarding the decision-making process which I shall express today are based in large measure upon my observations of many successful executives, in the public utility field and in other lines of business. I am indebted to these men for many valuable lessons and for much sage counsel. Naturally, my opinions are colored to some extent by my own experiences—in journalism and in law, as well as in business.

When I became associated with the Georgia Power Com-

Address presented August 7, 1958 at the Seventh Utility Management Workshop, Arden House, Harriman Campus, Columbia University. Mr. Branch is president of The Southern Company.

pany some years ago, I was almost as naïve as my young son
who asked me whether electrical conductors punched tickets.
However, I was extremely fortunate in having as associates
men who knew the dangers of "ivory tower" decisions, which
are often unrealistic and difficult or impossible for the man
in the field to carry out.

As a reporter I had been taught the importance of assembling all, not merely some, of the facts; of examining every
situation carefully; and of communicating my thoughts to
others accurately and understandably. As a lawyer, I had
learned to make thorough analyses, to anticipate the unexpected, and to foresee objections to everything.

Thus, from my own experience and from the experience of
others, I have constructed certain guides and principles for
decision-making. My presentation will cover three stages of
the decision-making process—it might be called a 3-D approach.

The first stage is the *diagnostic* stage, in which all the pertinent elements are considered.

The second is the *determination* stage, in which the selection
of an objective and course of action (the decision itself)
takes place.

The third is the *desired-results* stage, in which the decision
is implemented.

The first two stages may require only minutes or they may
require weeks or even months, depending on the particular
situation. Like the three-stage rocket, these two stages are but
a means to an end. It is the third stage which determines the
ultimate success or failure of the entire decision process.

Before proceeding to a detailed discussion of these three
stages, let me generalize for a moment. It would be a great
relief if a "perceptron" could take over the decision-making
function, leaving business executives free to become, say, good-
will ambassadors of their firms. But the day of pushbutton

ease has not yet fully arrived, so I am afraid the responsibility is still ours. Few executives honestly enjoy the process. We are all sufficiently akin to the turtle to develop anxieties about sticking our necks out. In addition, so much has been written on the theory of decision-making, the dynamics of decision-making, the psychology, sociology, even astrology of decision-making—and, just recently, on the undoing of faulty decision-making—that the operation has taken on the aspect of a cult.

The boys in operations research want to reduce every decision to a fixed formula and to a so-called scientific approach which will do away with guesswork and old-fashioned instinct. "Methods," often conflicting with each other, are becoming so prevalent that they undo the very reason for their existence: to rid the process of confusion and emotionality.

I have found it useful—and perhaps you will also—to combine what is good and helpful of these formulas with a large portion of common sense and a dash of *educated* guesswork, then sit back and relax, even sleep on it. This was a technique reportedly used by Franklin D. Roosevelt. He would read everything on a subject and absorb it like a sponge. He never seemed to be making a conscious decision, because he would go to bed with all that knowledge stored in his brain and, when he awoke in the morning, the decision had made itself. I am sure you, too, have experienced the extra intelligence and insight that comes with the morning sunrise. A man who considers decision-making a formidable ordeal or who approaches it in an unrelaxed frame of mind rarely makes as sound decisions as the man who can free himself of the tensions which often surround and interfere with judgment.

Another generality: Decision-making cannot be dodged or deferred indefinitely without serious damage to and demoralization of a business. The man who constantly avoids making decisions, simply because he cannot make up his mind or cannot bring himself to take a stand, makes a poor leader, although, in a less demanding position, he might be a valuable employee.

On the other hand, there is such a thing as deliberate avoidance of a decision, or what might be termed "the decision to make no decision." If done for a purpose, this may be a positive and prudent exercise of executive judgment. In some situations procrastination may be a virtue; if the delay gives more time to gather necessary facts, it is certainly preferable to making a decision on the basis of incomplete evidence. But such deferment must be positive, not negative. And it should never be indulged in merely out of timidity or to avoid risk. A certain amount of risk is always present, else no decision would have to be made. Besides, hindsight always has 20/20 vision. A second-rate decision, vigorously and enthusiastically pursued, in many situations will be preferable to a lackadaisical approach while seeking the perfect course of action.

One last generalization: The kaleidoscopic nature of the decision-making process requires flexibility—but not so much as to amount to vacillation or indecisiveness. The right degree of flexibility recognizes that the elements involved in making decisions are not likely to be the same with every problem, and that one's methods and approaches may have to be modified. Flexibility means understanding and accepting or rejecting an idea or a proposed solution on the basis of its merits rather than on whether or not it conforms to one's own rigid preconceptions. A necessary part of sound decision-making is to clear the mind of predilections, just as a judge and jury are expected to do in a courtroom trial.

I

Now, to get to the specifics of what I have termed the 3-D approach to decision-making:

With any problem—be it medical, legal, military, or public

utility—an accurate estimate or diagnosis of the situation is the beginning stage. Here one seeks to identify the problem and the key factor involved. This includes marshaling *all* the known facts from *all* available sources.

Before attempting a solution it must be clearly determined that the right problem is being tackled. A good procedure is to write down what the problem is. There is something about putting one's thoughts on paper that helps reveal areas of vagueness or even of fallacy and helps to eliminate unrelated or secondary issues. Much of the working time of executives is spent in deliberating upon matters which are trivial, irrelevant, and unnecessary. Besides being a thief of time, debate over irrelevant details produces needless worry and frequently interferes with objectivity.

Once the specific problem and the related problems have been determined, it is wise to list all possible solutions. The failure to consider alternatives is probably the most frequent error in decision-making. A man may become so attached to one avenue of solution as to investigate it to the exclusion of all others; he will then conclude that this is the only solution. An executive may feel more comfortable with a certain alternative because he has had previous experience with it and tends to think it is right on that basis alone. Most of us tend to be vain about our own points of view and to think anyone who disagrees is either a fool or a knave. This is the sort of myopia that virtually guarantees error.

When each alternative has been listed, the next step is to forecast the probable results of each and to evaluate those results in terms of the ultimate goal which it is desired to attain. I cannot emphasize too strongly the importance of this phase of decision-making: that is, the phase of forecasting the likely results of a decision so as to eliminate undesirable side-effects in advance. As each alternative is being weighed, an effort should be made to maintain a consistency of viewpoint

and evaluation. Like the vain viewpoint, the shifting viewpoint can also lead to erroneous conclusions. The criterion for
evaluation should be the same for each alternative. A single
measure or common denominator should be used.

In forecasting probable results, absolute certainty is impossible. There will be uncertainties in every situation, so expect
and make allowances for them. Too often an executive, in
solving a financial or production problem, will say: "It looks
like our sales for the next five years will be so much," failing to
take into consideration what will happen to his solution if the
sales take a different turn.

In stage one, then, we have defined the heart of the problem, used all the facts to outline possible solutions, forecast
the results of each in terms of the objective, eliminated unrelated matters, and considered the ways and means of implementation. Thus far, we have tried to avoid making a decision
in favor of any particular alternative. While it is never possible to avoid being aware of the apparent superiority of some
alternatives over others, nevertheless in stage one care should
be exercised not to "jump to a conclusion."

II

That brings us to stage two—the time for decision. The word
"decision" literally means a "cutting-off," and this is exactly
what happens in this stage. In the first stage, the executive has
been able to solicit the help of his associates, he may have
gathered data prepared by statisticians or processed by computers, and he may even have employed consultants to advise
him. Now it is up to him *alone* to select the one alternative (or
combination of alternatives) that he considers to be the best
solution.

Here is where the men are separated from the boys! It is
easy to present guides for almost every stage of the decision-
making process, except for that suspenseful moment when the

cutting-off is actually accomplished. That is because there are no rules, as such; no one can tell you how to do it. You must depend on your knowledge of the facts, your experience, your judgment, and perhaps your intuition to tell you what to do. Ben Fairless, President of the American Iron and Steel Institute, says "You don't know how you make decisions. You just do it."

It takes a person of innate self-confidence, resolute courage, and boundless physical stamina to emerge continuously without scars from this stage of decision-making. However, there have been many men in the public utility business and in other businesses who have risen to meet the challenge of crisis and emergency—many of them sternly opposed every step of the way. One does not become a skilled executive overnight; the road to relative ease in decision-making is marked by trial and error.

I have already suggested that an executive should not make a final decision on an important matter when he is tense or tired. But, that is not intended to counsel dilly-dallying or to suggest that an executive can set aside a definite time and place—a sort of a decision-making sanctum sanctorum for uninterrupted thinking on important issues. The truth is that most executives are compelled to consider many problems simultaneously. Often they do not have time for more than a superficial analysis. However, an executive can learn to think "on the run" and also, with practice and experience, to examine preliminary considerations swiftly and almost unconsciously. John Pfeiffer in his book *The Human Brain* says: "We first use our higher brain to learn a skill and then, when it is learned, consign the skill to the lower or more automatic brain, which carries on in future situations."

In selecting between alternatives, some consideration should be given to the source of the alternatives and their probable objectivity and freedom from ulterior motive. Some sources are simply incapable of being objective. However, the executive in his final decision must, himself, be objective and free from bias. He cannot afford to be swayed by whether he, personally, likes or dislikes the person who suggested a particular solution.

In all stages of the decision process the executive must guard against fallacious reasoning. This is particularly important in stage two. Logical argument and abstract thinking have fallen somewhat into disuse. Clarence Randall says, in *The Cultivation of the Mind:* "Each advance in the technology of the visual aids tends to soften our capacity to think for ourselves. Just as we tend to abandon physical exercise in favor of spectator sports, so we tend to abandon intellectual exercise in favor of presentation of ideas by mechanical means."

The newsroom, the courtroom, and the laboratory are three places where caution against fallacious reasoning is constantly enjoined. It is no less important in executive offices of a business. Stuart Chase lists thirteen fallacies in his book *Guide to Straight Thinking.* I have already mentioned two that I have found to be particularly destructive of sound reasoning: one is the tendency to think in terms of the past (it happened thus in the past; therefore, it will happen thus in the future), the other is the insidious effect of personal prejudice in evaluating facts and sources of advice.

An executive should be aware that statistical data, no matter how impressively presented, can mislead as well as inform, and that averages are dangerous unless additional facts are known. Graphs, which some businessmen seem never to question, may be distorted to influence opinion. For example, rise and fall can be cleverly minimized by shortening the dimensions of the squares or exaggerated by lengthening them.

After a conclusion has been reached in stage two, some executives test it in this way. First, they make sure they are completely satisfied that they have made the proper decision and have thought of all possible alternatives and consequences. Then they put themselves in the position of a devil's advocate and argue against their own decision. They try to look at it as their subordinates, their superiors, and, above all, their critics may view it. If this sort of testing reveals flaws in their decision, so much the better. They can then correct the decision or even discard it without embarrassment or serious consequences.

I am sure most executives make it a practice, as I do, to discuss their major decisions with trusted associates. Their constructive criticism is invaluable and should be sought. At this point, "yes" men should be avoided like the plague. If an executive's ego needs bolstering, he should seek such bolstering outside the decision-making process.

III

The right thing to do has been determined in stages one and two. All that remains is to DO it! This is the "desired-results" stage. The best way to prepare for this stage, of course, is to have had it in mind from the beginning.

It is in this final stage that the most brilliant decision can be frustrated. For here the decision is like a 375-horsepower Thunderbird standing in the driveway: a product of careful planning and responsible craftsmanship, but not going anywhere until the ignition switch is turned on. Without the intelligent and enthusiastic support of the individuals who must carry it out, a decision not only fails to produce the results intended but it may actually do greater mischief than if it had never been made at all.

When stage three—the implementation stage—is reached, the decision-maker is no longer the dominant participant, manipulating fairly constant facts. He now becomes involved in the baffling, exciting realm of human relations. His dependence on the human element for the successful carrying out of his decision is so great that his every talent as a leader must now be marshaled and brought into play.

At this point two things are essential. First, an atmosphere of receptivity must be created by informing employees of the decision and soliciting their support; second, responsibilities for execution must be delegated.

Making a company-wide announcement of an important decision is, in itself, a move toward cooperation. Indeed, keeping employees informed is the only sure way to avoid inevitable and probably false rumors. It is the only sure way also to avoid hard feelings.

If the decision is a popular one, such as the granting of an extra day off at Christmastime, a simple official notice will take care of the receptivity problem. From most employees, the only unfavorable comment will be "Why didn't you decide to do this long ago?"

But where the decision does not so completely fit in with everyone's desires it is apt to be accorded a negative, perhaps even a hostile, reception unless measures are taken in advance to insure understanding and acceptance. A realist knows that people generally resist change and want what they do not have. Actually, intelligent resistance among employees is a desirable quality. It shows they are thinking about their jobs and their company rather than being disinterested and apathetic. Furthermore, the openly resistant person can be reasoned with; it is the silent disapprover who bears grudges and stirs up discontent.

Leadership is as indispensable to implementing a decision as it is to making a decision; and leadership, in both areas, depends on courage and character. I am convinced that the companies which are the most successful, which have the best year-in, year-out employee-management relations, share these common virtues: they are firm, they are fair, and they know what they are doing. They stick to their principles and everyone knows what those principles are. Employees like this because they feel secure. Unions like it because they know where they stand. Stockholders like it because they know their investment is in good hands. On the other side of the coin, companies run by officers who vacillate, who try to buy popularity and employee good-will, are usually kneedeep in trouble. Why? Because they try to "muddle through," deferring tomorrow's trouble until the day after tomorrow. They do not want to make anyone mad, so they make everyone mad!

The timid and incompetent company and the timid and incompetent manager are never respected. A decision-maker *must* have the respect of his subordinates. Of course, being human, he wants to be liked, too. But respect is more important, for if that is lost, all is lost. A leader's job is not always pleasant, but, when a man accepts promotion, he must be willing to set himself apart from the crowd. Actually, that is the way the crowd wants it. An executive cannot lead from the back seat. He has to make decisions and he has to make those decisions stick! The executive must be willing to stand by his decisions and refuse to retreat to safer, more popular ground. Blind stubbornness is never desirable, of course—but that is a different matter. The executive with the courage of his convictions will see his decisions take substance in the way he visualized them when he went through the "valley of decision."

Enlightened business organizations realize that in an enthusiastic, intelligent, industrious work force they have their most prized possession. What the people inside a company think is spread to the local community, thence to the financial community, and thence to customers, and even to legislators. The point that is sometimes missed by managers is that most employees are keenly desirous of doing a good job and want to know how they are doing and how they can improve. They are sincerely interested in the welfare of their company if they are made to feel that they are a part of it and that their contributions are appreciated. One recurring complaint from employees is that they are not told more about their company and given *specific* information on its goals and the manner of achieving them. Enthusiasm cannot be expected to flourish without inspiration. A company which neglects a suitable opportunity to make employees feel important has a difficult time in securing cooperation in the implementation of its policies and decisions.

The points I have just made are axiomatic. I have discussed them briefly to show that a favorable climate for implementing a decision is one which has been developed through years of inspiring leadership and good employee relations. Now let us consider the specific steps involved in implementation of executive decisions.

First is the timing and method of announcement. We have seen that unwise delay is damaging, but so is prematurity. One of the signs of an inexperienced or inept executive is a tendency to burst forth excitedly with a plan or solution as soon as it occurs to him. The plan may be a good one, but it may be rejected because it is proposed at the wrong time.

Road blocks should be eliminated in advance. Certain decisions lend themselves to pre-testing on a small scale whether the decision involves equipment or people. Any impracticalities are likely to show up, and these can be eliminated before a general announcement is made.

In most cases, the best method is to announce a major decision in person, in a group meeting if possible. The group conference permits the decision-maker to present his plan accurately and to make employees feel they have been taken into his confidence. It also permits questions to be asked and helps to avoid misinterpretations. Group interchange of ideas promotes enthusiasm and often results in valuable suggestions for carrying out the plan.

When presenting a new idea, a good rule is for an executive

to soft-pedal his enthusiasm for his own idea. This rule holds true for any phase of the decision-making process. Encourage the ideas of others and, if you still feel your own is best, put it over by firm, quiet suggestion rather than by unpleasant aggressiveness or imposing your will on others. This makes the listeners feel that they have had a part in making the decision rather than that it has been forced on them.

In announcing a decision, the reasons which prompted it should be enumerated and explained. If possible, it should be pointed out why alternative proposals were not selected. Emphasis should be placed on the way the change will bring about improvement. The undesirable aspects of the change should not be played down, since a decision or program, accepted with full acknowledgment of its advantages and disadvantages, is already well on the way to effective implementation.

Finally, the task is to delegate responsibilities of execution to subordinates. An executive is only one person and, hence, limited in what he as an individual can do to effect his decisions. By delegation of responsibility to others, he becomes many persons.

The extent to which an executive can delegate depends on his personality. Some men know instinctively how to get the best out of people. In every situation where individual personalities are involved, the ability to see through another's eyes is a valuable asset. For example, when an executive selects a subordinate on whom he will bestow the "honor" of a new assignment, he may think the subordinate should feel privileged to be given the new authority simply because that is how he feels about it. However, the subordinate may be unhappy with the added responsibilities and perhaps never become effective. Therefore, an executive must be sure he has won the subordinate's enthusiastic support before he leaves him alone to carry out a plan or program.

Once an assignment has been made, the executive should let go! But not desert. He should follow up his subordinate's progress, but let him do the job. If all goes well, the subordinate should be given the credit he deserves. If failures occur in the execution, the subordinate should not be allowed to lose self-confidence. The most effective knowledge frequently comes from making mistakes.

I have talked today about techniques which I consider helpful in decision-making. I have tried to emphasize the importance of creating an atmosphere in which people will want to help achieve the results desired by the executive. The essential key to handling any other human being is to understand and appreciate what he wants to accomplish. If his aspirations are the same as the executive's, the battle is won. Sometimes, however, his aspirations and even his methods may be different. In such a situation a wise executive will strive to mesh the two. This, of course, is an ideal—and not always easy. It can be accomplished best by treating the subordinate as a person whose goal, although different, is nevertheless important and not to be belittled.

When two men in an organization think exactly alike, the business can probably get along without one of them.

ACTION: THE REALIZATION

by J. Theodore Wolfe

WE DO NOT KNOW a great deal about the actual process of decision-making. One of my distinguished predecessors at this Workshop last year quoted Benjamin Fairless of U.S. Steel as saying, "You don't know how to make decisions. You just do it."

There is no question that much of the decision-making process takes place below the conscious level. Our subconscious minds can draw, without the slightest effort on our part, on the accumulated knowledge of all of our years of experience in solving problems and making decisions—good ones and bad ones. Someone has called this use of the subconscious the "saturation-incubation-illumination" process. We pack in the facts, let them cook a while in the lower brain centers, and suddenly along comes a pretty good solution. An explanation of how all this comes about we must leave to the experimental psychologists.

DECISION-MAKING: AN INTERRELATED PROCESS

The thoughts I will discuss today are largely my own observations of the elements that seem to contribute to the successful carrying out of decisions or, as it has been termed on your program, the "action" phase.

I should say, at this point, that I have a little difficulty in

Address presented at the Eighth Utility Management Workshop, August, 1959. Mr. Wolfe is President, Baltimore Gas and Electric Company.

seeing the decision-making process as one which lends itself to subdivision into a clear-cut sequence of events, though this approach may be useful as a means of analysis. On the contrary, it seems to me that the several phases of the process are closely interrelated. For example, in making a decision, the anticipated problems involved in putting into action what may appear to be a very well reasoned and logical conclusion are going to exert a considerable effect on the nature of the final decision. And once one decision is made, that is not the end of it in any but the simplest problems. A whole series of decisions often follows the decision which first triggered an action. These could take many forms, including terminating one course of action that had led to undesired results and formulating an entirely new and different course of action.

For this reason, while my assignment is to discuss the "action" phase of decision-making, I cannot but relate it in my thinking and in my comments to what has gone before.

My remarks this morning will fall into two broad categories:

First, a statement of three general principles which, if followed, seem to increase the probability that a decision will be accepted, understood, and carried out intelligently and enthusiastically by those responsible for implementing it.

Second, a consideration of several of the obstacles or road blocks which may be encountered after a decision is made, with a few illustrations of how they might be overcome.

GENERAL PRINCIPLES FOR SECURING EFFECTIVE ACTION

The first principle for securing effective action is the closest approach to a formula you will hear from me today. It can be expressed this way: *Participation* on the part of those who will be affected by a decision leads to *commitment;* commitment leads to *understanding and support* of the decision and the means by which it will be carried out.

This is a simple formula to state, but a difficult one to apply. Most of us are endowed with powerful unilateral impulses. Let us consider the equation again: *Participation* leads to *commitment,* commitment leads to *understanding and support.* The key word is *participation.* It is something which must be sought and practiced with sincerity. It cannot be used successfully, in a manipulative way, simply as a gimmick or technique to gain support of an executive's preconceived ideas.

My second principle, in which democracy and our business system are rooted, is a direct extension of the first. It is that the executive must be genuinely convinced that the aggregate of the thinking of many different individuals, whenever their experience is relevant to a particular problem, is likely to be better than that of one single person, no matter how great a genius he may be. I add the qualification that the experience of those who are consulted—who are asked to contribute their ideas—should be relevant, for otherwise there can be no real contribution to the quality of the solution. I am reminded, in this connection, of the epitaph said to be inscribed on the tombstone of Andrew Carnegie:

> Here Lies a Man
> Who Knew How to Enlist
> In His Service
> Better Men Than Himself.

When it comes to formulating the best course of action, we are in a sense all equals, even though the accountable executive retains the responsibility for the ultimate decision. The status barrier must be lowered enough to let ideas flow freely.

These first two general principles take the form, in business practice, of "consultative management."

There is a third general principle for securing effective action. I am convinced that the efforts of people are most productive when they are based on a clear understanding of the objectives of the organization. In simpler terms, employees

want to know—and work better when they do know—where
the business is supposed to be heading and how they can make
progress toward their personal goals by helping it get there.

This job of clarifying the objectives of the organization is
logically one for the higher levels of management. I cannot
think of many problems that give the chief executive a better
mental workout than trying to pinpoint the factors which seem
to produce success and then expressing them as a clear statement of objective. Yet it must be done if we are to have useful
participation, sound decisions, and purposeful action further
down the line.

There are, of course, many other elements which are important in translating decisions into action. Obviously, we need
a soundly planned organization, good communications, and so
forth. We must take into account the need for both timing
and balance. These are major subjects in themselves, however,
and I must limit myself for the most part to the three general
principles I have outlined.

OBSTACLES TO ACTION

If decisions are to be executed in the way the decision-
maker wants them to be executed—if he is to get the most
wanted consequences and the fewest unwanted consequences
—it is necessary to take into account the obstacles or road
blocks likely to be encountered after the decision is made, but
before the hoped-for results can occur. It may be helpful to
consider some of these.

THE "TIME SQUEEZE"

The "time squeeze" must certainly be listed as a prominent
road block. There are occasions, we all know, when decisions
must be made and acted on in a hurry. As many of you are

well aware, a hurricane, a heavy snowstorm, or some other emergency may create pressures on a utility's system that require a series of rapid decisions. These decisions may have to be made without complete knowledge of system conditions and with very limited opportunity for consultation with others. How effectively and rapidly these decisions are carried out will depend on how well the executive, when he had the time, developed a sense of spontaneous teamwork, loyalty, and spirit within the organization.

It is when the going gets rugged, of course, that an executive is called upon to demonstrate why he was made an executive in the first place. The experienced executive should be accustomed to thinking ahead to future hazards before they become "real and present dangers."

It is when the chips are down that the executive must exert a personal influence, too. It was said of General George Patton, when his armored divisions were locked in combat with the German armies during the Second World War, that he never allowed his troops to see him move toward the rear. He wanted to avoid the psychological impact of being seen heading away from the enemy. His method was very simple. He moved toward the front in an open jeep, or on foot. He returned to his command post in a light liaison plane.

Patton as an example for business leaders may seem farfetched. Yet I think there is a corollary here. When things are rough, the accountable executive should at least be around. While he may not have to *do* a great deal, he should be visible and accessible. This not only demonstrates his personal interest in seeing that decisions are made and energetically pursued; it has, as George Patton well knew, some morale value as well.

The problem of effective use of executive time is by no means limited to emergencies, of course. Most executives are, I am sure, troubled at times with the thought that there is more to do in a given day than any one human being can possibly handle, even if eight hours were extended to twenty-four. And truly, one executive cannot do it all himself. He must delegate. If he can do it all himself, he is by definition not an executive. This brings us to our second road block.

FAILURE TO DELEGATE

We have read and talked about the need to delegate authority and responsibility to subordinates until the phrase has almost lost its meaning. It has become a standard preachment in books and papers about how to be a good executive and is frequently confused with assigning work, which it is not, according to Mr. Webster. When we delegate, we pass on to a subordinate—we entrust to him—one of our own responsibilities. When we assign, we simply direct him to perform within his own job description, so to speak. To cite an example. A general foreman hands a foreman a routine overhead job, with sketches, drawings, and so forth, and says, "Ed, I'd like you and your crew to get started on this first thing tomorrow." In this case, he has assigned work to the foreman. On the other hand, if he says to the same foreman, "Ed, I'm going on vacation next month, and I'd like you to take a shot at making up the General Foreman's Report while I'm still around to answer any questions"—then he is delegating.

When we hear the advantages of delegation described, it is often in terms of what it will do for the delegator. It can do a great deal: provide time to think, use time more effectively, reduce the pressure of unfinished jobs; these are certainly important results of delegation for the executive who delegates.

Another value to the delegator has been pointed out by Morse G. Dial, Chairman of the Board of Union Carbide Corporation. It is delegation's value as a self-developer. Mr. Dial has said: "A man must broaden his character to be a manager, and 99% of this broadening is a willingness to delegate." [1]

All of the necessary decisions just cannot be carried into action unless there is real delegation as I have defined it, and the higher one goes in an organization the truer that becomes. Delegation does for the executive what Frank Gilbreth did for the bricklayer when he gave him a helper. The helper, by separating the good bricks from the bad ones and carrying and placing them at the proper working level, made it possible for the bricklayer to spend all his time—most of it, anyway— laying bricks rather than lifting them. An executive who fails to delegate will soon tire from lifting too many administrative bricks.

But there is another side to this question of delegation—the effect on the person to whom some of the authority and responsibility of the accountable executive is given. We have been told that the human resources are the greatest single asset of a business and the only resource capable of enlargement. All the other resources, as Peter Drucker [2] has pointed out, stand under the laws of mechanics, and the problem is to minimize loss (e.g., friction, line loss, interest on money loaned to a business, and the like).

From this we can see the value of delegation in developing the potential in people—to equip them to make and carry out their own decisions, and to grow into greater responsibilities. And it will give them a sense of personal worth and dignity, I believe, that salary and working conditions alone cannot do.

Delegation combined with participation can improve the quality of results. We think we have improved results, for example, in our budget planning. Some years ago our cycle for preparing the operating budget went something like this. Each

[1] *Business Week,* August 4, 1956.
[2] *The Practice of Management* (New York, 1954).

department head was required to price out his program for the coming year and to submit his budget estimate by such-and-such a date. The estimates were then reviewed at a higher level, certain recommendations were made, and a duly approved letter was sent to the department head saying, in effect: "Your budget estimate for the coming year is approved except for items 5 and 9, which have been eliminated, and item 10, which is to be postponed for at least one year."

Our procedure is now a little different, but bear in mind that the objective or decision is exactly the same, namely to eliminate nonessentials, keep expenditures in proper relationship to income, and improve profits. But, now, instead of standing aloof and issuing the pronouncement "Do this," we have tried to bring each department head into the act. We delegate the "action" part of the decision to him. We say, "Here's where we've got to come out. What are we going to do to get there?" The consequence: better results and time savings. The decision is the same: to make the best possible use of the available dollars in the production of profit. But the action to carry out the decision is different, since it involves active, thinking participation by those who have to live with the budget. Not only is better understanding achieved; I believe the chances are good that the budget in the aggregate is a better budget.

Delegation is not easy for some executives, particularly if they are relatively new in their jobs. There may be a reluctance to "let go" after a decision is made. They may fear that the decision will be misinterpreted and lead to "wrong" results, or that the indicated course of action will not be pursued by their subordinates with sufficient energy and intelligence. They may tend to hover, or to intrude at inappropriate times, with the result that action and initiative on the part of subordinates are discouraged rather than stimulated.

If you are managing managers, as I suspect most of you are, the solution, I believe, is the development of the ability to manage by objective—by making clear where you expect a subordinate to get and letting him figure out how best to get there. He should understand that the relative success of his actions is going to be measured by final results, and not by some sort of activity index that may or may not be productive.

PAST EXPERIENCE AND CONDITIONING

A third road block to effective action is our past experience, our early conditioning. You will recall that when I discussed the formula "participation leads to commitment, commitment leads to understanding and support," I went on to say that this does not always come naturally. Our early years in life usually have not equipped us to use a consultative approach at the appropriate times. We were simply told what was to be done, by our parents, our teachers, or perhaps by superior officers in the armed forces, and we were expected to do it. It is a natural and easy transition to apply this same unilateral approach in our dealings with subordinates.

Let me emphasize, as a parenthetical thought, that I do not want to give the impression that consultation is always the appropriate action for the executive. The great majority of decisions, including those where there is no serious impact on an individual person or group of people, must be made by one person. The limitation of time alone makes this necessary. And, as the critics of consultative management have pointed out, it can become a "leaderless activity" and a device for diffusing responsibility to the point where nothing gets done. Improperly applied, it could conceivably so discourage minority opinion as to result in the kind of "Organization Man" William H. Whyte is so exercised about. But it need do none of these things. My point is this: If we can learn the advantages and appreciate the limitations of consulting, we can also learn when it is appropriate to consult.

This problem of developing an appreciation of the value of consultation is one which the chief executive cannot solve simply by delegation, for it is his own behavior that sets the pattern. If he considers it desirable, for example, to have interested individuals or departments consult with each other on matters of mutual concern, he has got to do it himself. Yet, according to at least one study,[3] the opposite was often true among the executives who were interviewed. While they agreed verbally with the idea that consultation is desirable, they were personally inclined to act unilaterally. At the same time, they complained that their subordinates should have consulted more widely. Now for a fourth road block.

THE EXECUTIVE'S PRECONCEPTIONS

The executive's own attitude—his preconceptions—his conscious or subconscious bias toward one line of action, may contribute to lessened understanding, support, and enthusiasm on the part of those who must carry out the action. Whatever the executive's inner convictions may be, if he feels the problem is an appropriate one for consultation, he must keep his own predilections in the background until the decision is actually made, at which time his associates, if he has been really successful, will be convinced that it is their own decision which they have been asked to act upon.

We communicate, as you know, in so many ways—even by remaining silent. It is all too easy to communicate the feeling that you believe one course of action is preferable to another. A slight smile or a startled expression may be enough to discourage a worthwhile contribution.

The better role for the executive, when he really wants independent thinking from his associates, is to maintain as

---

[3] *Executive Action* by Edmund P. Learned and others (Graduate School of Business Administration, Harvard University, Cambridge, Mass., 1951).

neutral a mental stance as possible. He may even role-play a viewpoint different from his own, if he feels certain alternative actions have not been sufficiently considered.

FAILURE TO THINK IN TERMS OF HOW AN
ACTION AFFECTS PEOPLE

The action which follows decision affects people. We forget that at our peril. Sometimes it is impossible, or undesirable, to consult. But it is still necessary to weigh in our minds each of the probable alternatives against the reaction of the people who will be affected. Otherwise, a decision which seems to meet every test of logic and common sense may be completely nullified. Being "right" is not enough.

Do you remember the jingle of Jonathan Jay?

Here lies the body of Jonathan Jay
Who died defending his right of way.
He was right, dead right, as he sped along
But he's just as dead as if he were wrong.

If you will pardon another personal reference, I should like to illustrate from my early business experience how important it is to consider the effect of an action on people. Twenty-seven years ago, when I came to Baltimore for the summer to work with the Gas and Electric Company, still having a year of graduate study ahead of me, I had the great good fortune to be assigned to staff work in the executive department. My then boss (or perhaps I should say my tutor) was assistant to the executive vice-president. In other words, I was a staff assistant to a staff assistant, although he was a 100 percent executive in his relationship to me.

Well, he went away on vacation, leaving me to do some preliminary work on the appraisal of Department X. The very next day the executive vice-president called me into his office and asked me when the report on Department X would be ready. I said that I supposed it would be ready two or three weeks after my boss got back. He said: "No good," to that. "Write the report yourself and have it in my hands two weeks from today."

So, two weeks later he had the report. I forget the details, but this I remember: After suggesting that several activities of Department X be discontinued for the sake of economy—these were depression years—the report wound up with the observation that, while the department head was a very able man, if the work of his department were curtailed as suggested, it would be in order to reduce his salary by at least 25 percent.

I presented the report in person to the executive vice-president. He looked at the cover and asked me just one question: "Has Mr. Jones [the department head] seen this?" I said, "No, I thought it was confidential." With that, he took his pencil and wrote on a piece of paper "Mr. Jones: Any comment?"—clipped the paper to the report and tossed it in his outgoing mail tray. "That will be all," he said, and you know, I believed him. I thought that Jonathan Jay had nothing on me.

Well, I am going to remember for a long time to come that it is unwise to creep up on anyone with an unpleasant surprise. And the more critical the action that is to follow the decision, the more important it is to consider those who will be affected even if not to consult them; that is, unless you have an iron-clad promise that a report or recommendation is to be confidential, which sometimes is not feasible.

Certainly part of the problem of gaining acceptance of a decision is remembering that reasons and logical explanations are not enough in themselves to convince someone who feels his security or well-being is involved. If they were enough, the job of the executive would indeed be facilitated, for he could then confine his thinking entirely to facts, and not to emotions. But people are as they are—differently motivated, differently oriented, and possessed of the full complement of human emotions. And what is true of individuals is also true of groups. The premises on which customers base their conclusions are quite different from the premises of stockholders, and these in turn are different from the premises of employees. We can not change this greatly. We have to take it from there.

For my part, I am glad that this is true. Otherwise, I could turn over my job tomorrow to a professor of logic, a data programmer, and an EDP machine.

BROADLY APPLYING AN UNTESTED DECISION WHEN
IT IS NOT NECESSARY TO DO SO

There is a natural inclination, particularly when much time and effort have gone into a decision, to press forward to "get the show on the road." But unless the situation requires immediate, broad-scale action, there are advantages in pre-testing a decision by taking a more limited action.

Robert Burns observed that the best laid plans do not always work out as we hoped they would, and someone else noted that occasional slip between the cup and the lip. In many fields, the advantages of pre-testing have been recognized for many years. The aeronautical engineer has his wind tunnels and prototype models, the stage its rehearsals, and the military services their dry runs. Sales executives survey the public tastes and, having developed a product, test it for acceptance in a limited geographic area.

Similarly, the quality of a decision can be tested by limiting the action and hence the liability and cost of failure. And, as you may have read in a recent article in the *Harvard Business Review*, "Pretest Your Long-Range Plans," [4] this experimental approach will "not only reveal flaws but encourage bolder approaches to future planning. If a company has no experimental

[4] By Wm. J. Platt and N. Robert Maines Vol. 37, No. 1 (January–February, 1959), pp. 119–27.

means by which to make its planning mistakes inexpensively, it tends to adopt plans that have proved themselves in the past—and to avoid those which, although promising, do depart sufficiently from experience to pose severe risks. Conservative behavior is a natural consequence of the lack of valid experimental techniques."

The authors of this article were talking about planning the best use of material resources. But I think the same idea can be applied to problems involving people. I shall cite another example from the experience of our company.

After extended discussion about two years ago it was decided, not without some sincere disagreement, that a training program designed for newly appointed supervisors should first be given to our present supervisory forces—all those, that is, who had not actually participated in the development of the material used in the program. It seemed desirable for all supervisors to be thoroughly familiar with the materials used in the program, the way it was to be put on, and so forth. And, frankly, I thought that a review of certain fundamental principles of supervision might not be unduly harmful in one or two cases.

Well, the simplest and quickest way to go about a thing like that would have been to train the conference leaders and begin the meetings. But, as I said, there had been some honest disagreement. There was some fear that the supervisor of twenty or thirty years' standing might feel this was a reflection on his ability to do his job. And there was no way of being absolutely sure that the decision to have all supervisors participate, when put into action on a broad scale, would prove to be the correct one.

The line of action adopted in this case was to pre-test the program with a few selected pilot groups of supervisors, under the conditions that would exist in a broader program. Their reactions and their suggestions for improvement were obtained. Reassured by the results, we then put the program into effect for some 1,100 supervisors. This relatively slow start not only proved that the product was acceptable; it produced some useful ideas for improving the material and the methods of presentation.

OVERDEPENDENCE ON STATISTICALLY PREPARED INFORMATION

Another obstacle to effective action is the tendency to expect too much from statistically prepared information. Our success as a nation in applying physical laws to the improvement of our environment has perhaps led us to believe that measurement can be applied also to more subjective areas. Enthusiasts of automation (and I am told by my staff that no talk may be made these days without mentioning that word) seem to me to be claiming a great deal more for facts, figures, and information—even though they are rapid and concise—than is likely to be realized. Facts and figures must still be interpreted and, if necessary, discounted to fit the business enterprise and the human beings of which it is composed.

There is a natural tendency to hope that mathematics or statistics will produce some pat system for solving our problems. And if our problems dealt only with freight car loadings or material processing, they might. But, unfortunately, our problems for the most part are not "thing" or "material" problems, they are "people" problems. We have to avoid becoming so enamored of systems of mathematical measurement that we forget that it is still the ability to relate facts not only to each other, but to the total situation that prevents the executive from becoming obsolete.

"GROUP-TIGHT" THINKING

I do not know how expressive the term "group-tight" thinking is, but the thought I want to convey is this: we all have a tendency to limit mentally the effects of our decisions and actions to our own sphere of activity, whether it be as a member of an overhead crew or as a head of a department or company. Again, we are the product of our experience and have our own unique orientation. As young children, we first thought only in terms of the effects of our actions on ourselves. Later, possibly at the expense of some personal discomfort, we learned but did not always remember that our actions affected others—our classmates, our parents, and so forth. In our schooling, the courses were often presented as relatively unconnected fields of knowledge—finance, organization planning, engineering, and the like. Upon entering business, it is perfectly natural to continue this way of thinking in terms of one specialized activity—in terms of parts of the whole—rather than the whole itself.

The effect of this group-tight thinking is a tendency to interpret decisions passed on for action in terms of the effect of the action on our own sphere of responsibility rather than the effect on the entire organization and, indeed, the entire community. We must somehow overcome this and fit together in the minds of all members of our management team the various parts of our business, so that each manager can better project the results of his decisions and actions on company results.

Here I come back to the need to clarify the objectives of the company and ways in which progress toward those objectives can be measured. There is no good, for example, in achieving a $1,000 monthly cost saving in an electric operating department by eliminating a foreman's report, if the direct result will be a $2,000 additional monthly cost to the clerical department which becomes responsible for the record-keeping.

We established our corporate objectives specifically, and in writing some years ago. If an over-all orientation to the objectives of a company can be achieved, it should become easier for all managers to project the results of their decisions and actions in terms of their total effect on company operations, and to see themselves as members of a single, unified company team.

There remains only the question of measurement. How can we tell how well we are doing? How can we tell how close we are coming to achieving these objectives?

Well, as I have indicated, statistics have their limitations. There are many intangible but highly important accomplishments which we cannot really measure. We can feel them but are unable to measure them, except in a general way. Customer relations would be a case in point.

There is, however, one very specific economic yardstick, and, after all is said and done, it is still the first job of management to produce satisfactory economic performance. It is the yardstick used by the financial community to determine a company's entitlement to capital funds, in competition with others. I have in mind the earnings per share on the common stock of the corporation. If utilities are to grow as they must grow, all of our managers must understand the significance of a sound earnings record in obtaining new capital and appreciate that their decisions and actions have an ultimate effect on earnings. I think this is possible to achieve, and I suspect that "improving profits" may be a more positive and challenging goal than the somewhat more negative one of "cost control" or "cost reduction."

Now, so that you will not get the idea that I am merely prescribing this kind of brain-stretching for lower levels of the management team, let me say very quickly that all I have said applies with particular force to the higher echelons. But, here, the thinking about company objectives must be expanded to include consideration of the effect of decisions and subsequent actions in an even broader sense. It must take into account the effect of actions on the community of which the company is a part, on the other members of the utility industry, and even on the national welfare, in such matters as atomic power development and the question of public ownership of the power industry. State ownership and state planning are handicapped in precisely the same way as is a large business which is run as a one-man shop. It is impossible—I say that flatly—it is impossible for the plans of a single state agency to be as good as the sum total of all the long-range plans of the hundreds of companies that make up an industry, be it the production of electricity or the production of corn flakes.

CONCLUSION

To summarize briefly, I believe that decision-making is an integrated process, beginning with a need for action and ending, we hope, by hitting the center of the target aimed at. It cannot be neatly disentangled—it is an interrelated process. For this reason I have gone somewhat beyond the "action" phase. I have discussed a few of the many road blocks to effective action, and suggested some possible means of overcoming them.

The ultimate job of any manager—of any leader, for that matter—is to see that the correct decisions are made and are carried out, if possible with the understanding and enthusiasm of his associates. A decision is correct when it results in an action that advances an organization toward its goals or objectives—when it gets you where you want to go.

One good way to achieve understanding and enthusiasm is through the understanding and practice of consultative management. While it is difficult to capture group dynamics in a model or line drawing, I should like to share with you, as a sort of summary, my own imaginary model of how consultative management works.

First, think of a problem—a complicated problem—as a solid object having a number of polished facets. Each facet is of a different kind of metal, some precious, some worthless, many in-between. None are identified. Each reflects a certain amount of light and is best seen from only one position.

An executive is responsible for deciding which is the most valuable metal—which is the best solution to the problem. He rotates the object slowly, in as much light as he can bring to bear, being careful to expose all facets equally.

His associates, seated in different locations in the room, will simultaneously see different facets, depending on their orientation with respect to the object. As it continues to revolve, most of them will see other facets. One, however, may avert his eyes, the better to meditate on the first surface he saw, which he thought could not possibly be improved upon. Another may be strangely silent, remembering that he had stumbled over a similar object some months ago in his office and had suffered multiple bruises and contusions.

The object continues to rotate, and one man and then another describes what he sees, encouraging the others to come to where he sits so that they can examine the same facet together. "Gold? Or merely something bright and yellow?"

If they can agree that the facet is gold, the problem is solved —unless the presence of platinum is suspected and additional rotation seems in order. If they cannot agree, then the executive responsible for the decision must make his own evaluation, assaying the weight of the opinions he has heard together with his own knowledge of the characteristics of the metals.

This is the point of consultative management—"the object of the exercise," as our English cousins say. To identify every side of a problem, to weigh the alternatives, together, and to agree upon and select the best.

Now, if you were to ask me how a manager can acquire practice in putting decisions into action without risk to his business career, I would suggest to you that off-the-job activities of a charitable, civic, or community nature, in addition to being worth-while in themselves, provide an almost ideal training field. Activities of this kind are most successful when voluntary cooperation is enlisted by the person responsible for the activity. An executive who is functioning as, say, chairman of a charity drive or a church committee will very quickly learn that he cannot get cooperation—he cannot win support—by a system of commands or even direct delegation of his duties by the "you do this" method. He must accomplish his ends by persuasion and suggestion. If he is responsive to the lessons of experience, a man engaged in this sort of activity will learn the value of such phrases as "What do you think?" and the need to suppress the one-letter vertical pronoun.

What I say of charitable or civic organizations applies, of course, to many other forms of activity with business groups or committees, such as the American Gas Association and Edison Electric Institute and their equivalents in the telephone and other industries. They broaden the managers' skills in effectively carrying decisions into action through persuasion, influence, and example.

In touching on these aspects of leadership I have been reminded of a story which our personnel manager brought with him from his steel mill days. It involved a hard-boiled plant superintendent—a bull-of-the-woods of the old school. For years he had been tongue-lashing his men for the slightest infraction of the rules. Any suggestions on the part of his employees for a change in methods would have been regarded as rank heresy, to be instantly and forever repressed.

Well, in this particular steel mill, the supervisors, including the superintendent, had just been exposed to a course in "leadership." At the end of the final session, the question was put to him by the instructor: "Are you willing to try out some of these leadership principles we've been discussing?"

To this the old-timer answered: "All right. I'll be a leader. But the so-and-so's had better follow."

I wish I could leave you now with some bit of distilled

wisdom that would enable each of you to make the best possible decisions and always take the correct line of action during your business careers. I cannot. I would like to share with you, however, a little prayer which I have found to be a source of inspiration: "God grant us the serenity to accept the things we cannot change; the courage to change the things we can; and the wisdom to know the difference."

DECISION-MAKING AND THE BUSINESS CLIMATE
by Fred Rudge

WE ARE WITNESSING in America today a growth of conviction among businessmen that corporations should expand the direct and deliberate role they play in affecting the course of our society. It would be simpler to speak of a more active corporate role in "public affairs," but this term is becoming rather narrowly associated with direct political action, and much more than practical politics is involved here. The term *public progress* perhaps encourages a broader focus and permits us to define the business "climate" as the sum total of the social, economic, political, and industrial conditions under which business operates.

In attempting to weave together threads from the highly charged emotional area of concern for the business climate and from the cold intellectual fabric of scientific decision-making I feel supported by three brief passages from Dr. Livingston's fertile pen:

1. "It is quite generally accepted that there is a universal rational process which flows from information to consideration to decision and to action."

Address presented August 3, 1959 at the Eighth Utility Management Workshop, Arden House, Harriman Campus, Columbia University. Mr. Rudge is president of Fred Rudge, Inc.

2. "It is useful to understand how others see or estimate us and anticipate our behavior."

3. A consultant can make himself useful, though not necessarily popular, by occasionally "challenging them [managers] to dust off and reexamine their biases, preconceptions and habitual behavior patterns."

DECISIONING AND CLIMATE

The movement to expand the boundaries of corporate responsibility in the public process poses one of today's most pressing problems for management and portends some extremely difficult decisions. The matter is pressing because of the urgency building up within a large segment of the business community, an urgency which is both felt and expressed. The decisions are difficult for many reasons. How should, and how can, the corporation affect society, both through its own people and by acting externally in relation to its community, its state, and the nation?

A New Role. This is a new and unfamiliar area for direct corporate action. Traditionally, views of the corporation's role in society have been almost exclusively in terms of its economic function through production. The new view sees the corporation also in an educative role, as a source of information to all segments of the society—as an organization which seeks, in its own and in the public interest, to strengthen understanding and support of the free enterprise system.

The educational problem is one of great scope; it is diffuse and multifaceted. At what points does the corporation come to grips with it? Involved here are questions of the nature of corporate responsibility; of a desirable public image; the existence of current attitudes and expectancies of many groups of people with different "languages" and frames of reference;

many uncomfortable political realities; and the impact of sociological factors. There is, in short, a great deal more involved than the reiteration of "the economic facts of life" at the Adam Smith level of perception.

Managers Are Not Necessarily Good Educators. Decisions are difficult because of the generally undeveloped state of basic knowledge and information in this area among managers as a group. A good deal of the fundamental comprehension of factors involved in the creation and change of attitudes in masses of people is second nature to politicians, sociologists, and others professionally grounded in "people problems." Managers have learned less about these things.

There is the hazard in dealing with attitudes, of deciding (despite the best of intentions) on actions that will create even worse attitudes and result in the alienation of people whose support is crucial. There can be no question of the need for fuller comprehension of the needs of business as a core part of our social integrity; no question that the corporate community, like all other major segments, must speak for itself; no question that exposure of the interests of every group, majority and minority, to the action of public opinion is indispensable in an open society. There seems little question that the corporate community has been somewhat more shy in this connection than other key segments—the military, for example, or the formal education community, or the religious community. The hazard lies not in corporations' deciding to act, but in the possibility that managers may choose courses of action which will cause people to interpret the business goal as seeking more power than the public thinks it should have.

Different groups *have different and frequently misunderstood* frames of reference. Decision-making in this area is made more difficult by the existence of deeply rooted assumptions which are rarely put to the test. Developing new understanding in depth and new frames of reference for millions of people about the corporate responsibility in the public process obviously must take account of people's current orientations. In most cases this orientation is the product of past experience. For example: When management has communicated about issues in dispute between itself and the union movement, it has understandably been looked upon purely and simply as a protagonist in its own interest. Preconceptions on both sides are likely to inhibit decisions by management to canvass the much larger areas of mutual interest. Management's orientation breeds the assumption that no good can come of efforts to work together; labor's orientation breeds the assumption that such an approach must be a management trick.

Identification of Climate as a Function of Management is Pivotal. Finally, there are difficult decisions involved in providing leadership and structure within organizations for the planning and conduct of activity in the "climate" area.

There is no problem in establishing outside-the-line staff sections and providing them with lip-service support. This has been done and the effort has withered and died. Establishing built-in responsibility in this area, as a continuing function of management (like marketing, finance, research, and the like) is quite another matter.

All these considerations give substance to the climate movement as a management problem. I have chosen it as an illustration in the field of decision-making *per se* for two reasons. First, it is one in which a rational and ordered process of decision-making can certainly be applied but rarely is; and, second, it is an area in which my consulting organization has been having experience recently, to which we have given some thought, and from which I can draw some reference to real situations.

SUB-PROCESSES IN DECISIONING

Dr. Livingston has identified, as a basic sub-process in decisioning, the use of five steps or components:

1. Determining, at a decision-making level, that a change has to be made.
2. Weighing any obvious solutions against the desirability of getting more information before you decide what to do.
3. Figuring the hazards and difficulties of implementation.
4. Making the action decision itself.
5. Making sure that people know what the decision is and what they have to do about it.

Let us look at the problem of expanding a company's responsibility for contributing to the public process in the light of these five fundamental steps. In introducing each one I will quote Dr. Livingston's own words, which are both more erudite and more precise than mine.

Recognition. "Acceptance of the need to make a decision, probably involving change—recognition." The need is seen—but often in a narrow focus. Our research shows that many of the very large corporations are feeling pressure for action and share a sense of need for it. But a majority has not yet accepted the need for decisions that will make a real change in the corporation's way of life. The most common responses to pressure are (a) deferring the major decision to act directly, "letting George do it" through business associations; (b) stepping up of action by individual members of management on a personal basis but avoiding decisions to involve the company as an organization; (c) assigning certain relatively bland and non-risky kinds of activity to staff units, essentially as a useful spare-time occupation. On the other hand, the larger focus calls for reexamination of the corporate responsibility. Some few managements have accepted the need for decisions in this area which encompass a new framework of corporate responsibility.

These may have important effects on corporate image, internal and external relationships, management structure, profit and loss.

Judicial. "Evaluation of projected solutions vs. special information available—judicial." The newcomer will not find information ready-made for his use. At first blush, considerable data on individual corporate action to improve the "climate" may seem to be available. But a great many of the "proposed solutions" currently advocated are not really solutions as much as they are exhortations—various ways of saying "get in there and fight" or "you too can learn to be a practical politician" or "get your people to take an active interest in civic affairs." As for the special information available, most companies are finding that, practically speaking, this is pretty thin.

A fact-gathering job should be done by each corporation. Where the *need* for decision has been accepted, many companies have found that *making* the decision entails the need for developing information by themselves on a number of fronts, including some which, as a consequence of the information, are now reexamining "biases, preconceptions and habitual behavior patterns." This data-gathering has been prompted by managements' asking themselves some rather searching questions. What is our "market"? Who are to be our "salesmen"? How many of our people do we want to be active as "salesmen" in this area? And, whose help must we enlist within the corporation? One way to deal with this question is for the president to make a usual, straight-forward, essentially unilateral decision about the kind of action he wants and the setup he wants for getting it. One large company in the container business has directed its management people to make contact with public officials on certain issues, and has provided the information to be conveyed. This certainly reflects determination to act. Another approach to answering these basic questions was adopted by a major chemical company, which enlisted a task force of company people to figure out the corporate responsibility, policy, and approach in all areas of the development of a business climate. Purposely, the men picked for the task force were third-echelon, more aggressive, younger types. Among their conclusions were these: It's fine to cope with external factors but maybe we ought to concentrate on the people who work for us. Better understanding of the company will lead to better operation, better profits, and, simultaneously, greater comprehension of the "economic facts of life." Moreover, the task force reported its feeling, based on real inquiry and research, that less can be accomplished by telling officials and politicians what the company thinks than by providing some solid support behind politicians whose inclinations are "right." Employees, after all, are voters.

How can we motivate our "salesmen"? What information do we need to help us steer away from approaches that will not work in making these people our salesmen? One company task force explored this question, arranging for surveys to be conducted in three of its plants. This confirmed the perhaps obvious fact that people cannot be simply ordered to commit themselves to action in the climate area, and it permitted the company to assess degrees of interest, concepts of the problem and the difficulties, and other crucial attitudes among the people who had to be involved in any sustained, on-going process.

How tough a job of influencing attitudes lies ahead? What are the real attitudes in the "markets" on which we are trying to operate—internal and external? Gathering of "special information" has revealed a good deal of common misunderstanding and distortion. Most common, in the ranks of line management, are faulty assumptions about lack of concern and interest, down the line, in better operation (there is much more mutual interest than commonly supposed). Most common in the lower ranks are a number of stereotypes about "the corporation." One major company discerned 24 of these (the corporation is a power center not accountable to any public, it pushes the little fellow around, it would never increase wages if it weren't for unions, and so on). The implications of all this seem clear: A company can scarcely hope to be effective (or constructive) in its efforts as an educative source unless it has clear knowledge and objective understanding of the attitudinal forces currently working in each part of the "market." Obeisance to sacred cows and stereotyped ideas is not going to be very helpful.

Implementation. "Estimate of risk, probability of occurrence of events and difficulty of implementation—both organizational and personal. . . ." Looking first at the matter of implementation, there are conclusions to be drawn from corporate experience. What needs to be done to bring about real managerial involvement, a real commitment to action at all levels of management? The data would indicate some basic necessities: (a) more than exhortation is needed (top management people have been doing this to each other at the Waldorf for years with little practical result); (b) organization within a company's management must be on the "cell principle" (implying no Leninist subversion) rather than on the chain-of-command basis—this because attitudes cannot be dictated effectively; (c) top management's commitment to expanded responsibility for the company in the public process needs to be seen as serious and continuing, not an impulsive whim; (d) action decisions need to be specific, especially in terms of the ground rules involved; and (e) the kinds of action initiated need to be identified as integral with the company's operational best interests, not as an extracurricular intrusion.

In the matter of the "estimate of risks" there are also conclusions to be drawn from experience. For example, there is the risk of spreading managerial effort too thinly. The Sears approach of building community participation into the job specifications of local managers is a practical illustration of overcoming this kind of risk. Then, there is the risk that decisions on climate action, if approached on the chain-of-command basis, can be divisive within the company, resulting in lack of cooperation and emotional disturbance. Task forces on the "cell principle," which involve a talking-through process, illustrate an approach to overcoming this risk. Finally, there is the risk, already mentioned, of worsening attitudes, internally and externally, instead of bettering them. The central element in avoiding this risk is *not* to assume that you know what the attitudes are. Learn about them with the same objective acceptance you would give to other kinds of facts on which managerial decision-making depends.

The Decision. "The actual commitment—selection of course of action and assumption of responsibility for both results and consequences." In the "climate" area, full attention to steps two and three has made it possible for some companies to accomplish what Dr. Livingston calls "superior decisions" in terms of actual commitment.

In one of the companies referred to earlier there was found, down the line from top management, a solid base for action in terms of high orientation toward the company, acceptance of the need for broader corporate responsibility, and willingness among individuals to devote time and effort, in a sustained way, to an organized and rational program clearly linked to the company's interests. Throughout the company there was a strong inclination to establish a connection between good "climate" and good management. There was also awareness of possible pitfalls if the company rushed precipitately into the field of direct public political action; awareness that the managerial group, as a whole, is not free from political naïveté; that there are legal and other inhibiting factors; that there is danger of inter-company conflicts of interest on public issues; that there is a long background in the business community of being "against" everything that is happening, and that this will not be completely overcome until corporations develop more fully a positive philosophy in regard to the public process; that there is some danger of confusing the public with a wide range of "images" about corporate responsibility.

From these findings came decisions and actual commitments to company action which were in accord with reality, and which launched the company on a course of constructive action. These included commitments (a) to build internal understanding and support of managerial goals in a fashion calculated not only to have an ultimate impact on the external "climate" in the traditional sense but, also, importantly—and more immediately—to affect productivity, costs, and cooperation in the accomplishment of desired operational and organizational change; (b) to strengthen, through better planning and organization, the non-public efforts of management in the area of political contacts (lobbying); and (c) defer major action in the area of direct political education until a total and positive corporate approach is crystallized, understood, and supported throughout the organization as an outgrowth of the first commitment.

Other companies have made equally superior decisions and commitments, varying somewhat in accordance with varying results from making the first and second commitments. In doing so, they have demonstrated the truth of another of Dr. Livingston's maxims: "The theory of sequential decisioning considers the problem of the change in decision due to the change of information available"—both quantitatively and qualitatively.